Her Own Thinker

Canadian Women Writers as Essayists

ESSENTIAL ESSAYS SERIES 81

Guernica Editions Inc. acknowledges the support of
the Canada Council for the Arts and the Ontario Arts Council.
The Ontario Arts Council is an agency of the Government of Ontario.
We acknowledge the financial support of the Government of Canada

CHRISTL VERDUYN

Her Own Thinker

Canadian
Women Writers
as Essayists

GUERNICA
EDITIONS

TORONTO • CHICAGO • BUFFALO • LANCASTER (U.K.)
2023

Guernica Founder: Antonio D'Alfonso

Michael Mirolla, general editor
Julie Roorda, editor
Cover and Interior Design: Rafael Chimicatti
Guernica Editions Inc.
287 Templemead Drive, Hamilton (ON), Canada L8W 2W4
2250 Military Road, Tonawanda, N.Y. 14150-6000 U.S.A.
www.guernicaeditions.com

Distributors:
Independent Publishers Group (IPG)
600 North Pulaski Road, Chicago IL 60624
University of Toronto Press Distribution (UTP)
5201 Dufferin Street, Toronto (ON), Canada M3H 5T8

First edition.
Printed in Canada.

Legal Deposit—First Quarter
Library of Congress Catalog Card Number: 2023931221
Library and Archives Canada Cataloguing in Publication
Title: Her own thinker : Canadian women writers as essayists / Christl Verduyn.
Names: Verduyn, Christl, 1953- author.
Series: Essential essays series ; 81.
Description: 1st edition. | Series statement: Essential essays series ; 81
Includes bibliographical references.
Identifiers: Canadiana (print) 20230153283
Canadiana (ebook) 20230153488 | ISBN 9781771838023 (softcover)
ISBN 9781771838030 (EPUB)
Subjects: LCSH: Canadian essays—Women authors—History and criticism.
CSH: Canadian essays (English)—Women authors—History and criticism.
Classification: LCC PS8211 .V47 2023 | DDC C814.009/9287—dc23

Contents

Their Own Thinkers

> *There is another way to be, to think, to know ... Each time any one of us has a thought, others do so as well.*
> —Lee Maracle (Stó:lō),[1] *Memory Serves* (xiv)

> *i thought of this writing not as a series of (position) papers in academic argument, but as* essais, *tries in the French sense of the word.* Essayings *even, to avoid the ossification of the noun.*
> —Daphne Marlatt, *Readings from the Labyrinth* (ii)

The idea for this study formed as I stood before a large section of my bookshelves comprising a distinctive set of volumes: essay collections by women writers in Canada. More specifically, these were collections by Canadian women writers generally better known for their fiction and poetry than for their writing as essayists. Novelists, short story writers, and poets, from Margaret Atwood, to Dionne Brand, Nicole Brossard, Alicia Elliott (Haudenosaunee/Tuscarora), Margaret Laurence, Lee Maracle, M. NourbeSe Philip, Jane Rule, Gail Scott, Leanne Betasamosake Simpson (Michi Saagiig Nishnaabeg), Aritha van Herk, Miriam Waddington, and Adele Wiseman, among others—all had published collections of essays.

---

1 Indigenous identities are included at first mention of the writers and periodically thereafter.

When introducing Canadian women writers and their work in my literature classes I would refer my students to these essay collections. I suggested they read them to learn more about the authors' novels and poetry, as the ideas and development of their fiction works were often discussed in their essays. At the same time, by delving into the authors' essay writing, students could discover the many interesting insights and perspectives that they offered on a myriad of topics beyond literature. As essayists, Canadian women poets and fiction writers have written and published compelling commentaries and discerning analyses on a great variety of subjects. In addition to global concerns of the environment, human rights, racism, poverty, and violence, they have addressed national topics such as Canada's policies of multiculturalism and immigration, its history and treatment of Indigenous peoples, record of racism, systems of justice, as well as events and movements like the Writing Thru Race conference, Idle No More, and Black Lives Matter. Canadian women novelists and poets writing as essayists have been attentive and perceptive observers of Canada and the world.

Despite the topicality and contributions of their essay collections, this branch of writing by Canadian women writers has generally attracted little critical attention. A short review or article might appear in a newspaper or a journal but otherwise this body of work has fallen largely below the radar of most readers, even those devoted to Canadian literature. Was this a measure of Canadian women writers' contributions to critical and cultural discourse in the country? A tacit reflection of the writers' intellectual heft? Was the inattention a fair assessment? What *did* all this writing amount to?

Questions such as these were at the origins of the project that has led to this study and to its argument for greater attention to and appreciation of the contributions, insights, and value of essay writing by Canadian women poets and novelists. Along the way, these questions generated a graduate course, article publications, conference organization, papers, and proceedings, and finally *Her Own Thinker*.[2] The title came to me while reading Kristjana Gunnars's collection *Stranger at the Door: Writers and the Act of Writing*. In her Preface and Acknowledgments Gunnars names a series of writers and essayists who inspired various pieces in the collection, including Italo Calvino "because he positions himself at the cusp of various traditions and is *his own thinker*" (xiii, emphasis added). The same, I argue in *Her Own Thinker*, can be said of the women essayists discussed in this volume.

Her Own Thinker looks at the sizeable body of essay writing by Canadian women novelists and poets, with a primary focus on collections of essays, in particular those published since the 1960s. It explores the thinking, ideas, and perspectives that Canadian women fiction writers have chosen to express in essay form rather than in fiction form. It is no secret that writers' fiction and nonfiction frequently share themes and concerns in

---

2   The graduate course was at Wilfrid Laurier University; I would like to thank the students in that course for their interest in the topic, and to note early help from Sally Heath and Kristen Poluko in finding reviews of collections of essays by Canadian women writers. For later research assistance at Mount Allison, thank you to former student Amy Bright. The publications in question are listed under Verduyn in the Bibliography for *Her Own Thinker*. The conferences were *Discourse and Dynamics: Canadian Women as Public Intellectuals* (October 16-18, 2014), *Speaking Her Mind: Canadian Women and Public Presence* (October 20-22, 2016), and *Resurfacing: Women Writers of 1970s Canada/Refaire surface: écrivaines canadiennes des années 1970* (April 24-26, 2018). The conference proceeding is the online publication *HEAR HE(a)R! Canadian Women Writing*: https://mta.cairnrepo.org/islandora/object/mta%3A27096. Accompanying website: https://speakinghermind.ca/

common; as Nora Stovel (2020) points out of Margaret Laurence's essays, for example, the novelist often worked out issues in her nonfiction before taking them up in her fiction (xix). Writers' essays can and do illuminate their novels and poetry. *Her Own Thinking* is not a study of fiction works by Canadian women writers, however; it is an exploration of nonfiction writing that they have published in the form of essays collected into print volumes.

The post-2000 period has seen a proliferation of essay writing in non-print and uncollected forms, such as online blogs, Twitter threads, and other social media platforms. Canadian women writers have participated in these practices; poet Sina Queyras's online blog/literary journal "Lemon Hound" and Quebec author Catherine Mavrikakis's blogs are two examples.[3] There is a study to be done of these and other examples. In *Her Own Thinker*, however, the focus is on print collections of essays, reflecting my personal reading passion, which has always been for print.

The Project: "Too varied to be yoked"

The collections explored in the pages that follow address a wide range of issues and topics, "too varied to be yoked," to borrow a phrase from Miriam Waddington's collection *Apartment Seven* (ix). From the artistic to the political, these topics add up to a

---

3   Notably, Mavrikakis's blogs have been gathered and published as *L'éternité en accéléré* (2010), and Queyras's have similarly found their way into print as well, for example in *Lemon Hound* (2002) and *Unleashed* (2009). Indeed, following a focus on online writing and communication at the outset of the new millennium, there has been a resurgence of essay writing published in traditional book form.

long and formidable list.[4] Some topics recur across the collections, such as language and identity, writing and women's experiences as writers, the experience of colonialism, racism, and being an outsider. Together, these topics form a through-line in *Her Own Thinker*. Structurally, *Her Own Thinker* is both broadly thematic and loosely chronological in organization.

Writers and collections are grouped by overlapping decades in three waves of essay development—1960s/1970s, 1970s/1980s/1990s, and 1990s/post-2000. Writers' work can and does resist such organizational concerns, as essay collections by Lee Maracle, M. NourbeSe Philip, Dionne Brand, and Margaret Atwood readily demonstrate, each having published collections in more than one decade. As well, within collections there are gaps in time between the publication dates of individual essays and the publication date of the collection as a whole. Sometimes the gap is quite significant, as is often the case of collections by writers grouped in Chapter II. With birth years ranging from 1916 to 1939,[5] and publishing careers dating from the postwar period, essay collections by this group of

---

4   Even a cursory inventory impresses: abortion, appropriation, the arts, class, colonialism, culture, desire, the environment, ethnocentrism, feminism, gender, homophobia, identity, the imagination, imperialism, Indigenous rights, multiculturalism, music, nationalism, nuclear armament, power, waste, and war; patriarchy, PEN, philosophy, police shootings, politics, pollution, poverty, protest, race, the ROM's Into the Heart of Africa exhibit, sexism, transgression, trauma; violence, writing, and the writer's life and relationship with readers and critics, with theory, with time and space, with morality and death.

5   P.K. Page (1916-2010), Miriam Waddington (1917-2004), Mavis Gallant (1922-2014), Margaret Laurence (1926-1987), Phyllis Webb (1927-2021), Adele Wiseman (1928-1992), Jane Rule (1931-2007), Margaret Atwood (1939).

writers typically appeared decades later, in the 1980s and 1990s, or even after 2000. For instance, essays by P.K. Page, whose poetry and prose publications of more than thirty books began in 1944, were collected and published in 2007. Poet Phyllis Webb's essays appeared in 1995 and novelist Adele Wiseman's in 1987. Similar lags in time apply to essay collections by Miriam Waddington, Mavis Gallant, and Margaret Laurence. The passage of time between the publication of these writers' novels and poetry, and the collection and publication of their essays, reflects an oversight or under appreciation of their work as essayists. This is a lacuna that *Her Own Thinker* aims to address.

In broad strokes, *Her Own Thinker* unfolds as follows. Chapter I takes a brief look at the essay genre and its two primary Western traditions: the personal, informal French tradition, originating with Michel de Montaigne's 1580 *Essais*, and the more formal, empiricist English tradition, associated with Francis Bacon's 1597 *Essays*. It considers the essay genre in relation to the part played by writing in general in public intellectualism, which historically has been associated with men rather with women writers. Canadian women novelists and poets challenge this history in their practice of the essay, drawing on both the Montaigne and Bacon essay traditions while developing each in innovative and substantively new ways.

Chapter II considers collections by a group of women writers whose careers as poets and novelists were forged during the postwar years, including Adele Wiseman, Margaret Laurence, Jane Rule, Miriam Waddington, Mavis Gallant, Phyllis Webb, P.K. Page, and Margaret Atwood. These writers made use of the essay form to address issues and concerns that in many cases only decades later garnered sustained public attention, such as environmental pollution or Canada's colonial history and treatment of Indigenous peoples. In content, their collections were prescient and pressing. In form and language style, their essays tended toward the traditional. While a decade younger than this group of writers, Margaret Atwood is included in this chapter, her writing career having begun in the postwar period.

Chapter III turns to essay collections by a generation of authors whose publishing began in the 1970s and 1980s and who took less traditional approaches to the genre. Influenced by feminist, postmodern, and deconstruction theories of the 1970s and 1980s, these authors made creative innovations in their use of the essay and the form underwent striking changes in their work. This will be seen in collections by Daphne Marlatt, Gail Scott, Lola Lemire Tostevin, Erin Moure, Betsy Warland and Di Brandt, as well as Lee Maracle, Aritha van Herk, Kristjana Gunnars, and Bronwen Wallace. Prominent in these collections are the subjects of language and identity, sexuality, culture, and class.

Chapter IV concentrates on essay collections of the 1980s and 1990s and the post-2000 years, in which key issues include Canadian multiculturalism, racism, and immigrant and Indigenous experiences in the country. Important analyses of these and other topics inform collections by Himani Bannerji, M. NourbeSe Philip, Dionne Brand, Alicia Elliott, Leanne Betasamosake Simpson, and Tessa McWatt, as well as by ground-breaking writers of the earlier period, notably Lee Maracle.

Together, chapters III and IV account proportionally for the largest share of discussion of the collections considered in *Her Own Thinker*. In terms of length, they tally more pages than other components of the volume. This reflects the growth of Canadian literature during the decades covered in these chapters—the 1970s, 1980s, and 1990s. These years coincided with the significant expansion of "CanLit" as the numbers of writers and publishers increased in Canada, notably writers from previously underrepresented groups—women and members of "minority" groups—and "small" publishers, such as House of Anansi, Coach House, Guernica Editions, Douglas & McIntyre, and Dundurn, among others.

A concluding *envoi* looks briefly to the future and the use of the essay form by Canadian women writers going forward, in the hope that it will send readers off to discover for themselves newly appearing as well as previously published collections.

Throughout *Her Own Thinker* I quote often and at times lengthily from the authors' collections, sharing M. Travis Lane's view of the value of "ample quotation". In her essay "On Reviewing," Lane makes the case for quoting generously from a text in order to give readers a good sense of the text in full, that is, to provide text with context (con/text: text with text). Without this, Lane argues, a text's power cannot be fully felt (*Heart on Fist*, 22). Among other hopes I have for *Her Own Thinker* is that it might convey a sense of, perhaps even a feel for, the power, place, and importance of Canadian women writers' essay writing within the larger literary and cultural contexts of Canada and beyond.

A Personal Caveat

In approaching collections by writers from Canada's Indigenous, Black, and other racialized communities, for which the acronym BIPOC (Black, Indigenous, and people of colour) serves widely today, I have been conscious of my limits in reading and writing about their work. My own immigrant experience has long made me aware of difference and belonging, and of societal, cultural, and intellectual centres and margins. Nonetheless, this has been the experience of a white, cisgender settler that is in no way comparable to the experiences of racialized Canadians. I have benefitted enormously from the invaluable critical work and insights of BIPOC scholars and writers, including those discussed in *Her Own Thinker,* and I am deeply grateful for the signposts their work has provided me on my own scholarly path.

My research and reading for this book included essay writing by Quebec women writers, whose novels, poetry, and drama works I have followed and taught throughout my career.[6] In *Her Own Thinker,* however, I deal mainly with collections by women writers in English Canada. Chapter III includes a short section featuring a group of Quebec women writers whose work had particular impact and meaning for feminist writers in 1980s English Canada, as reflected in the collection *La théorie, un dimanche* (1988).

In addition, while Chapter I includes a brief look at women writers as essayists in earlier periods of Canadian literary history, my primary focus in *Her Own Thinker* is on collections of essay writing from the postwar years through the end of the 20th century and into the new millennium. These were decades of dynamic expansion in literary Canada. The Canadian cultural scene was enlarged by developing critical discourses and theories of feminism, multiculturalism, post-colonialism, and anti-racism. This led to the inclusion of more work by women and by authors from underrepresented communities. Publisher

---

6   In my essay "Giving the Twenty-first Century a Try: Canadian and Québécois Women Writers as Essayists" (Verduyn, 2013), I discuss recent collections by French-language as well as English-language writers. The French-language writers include Louky Bersianik, Nicole Brossard, Madeleine Gagnon, Lise Gauvin, Suzanne Jacob, Monique LaRue, Antonine Maillet, Catherine Mavrikakis, Madeleine Monette, Madeleine Ouellette-Michalska, Régine Robin, Lori Saint-Martin, France Théoret, and Louise Warren.

lists began to feature new names and works by writers of immigrant, Indigenous, Black, and other "minority" identifications.

These years coincided with my own career studying and
teaching writing by Canadian and Quebec women and many
of the subjects and events discussed in the essays are personally familiar and meaningful to me. There is resonance between
Her Own Thinker and Daphne Marlatt's description of her essay
writing as "Attempts to read my life and the lives of women
close to me … Attempts, in a rather immediate form of writing,
to read the complex interaction between cultural representations and self-representation" (*Readings from the Labyrinth*, ii).
Her Own Thinker thus comprises elements of the personal, "subjective" nature of the Montaigne essay alongside the more objective, analytic character of the essay tradition associated with
Francis Bacon. The collections discussed or mentioned across
the chapters are of both personal literary and academic interest
to me for having met, heard, and engaged with many of their
authors over the years.

This subjective feature of *Her Own Thinker* means that there
are likely to be authors and collections that some readers consider missing or overlooked. In all, I address some forty volumes,
which for easy reading reference are listed in a Primary Works
Cited at the end of the study before the more comprehensive
Bibliography. There is always room for additional work to be
done, however, all the more so given the introductory, overview
intention of *Her Own Thinker*, akin in a more modest way to
Margaret Atwood's project in *Survival* to identify and promote a
distinct body of writing, in this case Canadian women poets' and
novelists' essay writing. Closer in length and purpose to an *essai*,
as discussed in the next chapter, than to a definitive, full-scale
scholarly study, *Her Own Thinker* readily invites other studies.
There are ample possibilities for in-depth analyses of individual

collections or of individual essayists, for example, or for a full examination of French-language collections for English-language readers, or a study of essay writing during earlier periods of Canadian letters, or alternatively of the new collections that continue to appear in both traditional print and digital formats. There is also room for a project on essay collections by men writers in Canada. My bookshelves include thought-provoking collections by such authors as André Alexis, George Elliott Clarke, Charles Foran, Douglas Glover, Thomas King (Cherokee), Roy Miki, Mordecai Richler, Drew Hayden Taylor (Anishinaabe/Ojibwe), Fred Wah, among others. But in *Her Own Thinker* my interest—personal, literary, academic, and feminist—is in essay collections by Canadian women poets and novelists, and their imaginative, innovative, thought-full "attempts" to express their thinking and insights in the form of the essay.

The collections considered in *Her Own Thinker* are rich in content, varied in style, diverse in authorship, and produced by women from across the country's different cultural and Indigenous communities. They were written for multiple reasons: out of necessity, as paid book reviews and pieces produced to supplement precarious finances; out of generosity, for a fundraiser or a worthy cause; out of professionalism, for as Margaret Atwood reasons, "those who are reviewed must review in their turn, or the principle of reciprocity fails" (*Curious Pursuits*, xiii). They are written in response to requests to deliver keynote addresses, give public lectures, or speak at one occasion or another—a conference, an award ceremony, a retirement, a memorial service. They are also written out of sheer desire to "try" the form of short nonfiction—the essay—and to say something. The collections are original, insightful, and often provocative; their authors are astute, intelligent, and witty, even at times humorous despite the general seriousness of the topics, many of which remain unsettlingly relevant today as more and more Canadians confront realities of the country's history. In the spring of 2021, unmarked burial sites of Indigenous children on the grounds of former residential schools brought the terrible reality of Canada's Residential School system directly to Canadians. "What a society buries," Atwood wrote in 1973, "is at least as revealing as what it preserves" (*Second Words*, 147). In the hands of Canadian women writers, the essay genre is a uniquely creative, multifaceted form of writing with which, *Her Own Thinker* contends, they contribute in important ways to cultural, social, political, environmental, and intellectual thinking in Canada and beyond.

CHAPTER I

Mining the Essay

> *It is no accident that the essay became such an important genre for women in the last few decades ... we were participating, at last, in the making of literature (...) inscribing ourselves into a critical genre.*
>
> —Lola Lemire Tostevin, *Subject to Criticism: Essays* (9-10)

> *A collection of essays? series of musing? on issues of language, identity, collective membership and self-authorizing as a woman writer ... Try again. Repeated attempts to articulate the problem of naming and the inexhaustibly unnameable contradictions of a self writing her way through the cultural labyrinth she finds herself in.*
>
> —Daphne Marlatt, *Readings from the Labyrinth* (i, ii)

A full account of essay writing by women in Canada would require a multi-volume project. Essay writing by women novelists and poets in English and French Canada traces back to well before the postwar parameters of *Her Own Thinker*. The nineteenth and early twentieth centuries offer up numerous examples of women poets and novelists writing as essayists, as the proliferation of newspapers and magazines presented new publication outlets and opportunities. Novelist Lucy Maude Montgomery (1874-1942), best known for her Anne of Green Gables series, wrote a newspaper column for the *Halifax Daily Echo* along with other nonfiction work, which was republished in 2018 as part of the collection *A Name for Herself: Selected Writings, 1891-1917*.[7] Mohawk poet Tekahionwake (1861-1913), or by her English name, E. Pauline Johnson, published in the newspapers of her time as well. Her essay "A Strong Race Opinion: On the Indian Girl in Modern Fiction," which originally appeared in the Toronto *Sunday Globe*, 22 May 1892, has been anthologized many times since, and remains as meaningful and relevant today as in 1892 for its indictment of stereotypical representations of Indigenous women as undifferentiated "Indian maidens." One could also cite essays by writers Edith Maud Eaton (1865-1914), publishing under the pen name Sui Sin Far in a nod to her Chinese heritage; French Canada's Laure Conan, pseudonym for Marie-Louise-Félicité Angers (1845-1924); Emily Carr (1871-1945), Nellie McClung (1873-1951), and others of their generation who wrote essays and saw them published in print. More writers followed these early poet- and novelist-essayists, coming to the fore in the 1950s-1970s—Margaret Laurence, Adele Wiseman, Jane Rule, Miriam Waddington, Phyllis Webb, and P.K. Page, or in Quebec, Simonne Monet-Chartrand, Marcelle Brisson, Louky Bersianik (née Lucile Durant), Suzanne Lamy, Madeleine Ouellette-Michalska, Michèle Lalonde, and Madeleine Gagnon. In addition to their novels, poetry, or short stories, these women wrote and published essays—individually, but also for my purposes here, in collections.

Outside the scope of this study but worthy of note are the countless occasional, uncollected essays written by women

---

7   Edited by Benjamin Lefebvre, *A Name for Herself: Selected Writings, 1891-1917* (2018) includes Montgomery's newspaper column "Around the Table," which appeared under the pseudonym "Cynthia" from 28 September 1901 to 26 May 1902.

poets and novelists in Canada and Quebec, as well as excellent anthologies of essays assembled by women writers, such as Syilx Okanagan author Jeannette Armstrong's *Looking at the Words of our People* (1993), Mikeda Silvera's *The Other Woman* (1995), or Smaro Kamboureli's *Making a Difference* (1996). There is also a vast body of work by women whose primary mode of writing is nonfiction—writers and journalists like Myrna Kostash, Charlotte Gray, Naomi Klein, or in Quebec, Lysiane Gagnon, Hélène Pedneault, or Nathalie Petrowski.

Of further note is a sizeable body of secondary literature about essay writing. In Quebec, the essay has been the subject of numerous scholarly studies (Vigneault 1980, 1994; Belleau 1985, 1987; Przychodzen 1993; Gauvin 1994). In English Canada, Lynch and Rampton's *The Canadian Essay* (1991) presents twenty essays, of which six by women, preceded by a short but useful historical introduction. Sean Armstrong's *Far and Wide: Essays in Canada* (1995) compiles forty essays, eighteen by women, in five thematic groups. While both collections include essays by Canadian women, neither considers their essays in depth.

Studies of individual Canadian women writers' works typically focus on their novels, short stories, or poetry, with possible passing reference to their writing as essayists, or to their essays as secondary contexts for their works of fiction. By way of exception, Smaro Kamboureli's "Writer as Critic" series for NeWest Press is dedicated to essay writing by Canadian writers. The series features collections by women and men alike: Di Brandt, Lee Maracle, Daphne Marlatt, Erin Moure, Aritha van Herk, Phyllis Webb; Douglas Barbour, George Bowering, Frank Davey, Stan Dragland, Roy Miki, Stephen Scobie, Fred Wah. It is the former—Canadian women writers' essay writing—that is my interest in *Her Own Thinker*.

Concepts and History

I use the word essay—*essai* in French—but other designations circulate for the focus of this study. In French, an *essai* can be short or long, even book-length. The latter is often structured around a key organizing topic, as in Atwood's *Payback: Debt and the Shadow Side of Wealth* (2008) or Dionne Brand's *A Map to the Door of No Return: Notes to Belonging* (2001), rather than a collection of differently focussed essays. In English, the word essay typically denotes a relatively short piece of writing, with longer texts identified as creative nonfiction or literary nonfiction. Literary nonfiction has been described as "mixed genre" writing, encompassing biography, memoir, travel, adventure, sociology, anthropology, and so on. In *Going Some Place: creative non-fiction across the prairies* (2000), Lynne van Luven includes as creative nonfiction "poetic personal journals, meditations, memoirs, activist personal reportage, autobiography, personal essays on being an outsider, historical and literary travelogues, tributes to a particular person, celebrations of a distinctive place, and explorations of the past" (ii). For Betsy Warland, creative nonfiction refers to "all non-fiction and mixed genre writing shaped by literary sensibilities, devices and strategies" (*Breathing the Page: Reading the Act of Writing*, Author's Note, np). Terms such as these appear in the relatively rare reviews that essay writing by Canadian and Quebec women has elicited.

Some women essayists devise their own terms—Aritha van Herk's *cryptofrictions*, Nicole Brossard's *fiction-theory*, Bronwen Wallace's "arguments with the world," Carol Shields's "dropped threads," Daphne Marlatt's "musings with mother tongue," Betsy Warland's "concept essays," Dionne Brand's "essay poems," Lee Maracle's "oratory turned-essay," Lola Lemire Tostevin's "soundings," Margaret Atwood's "occasional pieces," and so on.[8] Written by Canadian and Quebec women novelists and poets, the essay is an innovative, multifaceted form of writing that closer examination reveals to be significant both in substance and size. In turning to the essay, Canadian women writers tapped traditional approaches to the genre and shaped a unique and powerful practice of their own.

Montaigne, Bacon: two models of essay writing

In Western literary history and convention, the essay genre has been largely associated with men, and with two different traditions tracing back to the 16th century, one by Michel de Montaigne in France, the other by Francis Bacon in England. Canadian women writers have taken both traditional and innovative approaches in their practice of the genre.

The essay genre has been the subject of extensive investigation by numerous distinguished international and national scholars alike. Critics such as Graham Good (*The Observing Self: Rediscovering the Essay,* 1988), Alexander Butrym (*Essays on the Essay: Redefining the Genre,* 1989), John McCarthy (*Crossing Boundaries: A Theory and History of Essay Writing in German, 1680-1815,* 1989), Ruth-Ellen Boetcher Joeres and Elizabeth Mittman (*The Politics of the Essay: Feminist Perspectives,* 1993),

---

8   Aritha van Herk's *cryptofrictions* (*InVisible Ink: crypto-frictions,* 1991), Nicole Brossard's *fiction-theory* (*La Lettre aérienne,* 1985), Bronwen Wallace's "arguments with the world" (*Arguments with the World,* 1992), Carol Shields's "dropped threads" (*Dropped Threads,* 2001), Daphne Marlatt's "musings with mother tongue" (*Readings from the Labyrinth,* 1998), Betsy Warland's "concept essays" (*Breathing the Page,* 2010), Dionne Brand's "essay poems" (*The Blue Clerk,* 2018*),* Lee Maracle's "oratory turned-essay" (*Memory Serves,* 2015), Lola Lemire Tostevin's "soundings" (*At the Risk of Sounding: Essays,* 2015).

and Cristina Kirklighter (*Traversing the Democratic Borders of the Essay,* 2002), among others, have provided detailed analyses of the essay as established by and developed since the time of Montaigne and Bacon. [9]

The essay traces back to the 1580 publication of Michel de Montaigne's *Essais.* Unlike the prevailing writing practices of his time, the French Renaissance writer took a personal approach to expressing thoughts and feelings on a wide range of topics, from human nature and life experiences, to political, social, and religious mores of the day, including European colonization of the Americas, which he deplored. The personal nature of this writing was matched by a more informal form and style, which combined facts and imaginative speculation in an unconventional departure from linear argumentation. The Montaigne essay was a more free-form open-ended exploration of thought and feeling in which writing was a substantive feature in itself and did not have to bring "closure" to a subject. Innovative for its time, the Montaigne-style essay has been seen by some writers as a freethinking, even liberating form of writing.

Where the emphasis of Montaigne's essays was on personal experience and process, Francis Bacon's *Essays* (1597) were more utilitarian in purpose, infused with facts and public purpose, and motivated towards a concrete conclusion and intentional action. Bacon eschewed the personal for the factual, presenting empirical and scientific observations of the world, and advice and guidance to readers in a purposeful, practical, and public way. The Bacon essay focused on observable facts to help

---

9 I provide an overview of this scholarship in an early exploration of essay writing by Canadian women writers, using the example of novelist Carol Shields's essays: "(Es)saying It Her Way: Carol Shields as Essayist" (Verduyn, 2007).

readers understand their circumstances and make practical decisions. "Bacon's essays were meant to reach a public audience that would act on his word," Cristina Kirklighter remarks; "[Their] didactic nature ... moves away from the inconclusive skepticism that pervades Montaigne's form" (10). Bacon's essays could be considered to have more potential for political impact than the more personal character of Montaigne's writings.

In sum, the French style essay might be described as personal, intimate, informal, or conversational, while the English essay could be characterized as impersonal, objective, methodical, rational, and pedagogic (Verduyn 2007, 2012, 2013). It bears noting that neither Montaigne nor Bacon themselves were bound by these delineations[10] and that essayists have not restricted their practice to these historical forms. In their essay writing, Canadian women poets and novelists have not overly concerned themselves with historical distinctions between French and English traditions, between Montaigne's and Bacon's practices of the essay. They have combined elements of each in a development of the genre to meet personal and political needs.

The essay has evolved and taken on different forms since the times of Montaigne and Bacon. Graham Good (1988) traces the genre's development "in the direction of formlessness" (1),

---

10 As I noted in "(Es)saying It Her Way: Carol Shields as Essayist" (Verduyn, 2007), Montaigne drew on empirical evidence and observation to argue the merits of experience. Similarly, Bacon resisted oppressive literary traditions; his essays were based on objective study and not the religious authority that formed the basis for claims about moral conduct in earlier eras (Good, *The Observing Self*, 46). At bottom, both essayists were motivated by and interested in knowledge that was derived from experience and observation rather than from pre-ordained doctrine.

beyond rules of genre and tradition toward an openness and freedom of practice as even a "non genre" or an "anti-genre." T.W. Adorno saw "the essay's freedom from specialization and genre boundaries as one way to destabilize [these] hierarchical divisions" (Kirklighter, 3). In Dobrée's assessment the essay is "the most adaptable of all forms" (47) and in Good's view it is a highly "democratic" genre (186), accessible to historically "non-traditional" writers including women and minorities.

Ruth-Ellen Boetcher Joeres and Elizabeth Mittman challenge this perspective in *The Politics of the Essay: Feminist Perspectives* (1993). For the first three hundred years of its existence as a genre, they point out, the essay was considered out of bounds for the woman writer and her concerns, even though the genre itself has been ascribed "feminine" qualities:

> Whereas essayists, the actors and agents, are almost always defined very clearly as "masculine," the essay itself is placed over and over again into a space that is uncannily feminine, at least as the qualities adhering to the "feminine" have been defined since the eighteenth century. Essays are called a mixture of anecdote, description, and opinion. Essays are said to focus on a little world, on details. Essays seem, according to Theodor Adorno, to form patterns of relationships "rather than a straight line of necessary consequences ..." Essays stress process rather than product.
>
> (*The Politics of the Essay: Feminist Perspectives*, 19-20)

Joeres and Mittman describe the essay's progress "from the genteel world of French aristocracy ... into the hands of women writers, many of them ardent and committed feminists" (17). This is an apt characterization of Canadian women writer-essayists of the postwar period. They articulated their conviction in the power of language and writing to effect social change. They demonstrated this as much through their essay writing as through their fiction and poetry. "It is no accident that the essay became an important genre for women in the last few decades," Lola Lemire Tostevin observed. "Through feminist awareness many women writers faced the realization that previously held assumptions—whether universal, social or cultural—were changing ... there were so many new ideas being tossed about that many of us felt we needed another genre to help us clarify the nature of our enquiries, to help us formulate and record our individual and collective ideas" (*Subject to Criticism: Essays,* 9). For Joeres and Mittman the essay is "perfectly designed for feminist projects" (20):

> To choose deliberately the form of the essay is to step away from a path of obedient submission to the academic world ... it is to say that we value the form in which we present our thoughts as much as we do their content. It is to say that we do not choose to imitate everything the male university has taught us and has told us is correct. It is to assert ourselves. It is to acknowledge that we are above all determined to connect with each other, with an audience, and to communicate with that audience. And on a practical level, it is to select a form that brings us closer to fulfilling the feminist aim of reaching and connecting with a widely based audience. (20)

If the feminist essay did not reach quite as widely based an audience as Joeres and Mittman envisioned, the genre nonetheless presented a fertile form for women writers to reconsider, reshape, and use for their own purposes and expressions of thought and ideas about the world, their circumstances, and their experiences.

In *Writers as Public Intellectuals,* Odile Heynders (2016) explores the different ways in which writers comment on the political, social, and cultural contexts in which they write. For Heynders, who indicates that the adjective "public" was originally an American addition (4), this context is Europe. *Her Own Thinker* makes the case for women writers in the context of Canada. Heynders shares Baert and Shipman's distinction between the public intellectual and the intellectual: "The *public intellectual* addresses an audience beyond intellectual peers, whereas the *intellectual* mainly interacts with other intellectuals" (4, italics in original). Heynders's aim is "to show that authors performing the role of public intellectual discuss ideas and opinions regarding society, while using literary strategies and devices" (20).

There is a historical link between the public intellectual and writers, though it is one that has but rarely been applied to women, let alone to women's essay writing. Heynders notes ruefully that "the female intellectual is time and again neglected and even considered non-existent" (55) and offers two explanations for this:

> First, the gender bias in society has overlooked the activities and output of female intellectuals, focusing on the dominance of the male public lecturers, commentators and writers. Second, there seems to be a certain unwillingness of women to participate in the conversation about intellectuals, and to perform the role of the intellectual appearing in the media as a convinced, provocative and encouraging speaker. This, it is argued by some theorists, has mainly to do with an aversion to universality – the Julien Benda position ... and to the role of the intellectual as educator or as someone fighting down opponents, while being hard, outspoken and radical. (55-56)

Heynders introduces the concept of "public private voice" (52) to express the "multi-perspectiveness" that she discerns in essay writing by women writers and how it uses their personal histories to prompt readers to think of their own responsibility. She further clarifies that "the public private voice ... entails the critical representation and encapsulation ... of several voices, that is: of ideas, expressions and personal feelings of several individuals worded in specific discourses and idioms. The public intellectual can speak, so to say, with a double tongue" (57). Double- and/or multi-vocality and perspectives describe a number of collections in *Her Own Thinker*, Margaret Atwood's *Negotiating with the Dead: A Writer on Writing,* Phyllis Webb's "multi-person" essayist in *Nothing but Brush Strokes,* and Lee Maracle's *Memory Serves,* among others.

The subject of the public intellectual has been and continues to be the focus of extensive critical discussion. It is taken up in depth in books by international scholars such as Julien Benda (*The Treason of the Intellectuals,*1928), Russell Jacoby (*The Last Intellectuals,* 1987), Edward Saïd (*Representations of the Intellectual,* 1994), Richard Posner (*Public Intellectuals: A Study of Decline,* 2002), Frank Furedi (*Where Have All the Intellectuals Gone?* 2004), among others.[11] In Canada, articles and essays by Michael Ignatieff (1997), Neil McLaughlin (2011), Mark Kingwell (2012), Kenneth Dewar (2020), and the contributors to a collection edited by Nelson Wiseman, *The Public Intellectual in Canada* (2013), have explored the subject. Writing about—let alone speaking as—the public intellectual has been

---

11 For example, Habermas (1962), Gramsci (1971), Foucault (1972), Debray (1981), Bauman (1987), Bourdieu (1991), Saïd (1996), Melzer et al. (2003), Collini (2006), Misztal (2007), Berman (2010), Lacroix and Nicolaidis (2010), Baert and Booth (2012), Baert and Shipman (2013).

predominantly the purview of men.[12] Wiseman's collection includes only four women: Sylvia Bashevkin, Janice Gross Stein,
Maude Barlow, and Margaret Somerville. An earlier investigation into the public intellectual in Canada conducted by the
National Post (26 October 2005) features twenty-two individuals of whom, again, there are only four women: Margaret
Atwood, Naomi Klein, Irshad Manji, and Margaret MacMillan.
Canadian women have rarely figured on lists of public intellectuals, as Wiseman acknowledges. More noticeable yet is the
absence from such lists of members of Canada's racialized communities. "The faces and preoccupations of Canada's public intellectuals," Wiseman admits, "have not changed as rapidly as
have the faces and concerns of Canada's evolving society" (245).
The under-recognition of Canadian women writers as essayists
is part and parcel of their absence from roll calls of the country's
public intellectuals.

Background to the present

Confronting this lacuna, two conferences—"Discourse and Dynamics: Canadian Women as Public Intellectuals" (2014) and
"Speaking Her Mind: Canadian Women and Public Presence"
(2016)— that Aritha van Herk and I organized highlighted the
intellectual work and contributions to public discourse that
Canadian women have made and continue to make in a wide

---

12 CBC Radio's Massey Lecture series, for example, has featured more men
    than women speakers. While a woman gave the first lecture series—
    Barbara Bard in 1961—she was followed by only one woman, Jane Jacobs
    in 1979, in the period 1961 to 1981. Between 1981 and 2001 there were
    15 men versus 4 women lecturers. The period 2002-2022 saw a better
    balance with 12 men and 9 women lecturers.

range of fields, from aerospace engineering to urban renewal. Conference participants, among them scientists, journalists, social workers, musicians, writers, and academics, expressed broader and more inclusive understandings of the work generally attributed to public intellectuals. They spoke of desire for making an impact on unequal social, legal, political, economic, or cultural situations, and for contributing to knowledge, discourse, and social change, rather than for recognition or lofty titles as public intellectuals. The conferences produced the co-edited collection of essays "*HEAR! HEaR! Voices of Canadian Women.*" An online publication,[13] this collection features many different views of Canadian women from across the country and its diverse cultural communities. Their voices may be "heard" in essays and excerpts from the conference discussions of public intellectualism, as considered by Margaret Atwood, Sylvia Bashevkin, Françoise Baylis, Cherish Violet Blood (Blackfoot), Dionne Brand, Nicole Brossard, Measha Brueggergosman, Rita Shelton Deverell, Denise Donlon, Mary Eberts, Charlotte Gray, Shari Graydon, Sylvia Hamilton, Smaro Kamboureli, Antonia Maioni, Lee Maracle (Stó:lō), Lorna Marsden, Judy Rebick, Natalie Panek, Francine Pelletier, Naomi Sayers (Ojibwe), Janice Gross Stein, Fibbie Tatti (Dene), Lori Turnbull, and Sheila Watt-Cloutier (Inuit).[14]

---

13 The collection is available at https://mta.cairnrepo.org/islandora/object/mta%3A27096

14 Academic essays by Bridgette Brown, Diana Brydon, Carole Gerson, Sarah Galletly, Marjorie Johnstone, Neil McLaughlin, Iga Mergler, Mélanie Méthot, Heather Milne, Erin Ramlo, Sarah Spear, and Wendy Robbins, about, among others, Samantha Nutt, Lisa Robertson, Pauline Johnson, Gwethalyn Graham, Idola Saint-Jean and Flora MacDonald Denison, Emily Murphy and Alice Jane Jamieson, E. Maud Graham, Florence Randal, Margaret Gould, Marian Engel, and Margaret Laurence.

Her Own Thinker sharpens the focus on this multidisciplinary host of Canadian women to spotlight women writers whose body of work includes collections of essays. The broader study and theoretical debates about the public intellectual is not the project in *Her Own Thinker*. Rather, it appraises the importance of Canadian women writers' essay collections and their contributions to Canada's intellectual enterprise and cultural record. That stated, Heynders's identification of the traits of "sensitivity, anticipation, the thinking through of alternatives, imagination and courage" as the "main conditions for taking up the role of the public intellectual" (11) describes the work of many Canadian and Quebec women essayists, as closer reading will show. The idea of the intellectual, public or otherwise, then, forms part of *Her Own Thinker*. However, its primary goal is to explore and weigh—as in the Latin root of the word, *exigere,* to weigh or measure—"essaying" by Canadian women writers, in particular those better known as novelists, poets, or short story authors, whose *oeuvre* includes published collections of essays.

Her Own Thinker works at the intersection of the essay's twin potentials and attractions. The genre's dialectical form has offered women writers an effective instrument of social, feminist articulation. The genre presents an invigorating, inventive means for exploring topics and expressing views in nonfiction form. In essence, the essay genre has been and continues to be a form for writers both to address substantive social and political issues and to develop new literary forms. As will be seen throughout this study, Canadian women writers have used the essay form purposefully and creatively to engage society and to reconstruct women's ways of articulation.

Margaret Laurence's collection of essays *Heart of a Stranger* (1976) is an early illustration of this dual role and twofold function. With respect to substantive issues, Laurence's experiences in Africa, in British Somaliland 1950-1952 and in Ghana 1953-1957, provided her with perspectives that anticipated postcolonial cultural critique that subsequently emerged only later in the century. These perspectives eventually worked their way into her creative writing. But they first appeared in essay format, as she observed in her essay "The Poem and the Spear":

> I wrote this essay for my own interest in 1964, just after the publication of *The Stone Angel*, when I could not yet get back to doing any fiction … I was making some attempt … to understand the plight of a tribal people faced with imperialist opponents who do not possess superior values, but who have greater material resources and more efficient weapons of killing. A long time later, this same theme came into my novel, *The Diviners*, in the portions which deal with the Highland clans and with the prairie Métis.
>
> (*Heart of a Stranger*, 44)

Laurence examined a variety of significant topics using the essay form, from colonialism and imperialism to the environment and nuclear disarmament; from equality and justice for women to the analysis of disadvantaged groups in society.

An equally weighty list of topics appears throughout essay writing by Canadian and Quebec novelists, poets, and short story writers. In her collections, Margaret Atwood has dealt with global warming, Sharia law, Canada-U.S. free trade, Canada's cultural policy and foreign policy, Canadian identity, the North, and debt. Dionne Brand, M. NourbeSe Philip, and Himani Bannerji have addressed issues of racism, Canadian multiculturalism, identity, and belonging. Bronwen Wallace's *Arguments with the World* (1992) engages the issues of domestic violence, social injustice, power, and politics. In various combinations, these topics have been expertly explored in essays by Lee Maracle, Nicole Brossard, and Di Brandt among others. For them, the essay genre has served and continues to serve a twofold purpose as witness to the world and as a form for continued exploration of writing itself. "Writers are eye-witnesses, I-witnesses," Margaret Atwood reflected in "On Being a 'Woman Writer,'" *Second Words: Selected Critical Prose 1960-1982,* 203).

"The essay is an act of personal witness," Graham Good states in *The Observing Self: Rediscovering the Essay* (1988); "The essay is at once the *in*scription of a self and the *de*scription of an object" (23). Canadian women poets and novelists have been drawn to this function of the genre, and to how the form has provided them with opportunities to be experimental in their craft. Witnessing, writing, and reflecting on writing are recurring themes throughout *Her Own Thinker.* Canadian women writers' essay work in this regard has been highly innovative. The essay form has been used to cross borders between genres, between the personal and the political, the public and the private. It has incorporated memoir and photographs, poetry and philosophy, and blended fiction with critical writing. Aritha van Herk's essay "Blurring Genres: Fictioneer as Ficto-Critic" (*In Visible Ink*, 1991) captures and expresses what many Canadian women writers achieve in their essay writing: a combination of fiction and criticism.

The expansive, experimental, hybrid nature of essay writing by Canadian women writers readily exceeds the familiar definitional sense or terrain of the "essay," which critics agree is a difficult genre to define (Scholes and Klaus, 1969; Good, 1988; Butrym, 1989; McCarthy, 1989; Joeres and Mittman, 1993; Kirklighter, 2002). For McCarthy (1989), the essay is an "enigmatic and elusive genre which seems to defy definition" (*Crossing Boundaries*, ix), associated as it is with "the facetious, the trivial, and the anecdotal on the one hand and with the learned treatise and useful, effective expository writing on the other" (Butrym, *Essays on the Essay*, 4). Butrym comments on the essay's ability to "draw us by indirection out of ourselves," a trait that permits individuals to "speak to each other across the boundaries of our narrower selves" (*Essays on the Essay*, 1).

Notwithstanding its malleable, innovative form, practitioners of the essay—in Canada and elsewhere—have seen it to be a highly disciplined enterprise; "its freedom from conventionalized form and thought," Scholes and Klaus (*Elements of the Essay*, 1969) observe, might create a sense of the essay as a "free-for-all form of writing" (166). In fact, however, the essay "calls for different ways of writing and different ways of reading" (173). It is not to be confused with article or theme writing, Scholes and Klaus emphasize; it "calls for using and understanding language as a symbolic form of action" (173).

Her Own Thinker explores how Canadian women writers have used the essay genre as a substantial instrument of social articulation and a means to call for purposeful action as well as ways to explore new and appropriate forms of writing to these ends. The essay format has been a valuable means for Canadian women writers, and their communities, to address substantive social and political issues as well as to develop new literary forms.

The Essay as Experiment: Try, try, and try again!

Discussion of the essay often plays upon the word itself and its various associations in English and French. To write an essay—to have a say. *Essayer*—to try, to attempt. *Essai*: a try, an attempt. There is another French word for a "try" or an "attempt"—*une tentative*—which Phyllis Webb cleverly considers in the introduction to her 1995 collection of essays *Nothing but Brush Strokes*. In its English pronunciation, the word tentative summons notions of uncertainty or hesitancy though not necessarily in a negative sense. Tentative could evoke a positive conceptual sense as "exploratory" or as "working toward" (insight or understanding, for example), finding, even feeling, one's way, through the dark toward the light.

These notions and metaphors recur with striking frequency in the reflections on essay writing offered by the women writers included in this volume. Of her essays in *Spaces like Stairs* (1989), Gail Scott comments that they do not make "*firm* [emphasis added] statements about writing in-the-feminine. They are, simply, (and not so simply) the story of a writer's journey among the literary, theoretical, political signposts of a certain period (the late 70s and 80s) in a certain place (Quebec)" (10-11).

For Erin Moure in *My Beloved Wager* (2009), the essay is "not pronouncement but the fragile terrain of a practice, an *essai* or *try* articulated from inside the work of poetry. Essaying is part of the work of poetry, part of my practice of writing and reading it," she states (10, emphases in the original). The essay "surges as a form proper to poetry" Moure further proposes (263), a practice of writing that for her and her contemporaries is "influenced by feminism and has a stake in it" (11). Poetry is integral to Di Brandt's critical writing (*Dancing Naked*, 114) and to that of Kristjana Gunnars, Betsy Warland, and Dionne Brand, among others whose essay writing could be described as Moure describes hers—as "moving (trying, leaning) toward … dislodging the invisible seams that cover up how language works to support dominant order" ("Breaking Boundaries:

Writing as Social Practice, or Attentiveness," *My Beloved Wager*, 56). This description recalls Gail Scott's thoughts above, as for her, writing is about "dislocating thinking" (Moyes, 227) and the essay form is "the way to write our new awareness into transformed ideology" (Gail Scott, *Spaces Like Stairs*, 109).

For Lola Lemire Tostevin, feminist writers' turn to the essay form was "being pulled into unexplored territory, our writings often translated from the unknown as we attempted to redefine the boundaries between and beyond cultural and gender differences … [The essay offered] a critical genre [and] a vehicle through which we can explore the different facets of new territory while creating new levels of understanding" (*Subject to Criticism,* 9-10). In their practice of the essay Canadian and Quebec women writers began "to cross genres, interweave different levels of discourse," Tostevin writes: "The essay was suddenly invaded by poems, personal anecdotes, autobiographical fragments. Abstract and master concepts were displaced" (10).

Canadian and Quebec women writers developed a "new sense of what the essay is," Gail Scott prefaces her collection *Spaces like Stairs*: "a form deriving not only from the ideological, but also, the self-reflexive and the fictional. In other words, a text where the everyday, the political, the cultural meet, risking syntax in the process of positing and dissolving 'meaning' (notably the traces of male dominance), and the (traditional female) subject" (*Spaces like Stairs*, 10). Risk, and the benefits and breakthroughs that can come of risk, recurs as a theme in essays by Canadian women writers.

Risk and political expression/practice

In her Preface to *La Lettre aérienne/The Aerial letter* (1985/1988), Brossard declares:

I believe there's only one explanation for all of these texts [essays]: my desire and my will to understand patriarchal reality and how it works, not for its own sake, but for its tragic consequences in the lives of women, in the life of the spirit. Ten years of anger, revolt, certitude, and conviction are in *The Aerial Letter*; ten years of fighting against that screen which stands in the way of women's energy, identity, and creativity. (35)

In a similar observation of Dionne Brand's extended essay *A Map to the Door of No Return* (2001), Elisabeth Harvor (2001) remarks "there's nothing tentative about how she writes. Her writing is swift, declarative"; the book is "part literary exegesis, part notebook, part history lesson, part war reportage, part tirade." Donna Bailey Nurse (1992) notes the outspoken nature of M. NourbeSe Philip's *Frontiers: Essays and Writings on Racism and Culture* (1992), while Lee Maracle is forthright in *I Am Woman* (1988) that her point of view is "couched not so carefully" (vii) in the essays that make up her collection: "The text is an emotional one, free of the humour and joy that punctuated the struggle for being which this book represents. I do not apologize for that" (viii). Like Maracle, other women writers in *Her Own Thinker* have turned to the essay to "have a say" in a public way, including those in the collection *Luminous Ink: Writers on Writing in Canada* (2018)[15] who deal directly with

---

15   These women writers include Eden Robinson (Haisla Heiltsuk), Lisa Moore, Madeleine Thien, Marie Hélène Poitras, Sheila Fischman, Hiromi Goto, Heather O'Neill, Nicole Brossard, Judith Thompson, Margaret Atwood, Lee Maracle, Pascale Quiviger, Rita Wong, Camilla Gibb, Leanne Betasamosake Simpson.

lives being lived after and despite Contact; with Canada's history—the colonial past that haunts and still choreographs social relations in the present; with considerations of personal, familial, and communal relations—[with] the unsettling, the unresolvable, the unforgivable.

(*Luminous Ink: Writers on Writing in Canada*, xiv)

"The provocation of these essays," co-editors Tessa McWatt, Rabindranath Maharaj, and Dionne Brand declare, "is that the reader is invited, compelled, to reimagine Canada" (*Luminous Ink: Writers on Writing in Canada,* xv). This is the provocation of essays discussed throughout *Her Own Thinker.*

This study explores not only how women writers set out to reimagine "reality," and Canada as part of it, but also how boldly they do so, as highly intelligent, cultivated commentators, to use Zailig Pollock's description of poet P.K. Page as essayist (*The Filled Pen*, xiv). Pollock notes the role of imagination in Page's essays, which he sees as a sort of "autobiography of the imagination" (xiii), blending the personal and universal (xv). An essay could be personal yet connected to community and beyond; it could have public relevance and at the same time be open-ended. "An essay is a perpetual work-in-progress," Gail Scott states; "I like the immediacy of this: the way an essay (even more than fiction) precisely intersects the period in which it is written. The way it is marked, at a given moment, by its context, its community, both of which are also part of how the writer is and how she changes over time" (Scott, *Spaces like Stairs*, 9).

In their essay practice, Canadian and Quebec women writers have integrated elements of both historical traditions of the genre. Their "essaying" exemplifies the Montaigne tradition without forgoing the declarative, public nature of the Bacon tradition. In subsequent chapters, *Her Own Thinker* presents and explores how Canadian women writers use the essay format to find their voice and have a say, whether in essays that engaged in social issues, developed new forms of language and articulation, or fused both approaches.

CHAPTER II

Writing With Intent

> *As a poet who writes rhetorical essays, I appreciate the public*
> *voice that the craft requires, a way of articulating a clear*
> *position on events and issues. As a political person who writes*
> *poetry, I know the need for the intimate, inner argument that*
> *is the centre of the poem.*
> —Bronwen Wallace, *Arguments with the World* (6)

> *I had to engage through my writing with events taking place*
> *around me.*
> —M. NourbeSe Philip, *Bla_k* (25)

As a genre for expressing personal and political perspectives on
issues and events, the essay presented Canadian women writers
with the possibility of more public engagement than a poem or
novel might conventionally offer. This is how the essay served
Canadian women writing in the 1960s-1970s—by offering
them an influential way to engage and transform the world.
This was a period in Canada when the critical and literary scene
was still largely dominated by men's voices. "Writing in the
1960s was pretty much a guy thing, in Canada as elsewhere,"
Atwood summed up the reality of the times ("Introduction to
Ground Works," *Moving Targets,* 298). Looking back to that
era, this was not for lack of women's views on issues of the day,
as readily attested by collections of essays by Adele Wiseman,
Margaret Laurence, Jane Rule, Miriam Waddington, Mavis
Gallant, Phyllis Webb, P.K. Page, and Margaret Atwood. These

collections make eminently clear that they had substantial thinking of their own to share, both about the world in general and about the Canada in which they were trying to make a living as writers.

This chapter explores what was a formative period in the evolution of women's writing in Canada. It was a period in which Canadian women writers were running uphill, as the literary landscape tilted against them personally or professionally. In response, their essay writing tended to be at once personal and passionate and articulated in the more straightforward language of their generation. Unlike subsequent eras, the language and writing styles that these writers used were relatively traditional—in effect, in tune with the realities and the politics of the day. What was new and different, if not radically innovative, was the use of the essay form to express in no uncertain terms their sense of, and engagement with, the social issues that they faced, felt, and feared in daily life in their personal and community worlds.

Adele Wiseman—*Memoirs of a Book Molesting Childhood and Other Essays*

Adele Wiseman's provocatively titled collection of essays is an example *par excellence* of essay writing by women of her generation, those born like her after the First World War during the 1920s and 1930s, whose fiction works appeared largely during the 1960s and 1970s. Wiseman's nonfiction *Memoirs of a Book Molesting Childhood and Other Essays* (*Memoirs*), published in 1987, illustrates both the foresight and insight that Canadian women writers demonstrated in identifying issues, many of which remain pressing today, that they chose to write about in essay form.

"As fiction writers, witnesses, expressers, instruments of our culture," Wiseman wrote, "we took the creative leap into the issues of our age which others still had not defined clearly as issues, and which they have since begun to use our fiction to help them understand" (*Memoirs*, 88). The "we" Wiseman refers to here includes Alice Munro, Marian Engel, Margaret Atwood, Helen Weinzweig, Joyce Marshall, Rachel Wyatt, Sylvia Fraser, Mavis Gallant, Betty Lambert, Jane Rule, and Audrey Thomas (*Memoirs*, 87). "I could go on," Wiseman stated; "the interesting thing is that many of these writers were not writing under the banner of 'feminism'; indeed the feminist movement had not yet come into being when Margaret Laurence and I began to write" (*Memoirs*, 87-88). [16]

It is fascinating to re-encounter Adele Wiseman through her essay writing. She is perhaps best known today for her remarkable novel *Crackpot* (1974). Her first novel, *The Sacrifice*, was published even earlier in 1956 and won the Governor General's Award. Wiseman also wrote plays and children's stories. But it is her nonfiction essay writing that is in focus here.

Before *Memoirs of a Book Molesting Childhood,* Wiseman published the nonfiction book, *Old Woman at Play* (1978), a publication as unique as its subject. The title refers to Wiseman's mother, Chaika (née Rosenberg) Wiseman. A Jewish immigrant from Ukraine to Winnipeg, Chaika made a living from sewing. She managed to make play out of toil by turning scraps of cloth and other materials—from buttons to fish bones—into

---

16 I also cite Wiseman's observation here (*Memoirs,* 87-88) in the introduction to the special issue of *SCL/ELC: Studies in Canadian Literature/Etudes en littérature canadienne* (Verduyn, 2019) that was the outcome of the conference *Resurfacing: Canadian Women Writers of 1970s Canada* (26-28 April 2018), one of three conferences related to this essay project.

rag dolls for children. *Old Woman at Play* was Wiseman's tribute to her mother and the artistry of her doll-making. It is also a broader philosophical investigation into creativity and life. In understanding her mother's doll-making, Wiseman presents a far larger vision of how to look at the world with different eyes, to, in effect, "unlearn," as is said today of the need to recognize and respect difference.

> UNLESSON:
>
> Who has not heard of the hands of the artist? Long, slim, sensitive hands, of course. (...) My mother's hands are chubby and small, her fingertips are needle-toughened and sometimes painfully cracked. But they sew on with unselfconscious skill. And from them a world emerges, my mother's world. For if you're lucky, as I think my mother has been lucky, at some time during the indenture of your lifetime, nature may give you the freedom, within your limited means, to transform your means, the freedom to create. What is freedom?
>
> (*Old Woman at Play,* 24-25)

At first glance, *Old Woman at Play* is highly personal in character. But Wiseman's writing was also highly "public" in its purpose.

In *The Force of Vocation: The Literary Career of Adele Wiseman* (2006), Ruth Panofsky presents the novelist as a "public author," in keeping with James West's definition: a "serious literary artist who meant also to reach a large audience through the publishing apparatus of the time and who wanted to earn a living by writing" (5). Panofsky broadens and assesses the scope of Wiseman's career by focusing on the author as an active agent of her own artistic and literary career, negotiating with publishers (ix) and with the ins and out of publishing (xiii).

In *Her Own Thinker*, the focus is on Wiseman as essayist and on the issues she chose to address in the collection *Memoirs of a Book Molesting Childhood*. Many of these were topics that she explored in her fiction as well: the experience of immigrants in Canada, particularly those of Jewish heritage; the economic struggles of society's marginalized; and the creative life and the challenges it presented for women. In her essays as in her fiction, Wiseman wrote about issues well ahead of society's broader attention to them. Two issues that stand out by way of example are the environment and Indigenous knowledge.

Both subjects are addressed in a feisty essay that Wiseman wrote upon being invited to speak at a 1986 Canadian Studies conference in France at the University of Dijon. The topic of the conference was "Man and the Forest," the gendered nature of which, if not untypical even in the 1980s, Wiseman queried, proposing "Man, Woman, and the Forest" as a minimally better option, and choosing for her own essay the title "And the Forest?"

Wiseman is clever and humorously self-deprecating in the essay as she muses on just how she, a fiction writer without formal academic credentials, could possibly contribute to a scholarly conference. Behind the self-deprecating humour, however, is a commanding commentary on environmental damage, in particular damage to forests, and the impact of this damage for Indigenous communities. "It is simply not possible to have the degree of innocence anymore," Wiseman declares, "about who was doing what to whom, in the Canadian bush" (*Memoirs*, 136). Forests are being mowed down "because we have given over the power to do so" and because "while it lasts it's a good cash crop for the despoilers." But, she points out, using terms of her time, "the logging companies are harvesting the sacred ancient forests of the Haida Indians on the Queen Charlotte Islands" (*Memoirs*, 139).

Like her friend and contemporary Margaret Laurence, Wiseman wrote with early awareness about the conditions endured by Indigenous people in Canada. Consultations with her "living footnotes," as she dubbed the various Canadian writers with whom she spoke about her conference paper, suggested that Canadians were broadly indifferent to the fate of forests and to Indigenous lives. This indifference, Wiseman declared, "is a tacit consent to their destruction, as it has been to the destruction of the Indians who originally lived in symbiosis with them [the forests]" (*Memoirs*, 143).

> We have laid claim to the natural kingdom and yet we deny responsibility and turn aside as the axes ring out. It is not a question any longer of how we regard our forests, or whether our bias is scientific or religious, pragmatic or idealistic. It is a question of recognizing that we are inextricably a part of the natural order, and that in devouring its gifts we are doomed to devour ourselves.
>
> ("And the Forest?" *Memoirs*, 143)

To underscore her view, Wiseman invoked work by fellow women writers Marian Engel and Margaret Laurence:

> Marian Engel's mangy bear is a pretty precise rendering of the state of our wilds today. I have hesitated to say all this because after all a literary conference may not be considered an appropriate place for such a radical dose of reality. But everywhere I have travelled across the country I have met with writers somehow trying to come to grips with their sense of a heritage betrayed, the guilt of unconfronted history, of unacknowledged motives for the continual betrayal. Shortly before I came here I

was talking to Margaret Laurence about this trip. I said, "What would you say about MAN AND THE FOREST?"

And she replied, "Tell them that well over a hundred years ago Catharine Parr Traill wrote that she felt our settlers were cutting down too many trees."

("And the Forest?" *Memoirs*, 137-138; caps in the original)

Wiseman was critical of scholars who are "comfortable with the prevailing religious, philosophical, and scientific thought of the time, but do not question the unacknowledged system of assumptions and permissions behind that thought, which has usurped the power to regulate and modify our behavior toward the wilderness as toward much else in our day" ("And the Forest?" *Memoirs*, 136). She felt strongly that "We must bear witness to an entirely different relationship to our woods. The old accounts no longer fit the current models" (*Memoirs*, 136).

Wiseman and other women writers of her generation—Laurence and Engel among them—saw clearly and wrote forcefully about the interwoven nature of marginalization and poverty for those outside the center or bases of power. These include in particular the Indigenous, immigrant, and economically disadvantaged populations across the country, in both urban and rural communities. Intersectionality[17] was not a term in wide circulation at the time but Wiseman and her contemporaries understood how human experience and identities were subject

---

17 Brought into scholarly and popular discourse by Kimberlé Crenshaw's 1989 address to a University of Chicago legal form, "Demarginalizing the Intersection of Race and Sex: A Black Feminist Critique of Antidiscrimination Doctrine, Feminist Theory and Antiracist Politics," intersectionality forms part of discussion in *Her Own Thinker* Chapter IV.

to multiple interconnected social, political, and economic structures and systems in different and widely discriminatory ways.
Wiseman, for example, points to David Adams Richards's work,
its "tormented tales of impoverished human souls of the east-
coast Miramichi area, poverty and decadence in an impoverished bush, the legacy of those who ... strip the land and get
rich quick and get out, or remain as the power base of the
country's rulers" (*Memoirs*, 136).

Wiseman's "memoirs" recall the "outsiderness" of being Jewish. Drawing on first-hand experience growing up in the impoverished multi-ethnic neighbourhood of North End Winnipeg
at a time when anti-Semitism was widespread, she remembers
"the peculiar nature of the reading life of the Jewish child in
the gentile world" ("Memoirs of a Book-Molesting Childhood,"
Memoirs, 15): "I found myself as distasteful in 'their' writing as
in 'their' country, in 'their' city, in 'their' street, in 'their' lives"
(15). At school, she found life less alienating "as long as we had
not yet played the 'what are you?' game" (16):

> What are you? English? Scotch? French? German? Polish?
> Icelandic? Ukrainian? I could have got away with Ukrainian,
> for a while at least, on the technicality that my parents came
> from the Ukraine. But I wouldn't. And because of my pigtails,
> I would have pretended to be "Dutch, I'll bet you're Dutch!"
>
> "No, I'm Jewish," I'd have to steel myself to say, finally, and
> watch myself turn into an instant monster in their eyes.
>
> ("Memoirs of a Book-Molesting Childhood," *Memoirs*, 16)

Decades later, in her collection *Shame on Me: An Anatomy of
Race and Belonging* (2019), Tessa McWatt recalls the same question being asked of her at school in the essay "What Are You?",
the experience as jarring and impactful for her as for Wiseman

so many years earlier. Notwithstanding schoolmates' attitudes toward her, "they couldn't seem to leave me alone," Wiseman noted; "When they couldn't find me they searched me out in order to tell me to go back to Jerusalem. They seemed to need their strange version of me to hate" (*Memoirs*, 15).

Wiseman was not alone among her peers in writing about marginalization of Jews in Canada. Miriam Waddington, who also grew up in a North End Winnipeg Jewish family, took up the topic in her collection of essays *Apartment Seven* (1989). The author of over a dozen collections of poetry, Waddington wrote in her essays about how Canadian society of the 1920s and 1930s "brainwashed every schoolchild with British Empire slogans, and promoted a negative stereotype of all Eastern European immigrants, but especially of Jews" ("Mrs Maza's Salon," *Apartment Seven*, 5). For her, being Jewish meant that:

> Then, as now, I felt an outsider as far as English Canadians were concerned. The message that had come through to me in public school in Winnipeg, and again in high school in Ottawa, was that to be a Canadian was to be English, to have your mother in the IODE and your father in the Rotarians. English was definitely top dog in Canada until after the Second World War. But I was Jewish ... and no Jew could get a job teaching English in a Canadian university until after the Second World War.
>
> ("Outsider: Growing Up in Canada," *Apartment Seven,* 40)

Waddington's Russian-Jewish immigrant mother was most certainly not in the IODE—the Imperial Order of Daughters of the Empire—nor was her father a Rotarian. In her 1969 essay "Canadian Tradition and Canadian Literature," Waddington is keenly aware that Jews were not the only targets of discriminatory attitudes and "ugly aspects" of Canadian history; so too were Indigenous peoples, the poor, immigrants, and prisoners:

> There are also many ugly aspects of our history that have never been accounted for in literature. Some of these aspects are still buried in the suppressed radical tradition, which has somehow failed to appeal to the Canadian literary imagination. The story of the long struggle of the dissenting minority against the forces of colonial conservatism, and of the inevitable defeats on political, social, and personal levels, has never really been told. Our poor people, our Indians, our lonely immigrants, our prisoners, our Métis in Manitoba—few of these have found a place in serious Canadian literature; they are only just beginning to find a place in our culture through the mass media.
>
> ("Canadian Tradition and Canadian Literature," *Apartment Seven,* 97)

Waddington's comments strikingly include the plight of prisoners and, like Laurence's and Wiseman's, foreground the circumstances of Indigenous communities and immigrants in Canada. The impact of immigrants as settlers on the lands and experiences of Indigenous peoples had not yet emerged as a focus of concern in the country. Yet it hovers just below the surface in Laurence's reply, seen above, to Wiseman's question about her paper for the conference "Man and the Forest." Wiseman was articulating this awareness long before more recent attention turned to the immigrant settler impact on Indigenous Canada. At that time, being an immigrant or having descended from immigrants was the focus—if the theme was considered at all. Wiseman's *Memoirs of a Book Molesting Childhood* certainly considered the immigrant experience. In her essay "The Writer and Canadian Literature" she not only examined the "insider-outsider" status of Canadians as she observed and personally experienced it, she also held that literature had a part to play in the process:

> I myself believe that an immigrant population is perforce a traumatized population. Nevertheless, an immigrant population which is encouraged to believe it brings something of value to the new society may thereby be enabled to do just that.
>
> With such a problematic cultural course, we can certainly look forward to some vivid expression from the various components of our mosaic; indeed, some of our finest writing to date has been done by writers who are examining their own particular cultural heritage and, as it were, placing themselves and their backgrounds into the general pattern of the living mosaic, and seeing what happens. The voices are beginning to be heard from every corner of the land, mapping our external and internal places, capturing the spirits of the inner and the outer country.
>
> ("The Writer and Canadian Literature," *Memoirs*, 88-89)

Wiseman's concerns for the environment and for Indigenous peoples in Canada were central to the essay that she wrote for the conference "Man and the Forest." But she also raised the issue of gender as it impacted women's lives, in particular the lives of women writers. Wiseman tackles the topic head-on in "Word Power: Women and Prose in Canada Today."

This is an essay that reads even more forcefully decades after it first appeared in print in *Memoirs of a Book Molesting Childhood*. Wiseman is both personally feisty and empirically factual on the differences between men's and women's experiences as writers in Canada. From a declarative opening statement that she has "no intention of setting up sexual rivalry as a basis for literary discussion" ("Word Power," *Memoirs*, 45), she moves on to an equally adamant declaration that it is also not her aim to depict women writers as victims or without agency or privilege. On the contrary, the first part of the essay discusses postwar conditions in Canada that were favourable to men and women writers alike. These included opportunities for work and education and the privilege and freedom of mobility—luxuries, Wiseman stated, that she and other Canadian women writers enjoyed alongside fellow Canadian writers. "We too experienced the freedom and the sense of enlargement that is related to the privilege of being able to go where you want to in the world" (53). Wiseman herself travelled to and worked in London and Rome. These experiences allowed her to realize that not only was the world different for most of the people among whom she lived but also that "you learn who you are [and] you see your own country through different eyes, from different perspectives" (52). Wiseman recognized and acknowledged the advantages that Canadian women writers like her shared with men. At the same time, she was cognizant of the differences between their experiences as writers and of the personal and professional costs to women of those differences.

> Few of us have "wives" and secretaries or even the comfort of existing in a setting where it is considered acceptable to try to ease our multiple day-by-day burdens in order to enable ourselves to be free simply to write.
>
> ("Word Power: Women and Prose in Canada Today," *Memoirs*, 53-54)

Her essay presents a comparative "statistical" analysis based on "a fictional baker's dozen of female writers of poetry and fiction … and the same number of imaginary male writers" (54) and their different experiences across a wide range of areas, from their marital histories and financial situations, to what household and childrearing duties were expected of them, whose work got reviewed in newspapers and journals, who, in last analysis, was considered a writer. "I must emphasize," Wiseman added, "that all of these hypothetical women writers are sexual women" (56) though the writer who "wants to live her life fully … is constantly faced with largely artificial choices and has her guilts set out for her" (54).

> No one has ever suggested to our male counterparts that they must choose between devotions and suffer guilt if they appear to make what is considered the wrong choice. Indeed, it is considered somewhat heroic and even a sign of genius in a man if he behaves with irresponsible selfishness in his personal life. He is considered redeemed by his utter devotion to his art. The exact reverse is usually true for a woman artist.
> ("Word Power: Women and Prose in Canada Today," *Memoirs*, 54)

Wiseman's thoughts in "Word Power: Women and Prose in Canada Today" reflect those of a generation tasked with describing what second-wave feminism would go on to theorize:

> The rights which male writers have always taken as their due are not yet readily accorded by society to their female peers (…) The writer who, for whatever reason, avoids the prescribed course of marriage and motherhood is an even more suspicious object, behung with guilt-inducing stereotypes

which often effectively neutralize, even for herself, the suspicion that she has gained something of freedom.

("Word Power: Women and Prose in Canada Today," *Memoirs*, 53-54)

Wiseman does not yet identify or expose the vocabulary of patriarchy that would become so prominent a project in the next decades. But her essay describes its impact on women. It also identifies Canadian women writers' resistance to patriarchal reality, particularly that of Margaret Laurence.

Adele Wiseman's essays comprise a classic early example of how a Canadian woman writer used the genre to engage in social reality—whether in addressing the pressing social issues that concerned her (environmental degradation, abuse of Indigenous communities, the immigrant experience) or in her personal experience as a woman trying to be a writer in a man's world. As illustrated above, the essay format served her well.

Margaret Laurence—*Heart of a Stranger*

As Adele Wiseman aptly observed, Margaret Laurence "jumped the gun on [feminist] theorizing ... [Her writing] put into imaginative form what [feminists] were theorizing about, before they had even begun to theorize" (*Memoirs of a Book Molesting Childhood*, 59). This was just one of several fronts on which Laurence anticipated and articulated the need for societal change, and for which she effectively employed the essay format.

Margaret Laurence's essay writing exemplifies the genre's double function of addressing social and political issues and exploring the writing experience itself. Laurence's attention to questions of gender, class, and cultural identity has been well and widely studied; less so, perhaps, her early concern about the environment and pollution, about nuclear power and waste, nuclear threat and war. Lynn McDonald's short but noteworthy article "Margaret Laurence and the NDP" identifies the novelist's active involvement with Energy Probe as a board member and founder of its international environmentalist wing, Probe International. Laurence sent letters to federal and provincial politicians alike about the nuclear arms race and about the environmental pollution caused by the nuclear industry. In the 1980 federal election campaign, McDonald points out, Laurence wrote a campaign letter for the NDP (National Democratic Party) that went out to some 300,000 people. The letter's priorities and language were vintage Laurence: civil liberties, a national energy policy, women's equality, funding for the arts and social services, Native peoples, Canadian unity and cultural sovereignty (McDonald, 24). These and a long list of additional concerns inform and energize the numerous essays that Laurence wrote. McDonald makes particular mention of "the everyday struggles of love and hurt, marriage and divorce, childrearing and old age, jobs and poverty" (24).

Laurence's nonfiction writing was extensive. In book-form alone it comprised her anthology of Somali poetry and folk stories, *A Tree for Poverty* (1954); an account of her life in British Somaliland, *The Prophet's Camel Bell* (1963); a literary study, *Long Drums and Cannons: Nigerian Dramatists and Novelists 1952-1966* (1968); the collection of essays, *Heart of a Stranger* (1976); and a literary memoir, *Dance on the Earth: A Memoir* (1989). These publications were in addition to her well-known novels *The Stone Angel* (1964), *A Jest of God* (1966), *The Fire-Dwellers* (1969), and *The Diviners* (1974), two volumes of short stories, and four children's books. Given the project in *Her Own Thinker* on Canadian women writers' collections of essays, the focus here is on Laurence's *Heart of a Stranger*.

In her foreword to the collection, Laurence explained that the title *Heart of a Stranger* was inspired by extensive life experience as "a stranger in strange lands." It is a title with resonance in later collections by writers such as M. NourbeSe Philip, whose essay "Echoes in a Stranger Land" introduces her 1992 *Frontiers: Essays and Writings on Racism and Culture,* or Kristjana Gunnars, in her 2004 essay collection *Stranger at the Door.* Laurence's years spent in Africa and then in England fostered her early understanding of colonialism, imperialism, and disrespect for the culture of the "other." Essays in which she critiqued these conditions predate the advent of postcolonial theory and its impact on literary studies. Laurence's essays further evidence her early grasp of Canada's problematic foundation on exploitative settler-Indigenous relations. The essay "Man of our People," for example, is as relevant and pertinent to Canada today as at the time of its publication in 1975, nearly half-a-century ago. The man and people of the title are Gabriel Dumont and the Métis of Manitoba. With one of the first usages of the term "settler Canadians," Laurence not only identities herself as one but exhorts Canadians as a whole to listen to and learn from the country's Indigenous peoples.

> Canadians who, like myself, are the descendants of various settlers ... must hear native peoples' voices and ultimately become part of them, for they speak not only of the soul-searing injustices done to them but also of their rediscovered sense of self-worth and their ability to tell and teach the things needed to be known. (...) We have largely forgotten how to live with, protect, and pay homage to our earth and the other creatures who share it with us—as witness the killing of rivers and lakes; the killing of the whales; the proliferation of apartment blocks on irreplaceable farmlands. We have so much to learn and act

upon, and time is getting short. Those other societies which
existed before imperialism, industrialism, mass exploitation,
and commercial greed were certainly far from ideal, nor can
we return to them, but they knew about living in relationship
to the land, and they may ultimately be the societies from
whose value we must try to learn.

("Man of Our People," *Heart of a Stranger*, 211-212)

Laurence recognized and readily acknowledged the difficulty
in trying to understand the concepts, customs, and life view of
another culture, and the damage that can be done by "the very
best intentions." This was her title for her very first published
article in 1964. Already then Laurence was clearly aware of the
issue of "white liberalism" ("The Very Best Intentions," *Heart
of a Stranger*, 36), including her own. She recognized that her
reluctance to disagree with her Ghanaian friend in their various
conversations and discussions was based on fear—her "fear of
damaging what I hoped was his impression of me—which was
actually my own impression of myself: sympathetic, humani-
tarian, enlightened" (*Heart of a Stranger*, 37).

The essay "The Very Best Intentions" still has a great deal
to say. Indeed, the ongoing relevance of Laurence's writing as
an essayist is demonstrated once and for all by the recent publication *Recognition and Revelation: Short Nonfiction Writings –
Margaret Laurence* (2020), a collection of 51 essays and pieces of
nonfiction edited by Nora Stovel. As Stovel remarks, the issues
addressed in Laurence's essays "are more pressing now than ever
before in this time of drastic pollution, climate change, and
nuclear buildups" (Stovel, xliii). Aritha van Herk echoes this in
her Afterword to the volume: "What is obvious in these essays
is that Laurence is no retro thinker, a writer to relegate to Canada's history, but a woman who was both of her time and ahead

of her time. Her support for unpopular causes, her sensitivity to racism and prejudice, her strong feminism and pacifism, her advocacy for peace and against censorship, altogether remark an imagination whose influence goes beyond momentary context" (Stovel, 294).

The organization of the essays in *Recognition and Revelation: Short Nonfiction Writings* into five sections illustrates the breadth and depth of Laurence's nonfiction writing: socio-political essays, essays on the environment and nuclear disarmament, essays about Canada and Canadian literature, personal and creative essays, and essays about her own writing. A handful of essays are from *Heart of a Stranger*. Two that are not and that underscore *Her Own Thinker's* focus on the value and contributions of Canadian women novelists and poets as essayists are "Ivory Tower or Grassroots? The Novelist as Socio-political Being" and "Listen, Just Listen."[18]

Stovel suggests that "Ivory Tower or Grassroots? The Novelist as Socio-political Being" is Margaret Laurence's manifesto. In it, Laurence posits the socio-political role writers can play and the central place of politics and religion in their writing. She illustrates this in the work of two writers—her own and that of Nigerian novelist Chinua Achebe. Using terminology of the times—the 1970s—Laurence describes both Achebe and herself as "Third World" novelists. "Yes, *Third World* novelists," she emphasizes ("Ivory Tower or Grassroots?" Stovel, 52), referring in her case to American cultural influence in postwar Canada, and in Achebe's case to the dispossession of Nigerian

---

18 Originally published in New (1978) and Geddes (1977) respectively, excerpts from these two essays here refer to their versions in Stovel's edited collection *Recognition and Revelation: Short Nonfiction Writings – Margaret Laurence* (2020).

culture under British imperialism. Despite the difference in their circumstances, in Laurence's situation "Canadian writers, like African writers, have had to find our own voices and write out of what is truly ours, in the face of an overwhelming cultural imperialism" ("Ivory Tower or Grassroots?" Stovel, 52).

This assertion may wobble in the wake of the race-conscious work that has appeared since "Ivory Tower or Grassroots?" was published in 1978, but the essay brings attention to the cultural and psychic damage to generations of Nigerians as a result of domination by British imperialism (Stovel, 53). "Taught as children to despise their ancestors and the old gods," Laurence writes, "they learned to despise themselves" (Stovel, 52). Laurence assigns primary importance to ancestors, valuing them in ways that resonate in the work of Indigenous writers such as Leanne Betasamosake Simpson discussed in Chapter IV. This is a striking feature of Laurence's essay writing, especially when read in the context of contemporary attention to Indigenous world views. "We need links with our ancestors," Laurence affirmed, "to determine who and what we are, to decide what we hope to become, and to know what sort of society will we try to form" ("Ivory Tower or Grassroots?" Stovel, 51).

Laurence perceived a critical place in the formation of society for writers, and for belief in writing and writing's connection with politics. By belief, she meant "something that has connotations both of faith and of politics," and by politics, she meant politics "with a small 'p'"—"something wider than the often-moronic exchanges in our (or any other) parliament, meaning a social commentary at the grassroots level" (all three quotes from "Ivory Tower or Grassroots?" Stovel, 51). Though she was referring to fiction when she stated that "it encompasses both history and belief, both social and spiritual themes … our dilemmas and aspirations, which are always in some way or other those both of politics and of faith" ("Ivory Tower or Grassroots?" Stovel, 60), the statement describes her essay writing as well. "Ivory Tower or Grassroots?" comments sharply and critically on British colonialism and its denigration and dispossession of the cultural life and very lands of Nigeria and Canada alike.

In colonial attitudes toward these and other colonized nations Laurence saw parallels with societal attitudes toward women, the "powerlessness of women, the tendency of women to accept male definition of ourselves, to be self-deprecating and uncertain, and to rage inwardly," a "whole history of imperialism, of being defined in others' terms, not our own" ("Ivory Tower or Grassroots?" Stovel, 58 and 57). In a "kind of kinship" ("Ivory Tower or Grassroots?" Stovel, 57) with Achebe and others in a struggle against externally imposed values and views, Laurence began to write out of her own cultural background. Her "Manawaka series" of novels was seeded in what she regarded as her "debt" to African writers, their "sense of themselves, an identity and a feeling of value" recovered from years of colonialism, and their coming to terms with their ancestors and their gods ("A Place to Stand On," *Heart of a Stranger,* 14; retitled "Sources" in Stovel, 3).

Laurence's essay "Listen, Just Listen" takes its title from advice Laurence was given by fellow novelist Rudy Wiebe in anticipation of her long-awaited visit to the site of the historic 1885 Battle of Batoche. "When you get there," Wiebe told Laurence, "listen. Just listen" (Stovel, 264). Laurence did just that, and what she heard, her essay recounts, were the voices of the Métis people who fought, died, and were ultimately defeated in defence of their ancestral land against the government of John A. Macdonald, Canada's first prime minister. The essay honours the Métis leaders and ancestors Louis Riel and Gabriel Dumont. It also expresses the strong connection that Laurence felt with the land and with "ancestral voices which arise out of many sources": "When I think of my own birth area of this land … In this one area alone, our names are Cree, French, Scots, Irish, Métis, English, Jewish, Ukrainian, Hungarian, Mennonite, Icelandic, German, and more" ("Listen, Just Listen," Stovel, 261). The essay is an argument for respecting and accepting difference, that of the people of Quebec, of Canada's Indigenous peoples, of all who have been "othered" and oppressed by colonialism. Laurence asks that we "listen to and hear one another, at the grassroots level … to right old wrongs and to learn about one another" ("Listen, Just Listen," Stovel, 264).

Laurence's faith was not in governments, but in influencing or replacing governments. Writing served that purpose for her. She felt that her responsibility as a writer extended into her life "as a citizen of my own land and ultimately of the world" ("The Artist Then, Now, and Always," Stovel, 232). She considered that she and other Canadian writers "must be prepared to make our government listen to and hear us" ("The Artist Then, Now, and Always," 233). Laurence's essays attest to her political, intellectual, and social engagement with Canada and its place in the world. Over and above letters sent to federal and provincial politicians, she wrote essays on the dangers of the nuclear industry and Canada's part in the nuclear arms race, the need for a national energy policy, injustices endured by Canada's Indigenous peoples, pollution of the Canadian environment, national unity and cultural sovereignty, and the possibility of Canada's role as an international mediator and peacemaker. Laurence's essays on these and other political and social concerns were "clear, balanced, and beautifully written," Aritha van Herk comments (Stovel, 291). "Laurence was not a writer who pronounced, or who dispensed unalterable opinions, but a thoughtful and considering observer of the world" (Stovel, 291-292). Her essays invite rereading and rethinking not only what we believe we know about Canadian writing, as van Herk suggests, but what we think we know about Canada.

As Adele Wiseman wrote in *Memoirs of a Book Molesting Childhood and Other Essays*, other women writers of her time "took the creative leap" into issues of the day as "witnesses, expressers, instruments of our culture" (*Memoirs*, 87). Not all of them produced collections of essays in book form, but among those who did were Jane Rule, Phyllis Webb, P.K. Page, and Margaret Atwood.[19]

---

19 A contemporary of these writers, novelist Marian Engel was also an essayist. A long-time admirer of Engel's work, I would have liked to include a section about her essay writing in this chapter, but her essays have not (yet) been collected into book form, which is one of the criteria I set myself for *Her Own Thinker*. By way of example of Engel as an essayist, I would refer readers to a series that she wrote for *The Toronto Star* in a column she called "Being Here." Appearing every Saturday for 43 weeks from 28 November 1981 until 25 September 1982, these weekly essays were wide-ranging explorations of, in Engel's words, "how personal experience extends itself into general experience" (*The Toronto Star*, 28 November 1981, F1). For a sense of what readers might encounter in these essays, here is what Engel wrote after reading Irving Abella and Harold Troper's book *None is Too Many: Canada and the Jews of Europe 1933-1948*: "Canadian policies have always been on the racist side. Since 1759, a concerted effort has been made to ensure that people from the British Isles kept control of the whole country. When any non-British group attempted to control its destiny, trouble ensued. There was the Riel Rebellion. There was the Rebellion of 1837, which took a stronger form in Quebec than here, though we don't hear much about that. Immigration policy always favoured Caucasian people and those, particularly, who were Christian and Protestant." (*The Toronto Star*, 25 September 1982: H1). There is a project waiting in collecting Engel's essays for *The Toronto Star* column "Being Here" into book form, similar to how Bronwen Wallace's essays for the column "In Other Words" that she wrote for the *Kingston Whig-Standard* from May 1987 to February 1989 were collected and published as *Arguments with the World*, edited by Joanne Page (1992).

Jane Rule—*Outlander*

In her fiction and nonfiction writing alike, novelist Jane Rule was forthright on the subject of sexuality, including her own. Her 1964 novel *Desert of the Heart* depicted the then still-illicit realities of lesbian lives and love, and she herself identified publicly as a lesbian—a "pre-movement lesbian," she pointed out, meaning before 1970s feminism and the developing discourse around sexualities ("With All Due Respect," *Outlander*, 175). Rule was committed to what she referred to as a visible life, despite the risks and even dangers of homophobia for lesbians. This was, she noted, the case for all members of minority, Black, and Indigenous communities whose visibility resulted in marginalization ("Closet-Burning," *Outlander*). She put sexual identity squarely on the writing table, as a selection of essay titles in *Outlander* makes clear: "Sexuality in Literature"; "Teaching Sexuality"; "Private Parts and Public Figures"; "With All Due Respect"; "Homophobia and Romantic Love"; "The Sex War"; "Fucking Pariahs on the Schoolroom Shelf"; "Closet Burning". Sexuality was still a relatively taboo topic when Rule raised it in her work and *Outlander*, while published only in 1982, was a bold break through barriers around the topic.

Outlander comprises short stories as well as essays, the latter collected from journals and publications such as *Fireweed*, *After You're Out*, and *The Body Politic*. The first essay in the collection, "Sexuality in Literature," is an early articulation of the need felt by many women writers for "a language adequate to express our sexual experience (…) and to describe negotiations far more complex than the entrance of a penis or finger into a vagina" (*Outlander*, 149).

> If we are ever going to understand ourselves as sexual creatures, at least some novelists and biographers, as well as sexologists, are going to have to learn to be accurate about sexual

experience, knowing the difference between fantasy and fact, between what ought to be and what is. Knowledge is a collective enterprise. Without it understanding is impossible. Ignorance is too often a murderous vulnerability.

("Sexuality in Literature," *Outlander*, 151)

Rule saw that her responsibility as a writer was to confront "the real world"; not the world as it ought to be but "as it is," she wrote in *Outlander* (153). For her that meant writing about difficult topics like rape, domestic violence, and child sexual exploitation. In the second essay of the collection, "Teaching Sexuality," Rule took up the controversial article "Men Loving Boys Loving Men" that appeared in *The Body Politic*, the Toronto gay and lesbian journal that ran from 1971 to1987. "I am convinced that censoring serious discussion of unconventional sexual relationships does nothing to protect those who might be exploited," Rule wrote about *The Body Politic* article, which she admitted posed "hard political questions" for her (*Outlander*, 157). As a subtle analyst of arguments that favour censoring erotic materials abusive of children and women, and of arguments that maintain censorship would drive such material into dangerous secrecy, like "so much child abuse" (*Outlander*, 152), Rule probed the complexities of private and public boundaries in human activity and the cultural conditioning that viewed sexuality as "the private parts" of life ("Private Parts and Public Figures," *Outlander*, 163).

She perceived this conditioning at work in literature, and in her essay, "Private Parts and Public Figures," she questioned the exclusion from biography of "the private parts" of life. For Rule, the job of the biographer was to present human beings in their wholeness (*Outlander*, 171). Her own biographical studies of writers Gertrude Stein, Willa Cather, Radclyffe Hall, and Vita

Sackville-West for her book *Lesbian Images* explored the complicated interactions of sexuality with class, faith, and psychology
("With All Due Respect," *Outlander*, 176-177). She drew attention to "the reciprocal pressures of sexuality and society, the
part money and privilege or lack of these play in sexual choice,
[and] how little 'masculine' and 'feminine' traits have to do with
sex at all but with power or lack of it" ("Private Parts and Public
Figures," *Outlander*, 170). "Sexuality itself," Rule reflected, "is
only one of dozens of tags by which we identify ourselves" ("Re-
flexions," *Outlander*, 203).

In "Homophobia and Romantic Love," Rule proposed that
"sex is not so much an identity as a language which we have
for so long been forbidden to speak that most of us learn only
the crudest of its vocabulary and grammar" (*Outlander*, 185),
pointing to the relationship between language and sexuality
that would animate much essay writing by feminists in the
1970s-1980s. She put patriarchy on her writing table too, cau-
tioning against viewing men's and women's relations as a sex war.
"What we have to fear and fight against is not each other but the
garbage in our heads that can make us see each other as symbols
of the establishment, as enemies rather than as people" ("The
Sex War," *Outlander*, 196-97). Rule stressed the humanity of
individuals. On that and that basis alone, everyone ought to be
able to exist and thrive within society, not be isolated and lan-
guish outside of it. She was aware of and wrote critically about
the outsider experience of lesbians in society, just as Adele Wiseman and Miriam Waddington wrote about the outsider status
of the country's Jewish communities and Margaret Laurence
wrote about Canada's marginalized Indigenous peoples.

Rule closed the collection *Outlander* with a short essay
called "Grandmothers," a title echoing the column "So's Your
Grandmother" that she contributed regularly to *The Body Politic*

until it ceased publication in 1987. The essay is a contemplative tribute to the aged and aging female body—the former Rule's grandmothers, whose lined "speaking faces" and swollen finger joints she recalls with deep love; the latter Rule's own body, at forty-six arthritic like her grandmothers' bodies, but like them, "intent on practicing life as long as it lasts":

> As my grandmothers taught me ... with their beautifully requiring flesh and speaking faces, so I would wish to teach the children I love that they are capable of tenderness and of strength, capable of knowledge because of what they can see in my face, clear in pain and wonder, intent on practicing life as long as it lasts.
>
> ("Grandmothers," *Outlander*, 207)

Outlander was not Rule's sole essay or nonfiction publication. Others include *Lesbian Images* (1975), *A Hot-Eyed Moderate* (1985), and *Loving the Difficult* (2008). These collections and their titles evoke the substantive content of Rule's essay writing. They reflect her lifelong concerns with and thoughtful commentary on difficult and often controversial issues and topics, such as censorship, sexual abuse, and social injustice, as well as her considered thoughts about the writing life, notably that of the woman writer, which was a central concern of the Canadian women essay writers of this period.

Notebooks, Brushes, and Pens
—Mavis Gallant, Phyllis Webb, and P.K. Page

In casting a critical eye on their country and in grappling with thorny issues of their day, Rule, Wiseman, Laurence, and Waddington were joined by three more of their writing generation,

Mavis Gallant, Phyllis Webb, and P.K. Page, all distinguished authors of multiple books of fiction and poetry.

Mavis Gallant is best known for her short stories, over one hundred of which appeared in *The New Yorker* magazine. Born in Montreal in 1922, she wrote and published her first short stories while working as a reporter for the *Montreal Standard* newspaper. In addition to her short stories, which have been assembled into a succession of different collections over the years, she published two novels and a collection of essays and reviews, *The Paris Notebooks*. Phyllis Webb, who worked as a CBC radio broadcaster and producer (she co-founded the program Ideas), published over a dozen volumes of poetry, beginning with *Trio: First Poems by Gael Turnbull, Phyllis Webb, and Eli Mandel* in 1954 and continuing through the 1960s and 1970s to the 1980s and the award-winning *Wilson's Bowl* (1980) and *The Vision Tree* (1982). P.K. Page was a successful visual artist under her married name P.K. Irwin, and the author of thirty books, including works of poetry, fiction, travel diaries, children's books, the autobiographical *A Brazilian Diary* (1987), and essays. The latter were collected and edited by Zailig Pollock and published in 2007 as *The Filled Pen: Selected Non-fiction*. Phyllis Webb's collection of essays, *Nothing but Brush Strokes,* was published in 1995 and Mavis Gallant's *Paris Notebooks: Essays & Reviews* appeared in 1986.

As the title suggests, the essays in Gallant's collection originated in notes that she took on events that shook Paris in the spring of 1968. "May 68," as the events came to be known, marked the beginning of nearly two months of civil unrest that included student protests and occupations of universities, worker strikes and demonstrations against government and employers, and general citizen critique of capitalism and consumerism. "If *The New Yorker* had not asked to see the record," Gallant recounts in her introduction to *Paris Notebooks*, "I might never have bothered to type up my notes or put them in order" (3). The "notes" make up the first half of the essays in the volume. Beginning May 3 and concluding June 4, they are divided into two parts and capture a city where life blazed and stopped:

> In almost no time, Paris became a city where it was impossible to buy a newspaper, go to school, mail a letter, send a telegram, cash a cheque, ride in a bus, take the Métro, use a private car (doctors excepted), find cigarettes ... sugar, canned goods, or salad oil, watch television or, towards the end, listen to a news bulletin. No garbage was collected; no trains left the city; there was no time signal, no weather report. Teachers stopped teaching, actors stopped acting. ... It was as though people on every level of society intended to bring matters to a halt, pause, and set off in a different direction. (2)

For some, May 68 pointed toward hopeful new social realities; for others, it signaled new and rich cultural expression with lasting traces in language, literature, art, and music. For yet others, Gallant suggested in her essays, national elections having put a conservative majority in government, May 68 became a collective memory, that of *soixante-huitards*—the sixty-eighters who participated in the events and the promise it held out to them (3).

The second half of the essay section in *Paris Notebooks* retains a French focus, with essays about writers such as Paul Léautaud and Marguerite Yourcenar, about French architecture, and about Gabrielle Russier, a high school teacher who was arrested and jailed in the 1960s for a relationship with a 16-year-old student, and who sadly committed suicide. "Introduction to *The*

War Brides," however, looked at the experiences in Canada of the women who met and married Canadian soldiers during the war—more than forty-one thousand, Gallant notes. These "war brides," who brought more than 21,000 children to Canada with them following the war, often encountered cultural poverty in their new surroundings. At the same time, many of the Canadian families receiving them experienced shock "as great as that felt by brides who found they had arrived into families where the only conceivable use for a book was as a doorstop" (156). Gallant's portrayal of cultural life in postwar Canada is sharply critical in this essay; if war brides arriving in Canada wondered or worried about the reputation that preceded them, Gallant wrote, Canadians ought to have wondered and worried "what sort of Canada" was offered to the newcomers (155). For her part, Gallant left Canada in 1950 to pursue a life of writing in Europe. She settled in Paris where she wrote the stories that established her as a doyenne of the form, along with the essays and reviews collected in *Paris Notebooks: Essays & Reviews.*

Poet Phyllis Webb's *Nothing but Brush Strokes* gathers material from the years 1970-1985 when she was in her forties and fifties. Her essay "Phyllis Webb's Canada" considers her country of birth from the perspective of middle age. Webb finds herself to be "more rebellious, more radical, less patient" (106) in older age, and more critical of Canada than her younger self, when she ran as the youngest candidate in a provincial election. At the time of British Columbia's 1949 election, twenty-two-year-old Webb was drawn to the CCF (Co-operative Commonwealth Federation) for its demand of "votes for Asiatics and native Indians": "That plank in the party platform," she later wrote in her essay, "was for me a springboard, and I jumped in" (107). Webb did not win, but the CCF's first Indigenous candidate did, which gave Webb hope for what the country could be.

Youthful optimism did not fend off later life disaffection, however. "Phyllis Webb's Canada" records her unhappiness with Canadian politics and society at large: "I'm disaffected from my governments (...) and from many of the institutions of the society which formed me" (106). Canada had become an "unreal estate" for Webb: "I am aware of this every time I switch on the news or watch the sun come up," she wrote. "The Earth is our real estate, our terribly threatened royal domain" (109). Political consciousness, amplified by her literary involvements, modified Webb's sense of being Canadian and her perspectives on the country. Ultimately this led to her late-life turn away from writing and toward the visual arts. This is uniquely illustrated in "The Mind's Eye, a Photo-Collage Essay" at the heart of *Nothing but Brush Strokes*. The eight glossy-paged, colour reproductions of abstract art works in the essay make Webb's collection of essays a distinctive volume.

P.K. Page's *The Filled Pen: Selected Non-fiction* also draws from the author's life and work as both a poet and a painter. Editor Zailig Pollock highlights the personal dimension of Page's *The Filled Pen,* pointing to her essays on her contemporaries, poet A.M. Klein and novelist David Adams Richards. "What sets her essays apart," Pollock writes, "is their essentially personal engagement with her subjects (...) their blending of the personal and (to use that word which is nowadays much derided) the universal" (*The Filled Pen*, xv). Essays such as "A Writer's Life," "Safe at Home," "Falling in Love with Poetry," and "Had I Not Been a Writer, What Would I Have Been?" chart Page's creative path and practice. They also fill in the backdrop of her artistic trajectory, the Canadian cultural context of her time blending with the wider international scene as life took Page from the centre, east, and west of Canada to Australia, Brazil, and Mexico. Essays like "Questions and Images" and "Traveler,

Conjuror, Journeyman" strike a philosophical note, fusing the "universal" nature of big questions about human experience and their personal meaning to Page, as Pollock suggests (*The Filled Pen*, xv). Of life's mysteries in "Questions and Images," Page reflects: "I don't know the answers … I begin to sense another realm—interrelated—the high doh of a scale in which we are the low. And in a sudden and momentary bouleversement, I realize that I have been upside down in life—like a tree on its head, roots exposed in the air" (*The Filled Pen*, 41). Of connections and correspondences between writing and painting, Page offers, in "Traveller, Conjuror, Journeyman": "The idea diminishes to a dimensionless point in my absolute centre. If I can hold it steady long enough, the feeling which is associated with that point grows and fills a larger area as perfume permeates a room. It is from here that I write (…) Expressed another way—I am a traveler" (*The Filled Pen*, 43; 44).

The writer or artist as traveler, and writing or the creative life as journey, are recurring tropes in Canadian women writers' essay writing. They are taken to further distance and development in collections by Margaret Atwood.

Margaret Atwood—*Second Words, Moving Targets, and Negotiations with the Dead*

The famous author of such internationally acclaimed, award-winning novels as *The Handmaid's Tale* (1985), *The Blind Assassin* (2000), and *The Testaments* (2019); of multiple collections of short fiction and of poetry including the recent *Dearly* (2020); of children's books and graphic novels, television scripts and libretti, anthologies and a dozen works of nonfiction, Margaret Atwood hardly calls for introduction. What calls for some explanation, however, is her inclusion in a chapter otherwise centered on writers of a generation that seems earlier than hers, that is writers born in the 1920s and 1930s whose writing careers developed during the 1960s-1980s. While work by Atwood continues to appear today, she began writing in the 1950s. Born in 1939, she published her first collection of poetry, *Double Persephone*, in 1961, and continued to write and publish a steady stream of work ever since, including nonfiction and collections of essays,[20] of which the 2022 *Burning Questions: Essays & Occasional Pieces 2004-2021* is the most recent example.

Atwood the essayist emerged at an early age, in the 1950s when she was a teenage reporter for her high school's Home and School Association meetings. In the 1960s when she was a university student, she undertook a more sustained practice of what she would dub her "curious pursuits" and "occasional writings," the subtitle of her collection *Moving Targets* in its UK edition: *Curious Pursuits: Occasional Writing* (Virago Press, 2005). Though younger than the others on Wiseman's list of fellow women writers, Atwood was similarly concerned with many of the issues that preoccupied them as essayists, such as the environment (her "environmental fretting," as she quipped, "considered lunatic-fringe" when she first expressed it in her Introduction to *Moving Targets,* 3), or the exclusionary social norms that constrained the life of a woman writer. Atwood

---

20 *Days of the Rebels 1815–1840* (1977), *Second Words: Selected Critical Prose 1960-1982* (1982), *Through the One-Way Mirror* (1986), *Strange Things: The Malevolent North in Canadian Literature* (1995), *Negotiating with the Dead: A Writer on Writing* (2002), *Moving Targets: Writing with Intent, 1982–2004* (2004), *Writing with Intent: Essays, Reviews, Personal Prose 1983–2005* (2005), *Payback: Debt and the Shadow Side of Wealth* (2008), *In Other Worlds: SF and the Human Imagination* (2011), *On Writers and Writing* (2015).

shared with writers included in this chapter an essay style less experimental or "deconstructed" in syntax and composition than that of essayists included in the next chapter.

As noted earlier, any one of the writers or collections in *Her Own Thinker* would warrant a separate or stand-alone study. Margaret Atwood and her extensive nonfiction writing certainly make a case in point. I have chosen to focus here on her first two collections, *Second Words: Selected Critical Prose 1960-1982* (1982), and *Moving Targets: Writing with Intent 1982–2004* (2004), and on one of her longer *essais*, *Negotiating with the Dead* (2002). *Second Words* and *Moving Targets* align with an Anglo-tradition of essay writing; comprising upwards of fifty essays each, they cover a wide range of topics in generally short pieces. *Negotiating with the Dead*, closer in nature to the French *essai* form of an extended work of thematically unified writing, originated as a six-part Empson Lecture series at Cambridge University.[21] Beyond being a personal favourite of mine, *Negotiating with the Dead* foregrounds a rich and critically important theme that, as noted above, threads through Canadian women writers' essay publications and resonates throughout *Her Own Thinker*: the writing life, more specifically Canadian women writers' experiences of that life.

---

21 Similar extended explorations of a central topic include Atwood's 1995 "essai" *Strange Things: The Malevolent North in Canadian Literature*, which was based on a lecture series that she delivered at Oxford University; the 2008 collection *Payback: Debt and the Shadow Side of Wealth,* a five-part exploration of the topic of debt for CBC Radio's annual Massey Lecture series; and Atwood's first book-length "essai," *Survival,* published in 1972.

Second Words: Selected Critical Prose 1960-1982

The essays in *Second Words* are organized in three parts corresponding to three periods of Atwood's life between 1960 and 1982 during which she published no less than five novels, a volume of short stories, nine collections of poetry (ten, if the 1976 *Collected Poems* is included), two children's books, two nonfiction works, a libretto, television scripts, book reviews, and essays.

Part I of *Second Words* spans the years 1960 to 1971. During this time Atwood made a conscious effort to review books by Canadians. She did this, she quipped, out of a Victorian Sense of Duty, one of the "dues for being a writer" (Introduction, *Second Words*, 12). It was a due that Atwood often found somewhat painful to pay, the pressure of deadlines necessitating "late nights up with the typewriter and the cups of half-drunk cold tea … the memories are not fond" (12). But a more serious—and generous—reason underlay this work: Atwood's commitment to the development of Canadian literature.

Writers and critics alike have recalled how precarious the country's literature was in the 1960s, how readily dismissed were its authors, how thin was its readership. Atwood has written often about that period of Canadian literature. A recent essay, "The Burgess Shale: The Canadian Writing Landscape of the 1960s," presented as the 2017 Kreisel Lecture at the University of Alberta, suggestively links the Canadian writing scene of the 1960s and the Burgess Shale—the fossil deposit in the Rockies known for the preservation of the fossil "soft parts." But Atwood's accounts of Canadian literature generated much earlier essays in the collection *Second Words*. It was not that Canadians did not read, Atwood wrote in "Canadian-American Relations"; "They just didn't read *Canadian* books" (*Second Words*, 382). Nor did they study them.

Most schools at the time did not offer the opportunity to study Canadian literature, and only some universities, Trent University where I was an undergraduate in the early 1970s being one, recognized Canadian literature as part of a literature degree. Atwood herself never took a course in Canadian literature. Given the breadth, depth, and vibrancy of Canadian literature today, the fact that it is nationally and internationally recognized, acclaimed, and studied, it is hard to imagine that it could ever have been absent from school curricula. And yet that was widely the case. As Atwood reflected in *Second Words*, the very idea of "thinking seriously about Canada had something shocking about it" ("Canadian-American Relations," *Second Words*, 384).

Serious thinking about Canada was what Atwood and her generation of writers wanted and set out to do. They began building their writing lives "at home" in Canada, Atwood wrote, rather than going abroad as so many of their predecessors had felt they had to do. "The colonial mentality was still in force," she pointed out; Canadian writers were widely assumed to be inferior to writers in London, Paris, or New York (*Negotiating with the Dead*, 67). Canadian writers also began creating publishing outlets of their own. "We started thinking in terms of Canadian publication for a Canadian *audience,*" Atwood recalled; "If we wanted to be heard, we had to create the means of production and maintain control over it" ("Canadian-American Relations," *Second Words*, 384). Looking back on this time Atwood noted "the change-over from British cultural colony to American cultural colony" ("Canadian-American Relations," 377).

The 1960s and 1970s were years of rising Canadian cultural nationalism. In her essay "Nationalism, Limbo and the Canada Club," Atwood wrote of realizing "the disadvantages of being a colony, political or economic, and the even greater disadvantages of being an Indian" (*Second Words*, 85). The essay has ties to *Survival: A Thematic Guide to Canadian Literature* (1972), which Atwood had started writing in 1965 but, given intervening commitments, returned to and completed only at the time of the essay "Nationalism, Limbo and the Canada Club." As its subtitle indicates, *Survival* was Atwood's attempt to provide a guide to Canadian literature for general readers and to "distinguish Canlit from Britlit and Amlit" (*Second Words*, 132). She proposed as a distinct characteristic of Canadian literature a victim-society relationship (132) featuring four basic victim positions, which she illustrated with examples from a range of Canadian literary works. *Survival*, Atwood emphasized in her introduction, was not, nor ever intended to be, a work of scholarly literary criticism. Nevertheless, it was targeted by a number of critics[22] who attacked it as lacking in academic scholarship despite Atwood's clear and repeated emphasis, as in her essay "Mathews and Misrepresentation," that such was never its purpose.

Survival's publication in 1972 marks the beginning of Part II of *Second Words*. Between 1972 and 1976 much of the writing Atwood did was in response to attacks she received related to what she summed up as "Women's Lib and Canadian Nationalism" ("On Being a 'Woman Writer'," *Second Words*, 201).

---

22 Perhaps most famously Robin Mathews in his article "Survival and the Struggle in Canadian Literature," *This Magazine Is About Schools*, VI, 4 (1972-73). But also George Woodcock, "Horizon of Survival," *Canadian Literature* 55 (1973); Frank Davey, "Atwood Walking Backwards," *Open Letter* 2:5 (1973), "Surviving the Paraphrase," *Canadian Literature* 70 (1976); and Barry Cameron and Michael Dixon, "Mandatory Subservience Manifesto: Canadian Criticism vs Literary Criticism," *Studies in Canadian Literature* 2 (1977), to cite just these examples.

These were two areas that many readers and critics associated with Atwood and her work. Her response to the attacks took the form of essays like "On Being a 'Woman Writer': Paradoxes and Dilemmas."

This essay tackles and critiques 1970s social and political assumptions and stereotypes about women writers in and beyond Canada. For example, Atwood pointed out, women writers were still subject to the "Quiller-Couch Syndrome". The British writer-critic Sir Arthur Thomas Quiller-Couch (1863-1944) had deemed there to be "masculine" and "feminine" styles of writing. The masculine style, he pronounced, was "bold, forceful, clear, vigorous"—of course, Atwood dryly commented—while the feminine style was "vague, weak, tremulous, pastel, etc." ("On Being a 'Woman Writer'," *Second Words*, 197). In a similar vein, "The Lady Painter, or She Writes Like a Man" stereotype, Atwood continued, holds that when a woman paints, writes, or thinks in a "good" way, it is because she has done so like a man (197). However outdated the stereotypes that Atwood inventoried in her essay may seem today they are reminders of what women writers confronted in 1960s-1970s Canada.

Atwood's essays make clear that being a woman writer presented paradoxes and dilemmas. On the one hand, a woman perceived to have "intellectual pretensions"—not just a woman writer but any woman—ran the risk of sneers and social ostracism ("On Being a 'Woman Writer'," *Second Words*, 191). On the other hand, what women writers had to say might be taken up by academics, intellectuals, and theorists, as Adele Wiseman astutely pointed out in her essay "The Writer and Canadian Literature" (*Memoirs*, 88). We like to think the old stereotypes have faded, Atwood warned, but even after years of the women's movement, old familiar images and icons linger ("Witches," *Second Words*, 331). In her own work these familiar figures were replaced by the image of women writers as "lenses, condensers of their society" ("On Being a 'Woman Writer,'" *Second Words*, 204), an image central to Atwood's practice of the essay. Like other individuals in society, women writers played a role in social change, and change came from looking clear-eyed at where and what one was. This could be difficult to do, Atwood pointed out; to look without flinching or turning away was not easy. But the writer is an observer, "an eye-witness and an I-witness," as she phrased it ("An End to Audience?" *Second Words*, 348), and must look. "The writer *bears witness,*" Atwood emphasized, and, bearing witness, "functions in his or her society as a kind of soothsayer, a truth teller" ("An End to Audience?" 348, 353). In declaring that "the writer testifies" Atwood presented and practised writing as "not mere self-expression but a view of society and the world at large" ("An End to Audience?" 349, 353).

Essays in Part III of *Second Words* expand on this view of the writer's relation with society. In the years 1976 to 1982 Atwood became increasingly involved with human rights issues, including those in Canada. The country's treatment of Indigenous peoples, the internment of Canadians of Japanese heritage during World War II, the 1970 deployment of the War Measures Act in Quebec (395), Canada's record on civil rights, these and other human rights issues—national and international— she wrote in the essay "Amnesty International: An Address," put the question of the role of writers and writing in societal change squarely on the table. Writing is many things, Atwood reflected in "An End to Audience?" A craft, an art, a profession, a vocation, a truth-telling, a naming, an act of faith, of hope, of imagination, writing was also, she was adamant, a witnessing.

"Writing will show you things you would never otherwise have seen," Atwood concluded in her Introduction to *Second*

Words; "I began as a profoundly apolitical writer, but then I began to do what all novelists and some poets do: I began to describe the world around me" ("Introduction," *Second Words*, 15).

Moving Targets: Writing with Intent 1982-2004

Atwood's essays take their place on the continuum of witnessing—seeing and (es)saying—the need for societal change. This work continued in her second volume of collected essays *Moving Targets: Writing with Intent, 1982-2004* (2004).

Atwood identified *Moving Targets* as a companion volume to *Second Words*. Both collections consist of "occasional pieces"—essays, book reviews (which, Atwood remarked (3), were still difficult but necessary to do), public talks, and tributes, on subjects of ongoing concern and importance to her. As before, these range from the environment to politics (national and international); history (global, personal, and literary); people, both real (aunts and editors) and fictional (Becky Sharpe and Bluebeard); writing and writers, notably those recently lost to Canadian literature: Marian Engel, Mordecai Richler, Matt Cohen, Timothy Findley, and Carol Shields. Like *Second Words*, *Moving Targets* is organized into three parts corresponding to three periods in Atwood's life and writing at the time. Part I covers the 1980s—*The Handmaid's Tale* years, ending with the fall of the Berlin Wall in 1989. Part II spans the 1990s and Part III ushers in the twenty-first century and its tragic 9/11 start.

Atwood introduced *Moving Targets* by explaining the title's two-fold meaning: moving as both emotion or feeling and moving as physical motion. "A moving target is one that moves you," Atwood put it simply; "I can't write about subjects for which I feel nothing" ("Introduction," *Moving Targets*, 5). The writer's response to the world could not be only intellectual, she maintained; it required "what used to be called the heart" as well ("Introduction," *Moving Targets,* 5). Moving also means not stationary, static, or unchanging. The targets of her essays, like the essays themselves, Atwood explained, were of a changing nature and character; "embedded in time, they flow along with it, they're changed by it," she wrote (5).[23]

Changing times formed the backdrop of the essays in *Moving Targets.* Introducing the first section, Atwood drew readers' attention to some of the historical events that took place between 1982-1989, including war in Afghanistan, the fall of the Berlin Wall, and a fatwa against the writer Salman Rushdie. Environmentally, the world was waking up to acid rain, greenhouse gases, deforestation, and pollution. Against this background Atwood worked on *The Handmaid's Tale.* She started the novel in West Berlin in 1984 and finished it in Alabama in 1985. The years 1982-1989 involved many relocations as Atwood took up different fellowships and writer residencies and endured the wear and tear of repeatedly setting up work and home in new places and spaces.

Atwood characterized the second part of *Moving Targets,* 1990-2000, as a "quieter" period of writing for her. Yet the decade leading into the millennium saw a steady succession of new

---

23 *Moving Targets* was the title of the collection's original 2004 Canadian publication with House of Anansi Press. The volume subsequently appeared in its near entirety with Virago Press in the UK in 2005, entitled *Curious Pursuits: Occasional Writing 1970-2005.* A year after that, it appeared in the U.S. under the title *Writing with Intent: Essays, Reviews, Personal Prose 1983-2005* with Carroll and Graff Publishers.

Atwood titles—ten in all.[24] Essays from this period present Atwood's thoughts and perspectives on writing by other authors
and offer insights into her own. In the form of reviews, after-
words, and introductions, she considered work by Thomas King,
Gabriel García Márquez, Lucy Maud Montgomery, Gwendolyn
MacEwen, Marina Warner, and Angela Carter. In "Nine Beginnings" she tackled a question that readers and writers, herself included, ask time and time again: "Why do you write?" Whatever
the answer—Atwood's essay offers nine possibilities—the writer
must always begin again, she wrote, and "it never gets any easier"
("Nine Beginnings," *Moving Targets*, 136). The essay "In Search of
Alias Grace: On Writing Canadian Historical Fiction" sheds light
not only on Atwood's novel *Alias Grace* but also on the period of
Canadian literary history in which she and her generation began
writing: "we found ourselves being fed large doses of anxiety and
contempt (…) concerning our own inauthenticity, our feebleness
from the cultural point of view, our lack of a real literature, and
the absence of anything you could dignify by the name of history (…) we were handed a particularly anemic view of our past,
insofar as we were given one at all" ("In Search of Alias Grace:
On Writing Canadian Historical Fiction," *Moving Targets*, 204).

Atwood's essays provide first-hand accounts of the state of
culture and literature in postwar Canada and the challenges that

---

24 *For the Birds* (children's book) 1990, *Wilderness Tips* (short stories) 1991,
Good Bones (short stories) 1992, *The Robber Bride* (novel) 1993, *Morning
in the Burned House* (poetry) 1995, *Princess Prunella and the Purple Pea-
nut* (children's book) 1995, *Alias Grace* (novel) 1996, *Strange Things: The
Malevolent North in Canadian Literature* ("essai") 1996, *Two Solicitudes:
Conversations (with Victor Levy-Beaulieu)* (nonfiction) 1998, *The Blind
Assassin* (novel) 2000.

faced writers and artists. The topic recurs throughout her work, and is dominant in the third and final part of *Moving Targets*.

Essays collected from the three years 2001-2004 appeared during a particularly intense period in Atwood's writing life and in the world at large. She worked on her novel *Oryx and Crake* and on two new children's books, *Roaring Radishes* and *Bashful Bob and Doleful Dorinda*. She wrote talks that she delivered as the University of Cambridge's 2000 Empson Lecturer, which came out in extended essay form under the title *Negotiating with the Dead: A Writer on Writing*. And together with the rest of the world she witnessed 9/11 and the subsequent American invasion of Iraq. In the last part of *Moving Targets*, essays such as "When Afghanistan was at Peace" and "Letter to America" convey some of Atwood's thoughts on violence and war as the world entered the new millennium. Her essay-introduction to a collection of experimental fiction, *Ground Works*, contrasted conditions of Canadian literary life on the threshold of the new century with those of the postwar period:

> Many of the conditions taken for granted today—that there is a Canadian "canon," that a Canadian writer can be widely known, respected, and solvent, that you can get a grant or a film contract or teach creative writing or win big prizes, that there are such things as book-promotion tours and literary festivals, that it is possible to live in Canada and function as a professional writer with a national, indeed an international "career"—these conditions scarcely existed in the writing worlds of the 1950s and 1960s.
>
> ("Introduction to *Ground Works*," *Moving Targets*, 295)

And yet, Atwood mused, Canada's postwar literary land-scape allowed for considerable optimism:

There was—strangely enough—a spirit of enormous optimism: not much was actual, therefore everything was potential. All was poised on the verge, about to happen. We felt, for a while, as if we really could stop being who we were often told we were—small, boring, hopelessly provincial—and, like the albatross, go straight from fledgling status to full soaring flight.

("Introduction to *Ground Works*," *Moving Targets*, 299)

Negotiating with the Dead: A Writer on Writing

Before any soaring to celestial heights could happen, however, Atwood's writing involved a journey to the Underworld. This is an experience that she explores at length in *Negotiating with the Dead*. This multi-part *essai* foregrounds a theme that repeats and resonates across the decades of Canadian women writers' essay publications and throughout *Her Own Thinker*, namely the writing life.

Elaborating on her earlier question in "Nine Beginnings"— Why do you write?—Atwood approached her new attempt– *essai*—at an answer in *Negotiating with the Dead* with three further questions: Who are you writing for? Why do you do it? Where does it come from? ("Into the labyrinth," *Negotiating*, xix).

These were the questions that writers as well as readers most often asked, in Atwood's experience. But the extent and variety of answers that she found compelled her to ask a different question, a single question that arguably anticipated the theoretical concept of affect: What did it *feel* like to go into writing (a novel), she asked (xxii).

Again, answers varied: writing was like being in a labyrinth or a cave or underwater; it was like groping in the dark, struggling with obscurity and obstructions, feeling one's way forward, toward light, toward an outcome. Possibly, Atwood proposed, writing had to do with darkness and a desire to enter, explore, and bring something out of the dark into the light. *Negotiating with the Dead,* she summarized, is about that kind of darkness and desire (xxiv).

The six parts of *Negotiating with the Dead* explore writing as motivated by a dark, deep-down fear and fascination with mortality and "by a desire to make the risky trip to the Under-world, and to bring something or someone back from the dead" (156). The journey discloses a set of characteristics: writers' double consciousness; tension between art for art's sake and art for a useful purpose; writers as participants in social and political power; the triangle of writer, book, and reader; and finally, "the narrative journey and its dark and winding ways" (xxvi).

Writers' double consciousness is their sense of being two entities within one body, Atwood suggested, "one that does the living and consequently the dying, the other that does the writing and becomes a name ... attached to a body of work" ("*Dedication*: The Great God Pen," 62). The writing entity is the "more shadowy and altogether more equivocal personage" who commits the actual act of writing ("*Duplicity*: The jekyll hand, the hyde hand, and the slippery double," 35). Writing with an eye on the lofty halls of art for art's sake, or writing with the ple-beian purpose of paying the rent, is a choice that at some point most writers face, men and women alike. For women of her generation, Atwood noted in chorus with Laurence and Wise-man, whatever the motivating choice, in society's eyes writing meant not being an "ordinary woman"—married with children ("*Dedication*: The Great God Pen," 83-4).

The fact that many women did manage both to write and have families did not spare them from having to deal with so-cietal conventions, Atwood remarked. While women writers were subject to social stereotypes that set them apart, writing nevertheless connected them with society. The relationship between writer and society recurs in *Negotiating with the Dead*. Atwood probed what could happen if, instead of the path of Art-for-Art's-Sake, writers took a path signposted Social Relevance ("*Dedication*: The Great God Pen," 90). Her answer was that it is not writers but rather readers who decide a work's social relevance. The essays in Atwood's *Negotiating with the Dead* suggest that whatever readers determine, writers carry on with their journey and descent into the world of stories, the "underworld" through which all writers must negotiate their way.

Among other women writers, Lee Maracle concurred with this vision: "To achieve clarity, we had to go back to the bottom of the sea, through all the layers of green to dark," the Stó:lō author wrote, "to consult with the mother of thought who lives there" (*Memory Serves*, xii). In her collection *Memory Serves*, Maracle elaborates: "Each oratory turned-essay here stands on its own, but read together they create a journey through our world and the underpinning thoughts, theories, and logic that drive the world *as I see it*" (*Memory Serves*, xiii).

Lee Maracle's essays are part of the discussion in the next chapter, where the essay journey is pursued in ways different from those travelled by Canadian women writers in the 1960s and 1970s. These later journeys try out—*essaient*—different forms and strategies of essay practice, particularly with respect to the re-development and use of language in women writers' engagement with society and the wider world.

CHAPTER III

Shapeshifting

> *An* essai *or* try *... Essaying is part of ... my practice of writing.*
> *In my work, I'm moving (trying, leaning) toward ... dislodg-*
> *ing the invisible seams that cover up how language works to*
> *support the dominant order.*
>
> —Erin Moure, *My Beloved Wager: Essays from a Writing*
> *Practice* (11, 56)

> *I want to look at the language—what it transmits, the state*
> *of being it describes, the mind, the philosophical orientation*
> *of the speaker. I want to look at the language, in this case,*
> *English, as vehicular—as transporting ideas of the normal at*
> *the level of syntax and feeling.*
>
> —Dionne Brand, *An Autobiography of the Autobiography*
> *of Reading (20)*

The feminism that Wiseman and her Canadian contemporaries had seen coming in the 1960s shifted into high gear in the 1970s and 1980s, fueled by new critical thinking and theories about human identity, language, psychology, sexuality, and culture. Of particular interest in the writing world were new structural analyses of and psychoanalytic perspectives on language. The work of French feminist theorists had special impact and influence among Canadian and Quebec women writers. Their publications disseminated widely among feminist writers in French-speaking Quebec while in English-speaking Canada access came through translation in books and anthologies like

New French Feminisms (1980). Edited by Elaine Marks and Isabelle de Courtivron, *New French Feminisms* made excerpts from key texts by French feminist writers available in English. The selections included works by theorists, psychoanalysts, and linguists such as Simone de Beauvoir, Marguerite Duras, Hélène Cixous, Luce Irigaray, Julia Kristeva, and Christiana Rochefort. These and other feminist authors analyzed and critiqued the patriarchal foundations of society and language and the phallocentrism of philosophical and psychoanalytic interpretations of human experience. Of the many new ideas and critical theories that circulated during this period, language was a core focus. Under the new theoretical scrutiny, language was revealed to be neither "natural" nor "neutral." Language was constructed and ideologically disposed to express the experiences of those in power. Historically, that meant men rather than women. Language was gendered.

Wiseman and her generation had convincingly identified the male bias of the writing life. The 1980s generation that followed extended the understanding of this bias to language itself. Language was the tongue of the fathers and the dominant discourse of the different areas of human life, from politics to religion, philosophy, psychology, history, literature, and so on. These were shaped, dominated, and determined by men's experiences and realities—patriarchal reality. Feminists sought to imagine a different reality, or more accurately, different realities, and different ways to express them. For feminist writers, language was the starting point—the beginning, as Daphne Marlatt wrote in her essay "musing with mothertongue"—of the search for a mother tongue, the language of women's experience of "reality."

The focus on language and theory and on re-envisioning reality through women's experiences and imaginations ushered in a unique period of contact and dialogue between feminist writers in English Canada and Quebec. In a rich and exciting exchange, Anglophone feminist writers like Daphne Marlatt and Gail Scott and Quebec feminist writers like Nicole Brossard and Louky Bersianik bridged the English-French language divide in Canada, reading and discussing literary theory and one another's work. This exchange was facilitated by both informal and formal get-togethers, such as two conferences at the outset of the 1980s: the 1981 *Dialogue* conference at York University, organized by Barbara Godard, a pioneering critic of feminist writing in Canada, and the 1983 *Women and Words/Les femmes et les mots* conference, coordinated by Betsy Warland, Victoria Freeman, and a group of women in Vancouver. Recalling these conferences in her essay collection *Readings from the Labyrinth*, Daphne Marlatt remarked how they brought together women writers, editors, publishers, translators, critics, and readers from across Canada's Francophone, Anglophone, Indigenous, Black, Asian, and other identity communities (*Readings from the Labyrinth*, 9). Together these women reached across barriers of language and differences in cultural backgrounds as they set about to redraw the boundaries of writing and genre, notably the essay genre.

Writers included in the previous chapter made use of the essay form to address a multitude of challenging topics. They raised issues of the environment, Canada's colonial attitudes toward and treatment of Indigenous peoples, social and cultural marginalization, and numerous other concerns still relevant to Canadians and to readers everywhere today. As cutting-edge as the content of their essays was, the form their essays took was relatively conventional. By contrast, essayists discussed in this chapter experimented extensively with the essay form, breaking it open with excerpts from other genres of writing.

By inserting into their essays extracts of poetry, critical theory, diaries, journals, letters, and legal documents, as well as visual materials such as photographs and drawings, they forged new forms of "essaying." Indeed, they created a new essay genre: "fiction theory."

Fiction theory, Gail Scott clarified in her collection of essays *Spaces like Stairs*, was not "*theory about fiction*, but rather ... a reflexive doubling-back over the texture of the text. Where nothing, not even 'theory' escapes the poetry, the internal rhythm (as opposed to the internal logic) of the writing" ("A Visit to Canada," *Spaces like Stairs*, 47). It was "a method of exploring a space, a gap ... between two or more ways of thinking" ("A Visit to Canada," 47). Fiction theory, together with new theoretical and experimental perspectives on genre and language, underpin and inform the recurring focus on writing in the essays by authors in this chapter.

The first half of the chapter considers collections by Daphne Marlatt, Gail Scott, Lola Lemire Tostevin, and Erin Moure, a group of writers who were intensely involved in the theoretical work and writing of feminist writers in Quebec. An example of this is the 1988 collaborative collection *La théorie, un dimanche* (in English translation *Theory, A Sunday*). A short section of this chapter is devoted to the collection.

The second half of the chapter turns to another grouping of essayists, Di Brandt, Aritha van Herk, Kristjana Gunnars, and Lee Maracle. These writers were equally engaged with critical theory and literary innovation, but also with difference stemming from cultural backgrounds that were neither Anglophone nor Francophone. Importantly, this difference involved not just Mennonite, Dutch, Icelandic, or other European cultural backgrounds, but Indigenous cultures. Lee Maracle's 1988 *I Am Woman: A Native Perspective on Sociology and Feminism* will stake the vital place of Indigenous women writers in the discussion of these and other Canadian women essayists.

The chapter concludes with poet Bronwen Wallace's *Arguments with the World* (1992). Closer in style to collections considered in the previous chapter, Wallace's essays span the topics prioritized by collections in this chapter as a whole, while looking back to those in the preceding chapter, and ahead to those in the next. In all, the range is sweeping, expanding the breadth and depth of Canadian women writers' essay writing.

Daphne Marlatt—*Readings from the Labyrinth*

Daphne Marlatt's essay writing presents elements of the Montaigne tradition of personal expression and "try" or "attempt". Marlatt describes her essays as repeated attempts at writing the self. She frames each essay in *Readings from the Labyrinth* (1998) with excerpts from her diaries written at the time of the essay, underscoring its personal, intimate quality. Marlatt immigrated to Canada as a child. Her family relocated from Malaysia to British Columbia when she was nine and she grew up in Vancouver. Her writing career developed in the context of the 1960s West Coast poetry scene, notably the experimental practices of the writers who founded *TISH* in 1961. A poetry newsletter, *TISH* was published until 1969, its mainly male contributors[25] and their poetics influenced by the work of such American writers and theorists as Charles Olson and Warren Tallman. Marlatt's multiple collections of poetry and her fiction

---

25 Among other writers associated with TISH were George Bowering, Fred Wah, Frank Davey, David Cull, Carol Bolt, Dan McLeod, Robert Hogg, Jamie Reid, and Lionel Kearns.

works such as *AnaHistoric* (1988) trace the trajectory of her writing from influences of *TISH* to involvement in Anglo and Quebec feminism. Joanne Saul has characterized Marlatt's writing as situated "between"—"between a masculine-oriented *Tish* poetics and a lesbian body-centered writing, between narrative and analysis, between truth and fiction, between a feminist 'me' and 'we,' between history and utopia" (Saul, 352). This is an apt description of Marlatt's writing, including of her essay writing. It also captures the impact of Quebec feminist writing on Marlatt's work. Quebec feminist writers, Marlatt observed in "So, to the Ambit," created a whole new literary genre, "crossing narrative with theoretical analysis and poetic language" (*Readings from the Labyrinth*, 170). This was the new genre "fiction theory," and Marlatt's encounter with it initiated her transition from "a male-mentored postmodernist poetic[s]" (1) toward a feminist poetics. From this period emerged her ground-breaking collection *Touch to My Tongue,* with its landmark essay "musing with mothertongue". [26]

In a brief introduction to the re-issue of "musing with mothertongue" in *Readings from the Labyrinth,* Marlatt recalls drafting the essay at a time when, "stimulated by the theoretical energy of feminist writers from Quebec" (9), she was rethinking her relationship to language and coming out as a lesbian (1). This was 1982, the year between the 1981 *Dialogue* and the 1983 *Women and Words/Les femmes et les mots* conferences, where Marlatt met Quebec feminist writers like Nicole Brossard, whose work she read, translated, and helped to promote in English Canada.

---

26 Originally published in *Touch to My Tongue* (1984) and reprinted in *Readings from the Labyrinth* (1998).

Brossard's critical examination of patriarchy resonated profoundly with Marlatt's own investigations into its workings across a wide range of areas, from language and literature to sexuality, psychology, philosophy, religion, to patriarchy's most powerful claim: reality. Brossard convincingly countered patriarchal reality in her important, thought-provoking 1985 *essai, La lettre aérienne* (*The Aerial Letter*, 1988). In this text and throughout her work Brossard argues that fiction and imagination are actually more real for women, more important to and vital for expressing women's experience, than so-called reality.

> Until now reality has been for most women a fiction, that is, the fruit of an imagination which is not their own and to which they do not *actually* succeed in adapting. Let us name some of those fictions here: the military apparatus, the rise in the price of gold, the evening news, pornography, and so on. The man in power and the man on the street know what it's all about. It's their daily reality, or the 'how' of their self-realization. You know—life!
>
> On the other hand, we can also say that women's reality has been perceived as fiction. Let us name some of those realities here: maternity, rape, prostitution, chronic fatigue, verbal, physical, and mental violence. Newspapers present these as *stories*, not fact.
>
> (Nicole Brossard, *The Aerial Letter*, 75)

Marlatt's "readings from the labyrinth" join Quebec and French feminists' essay writings in their critical interrogation of patriarchal reality, and of patriarchal language—"how it misrepresents, even miscarries, and so leaves unsaid what we [women] actually experience" ("musing with mothertongue," *Readings from the Labyrinth,* 12). Her essay "musing with mothertongue" was a response to the feminist call for "language that returns us to the body, a woman's body" (13):

> the beginning: language a living body we enter at birth … that body of language we speak, our mothertongue.
> ("musing with mothertongue," *Readings from the Labyrinth*, 9-10)

Like the mother's body, Marlatt proposed, language "births us" and "structures our world" (11). It is this very structuring that raises unavoidable questions for feminist writers, Marlatt included. How can patriarchal language, with its standard sentence structure and linear subject-verb-object syntax, convey the mothertongue and its "largely unverbalized, presyntactic, postlexical field," she asks, "where words mutually attract each other, fused by connection, enthused (inspired) into variation (puns, word play, rhyme at all levels), fertile in proliferation" (13). This is language that, as Marlatt readily notes, risks coming across as nonsensical in its intuitive leaps and breaches of usage, propriety, taboos and syntax. In this risk, however, lies a new "sense" in which imagination plays a vital role.

"imagining undermines the doxa" ("Her(e) in the Labyrinth," 191)

The importance of imagining new ways of thinking, seeing, and living, and the crucial role of language and writing for expressing new ways and realities, are recurring elements in essays discussed throughout *Her Own Thinker*. There are critical reasons for the importance of imagination and writing, Marlatt explains. One is that "the fully lived life of a lesbian, cannot be imagined within the confines of patriarchal thought" ("Lesbera,"

Readings from the Labyrinth, 44). Another is that the imagination is also linked to the immigrant experience. This is a theme richly developed by writers like Aritha van Herk and Kristjana Gunnars as we will see further on in this chapter. In Marlatt's work it appears in the essay "Entering In: The Immigrant Imagination."

Written in 1983, "Entering In" directs attention to topics and concerns that became increasingly important and prominent as the decade unfolded, namely Canada's colonial and racist history and the experiences and perspectives of the country's Indigenous, racialized, and immigrant communities. Marlatt names some of the writers who take these themes to greater depth in their work, such as Jeannette Armstrong, Lee Maracle, Sky Lee, Dionne Brand, and M. NourbeSe Philip. For all of these women, Marlatt observes, writing involves revising and reversing "old script" ("Old Scripts and New Narrative Strategies," *Readings from the Labyrinth*, 65), fostering "relatedness and community" rather than "individualism and the culture of the hero" ("Subverting the Heroic in Feminist Writing of the West Coast," *Readings from the Labyrinth*, 99), and developing strategies of resistance and subversion.

Essays in *Readings from the Labyrinth* establish the link between the central topic of writing and the title motif of the labyrinth. The essay "Writing Our Way Through the Labyrinth," for example, written for the special issue of *NBJ* (*Nouvelle Barre du Jour # 57*) *L'écriture comme lecture*, compares women's experience of writing "in a time when language has been appropriated by the neo-Freudians as intrinsically phallic" (*Readings from the Labyrinth*, 34) to "finding our way in a labyrinthine moving with the drift, slipping through claims to one-track meaning so that we can recover multiply-related meanings … using our labyrinthine sense" (35). The theme of writing weaves through the collection as a whole, returning Marlatt to Brossard and to the Quebec author's argument that, by writing, women become visible in public space. Each public space created by a woman's writing, Brossard contends, creates more public space for other women to inhabit. For Marlatt this is "reaching across what divides us in class, race and religion, our continual questing for what we share, even as we refuse to elide our differences for the sake of a 'unified voice'" ("Old Scripts and New Narrative Strategies," *Readings from the Labyrinth*, 66).

Crossing the cultural divide of French Quebec and English Canada, six women writers met on Sunday afternoons in Montreal every other month from 1983 to 1988 to share their thinking and writing. The meetings resulted in the unique collection of essays, *La théorie, un dimanche* (1988). This collection offers a sense of the work and ideas of Quebec feminist writers that captured the attention of feminist writers in English Canada like Daphne Marlatt and Gail Scott and that influenced the content, form, and style of both their fiction and essay writing.

In 2013, *La théorie, un dimanche* was published in English under the title *Theory, A Sunday,* the result of collective work by translators Popahna Brandes, Nicole Peyrafitte, Luise von Flotow, Erica Weitzman, Rachel Levitsky, Lisa Robertson, and Gail Scott. In discussing the collection in the next section, I have chosen to paraphrase the original French and to provide the latter along with the translators' versions in footnote form.

La théorie, un dimanche/Theory, A Sunday

The collection consists of an essay and a short piece of fiction by each of the six contributors—Nicole Brossard, Gail Scott, Louky Bersianik, Louise Dupré, Louise Cotnoir, and France Théoret. It opens with Nicole Brossard's essay "L'Angle tramé du désir" and her fiction excerpt "Eperdument"—in English translation "The Frame Word of Desire" and "Wildly".

Multiple award-winning poet and novelist Nicole Brossard holds a place of pre-eminence among writers who developed the essay as a space for critical and creative writing. As the French title of her contribution to *La théorie, un dimanche*—"L'Angle tramé du désir"—suggests, Brossard approaches the space of writing "on an angle," the better to see "reality" from a different perspective: a feminist perspective. From her very first publications in the 1960s through to present day, Nicole Brossard has challenged received wisdoms about reality and championed the possibilities of imagining a different reality. For Brossard, feminism requires "l'imaginaire"—the imaginary[27]—in order to move toward the "female unknown"—"l'inconnue," the "e" added to the French word "inconnu" to signal the feminine.[28] This movement involves struggle, Brossard warns, and demands action to change the social values and systems of power that keep women fighting—and writing—for space and place.

Space and place are key concerns in Gail Scott's essay for the collection. In "Une Féministe au carnaval"/"A Feminist at the Carnival," a woman writer recalls a summer picnic with some women friends during which she was struck by a sense of space opening up before them.[29] It becomes clear that this is the

---

27 "Sans espace mythique et sans ancrage imaginaire, le féminisme … ne peut être que ponctuel." (*La théorie, un dimanche*, 19). "Without a mythic space or an anchor in the imaginary, feminism can only remain something limited." (*Theory, A Sunday*, 24).

28 "Un mouvement continu vers l'inconnue." (*La théorie, un dimanche*, 24). "Continual movement towards the unknown [vers de l'inconnue]." (*Theory, A Sunday*, 29).

29 "Les femmes dans l'espace—femmes qui s'inscrivent dans l'espace, un espace qui s'ouvre devant elles." (*La théorie, un dimanche*, 42-43). "Women in space, the space of now, a now spiraling in some crazy, wild, hopefully erotic flight toward the future." (*Theory, A Sunday*, 39).

space of writing—a place here and present, where words mean action. Structured by feminist consciousness, women's writing is a place of community where body, spirit, and creativity can exist together and in the present, the here and now, not the nostalgic past or rose-coloured future promised to girls.[30] Gazing at the women writers gathered around the table of their Sunday meeting, their faces full of strength and intelligence,[31] Scott sees more than a space for writing; she sees a place of presence where women re-invent themselves through language.[32] The notion of writing as a space for re-invention, self-creation, and self-determination, if no longer "new" today, was newly in the hands of women writers at the time, like the six who assembled *La théorie, un dimanche/Theory, A Sunday.*

Louky Bersianik's essay, "La Lanterne d'Aristote"/"Aristotle's Lantern," first appeared in translation in *A Mazing Space: writing Canadian women writing* (1986), co-edited by Shirley Neuman and Smaro Kamboureli. Author of the unique novel *l'Euguélionne* (1976), a witty, incisive account of sexism through the ages as seen by an extraterrestrial, Bersianik's writing is

---

30 "En tant que *lieu* (la communauté) où le corps, l'esprit, la créativité peuvent exister ... au présent (par opposition à la nostalgie du passé ou au futur à l'eau de rose qu'on promet aux petites filles." (*La théorie, un dimanche*, 51). "This community that has fostered a feeling of the right to *be* in body, mind, creativity ... in the present, as opposed to ... presently." (*Theory, A Sunday*, 45).

31 "Autour d'une table, les visages pleins de force et d'intelligence" (*La théorie, un dimanche*, 51). Not translated in *Theory, A Sunday.*

32 "plus qu'un lieu d'où écrire ... une présence où nous pouvons constamment nous réinventer nous-mêmes ... par le langage" (*La théorie, un dimanche,* 58). "The potentially nourishing women's circle must not only be one that fosters one's (language's) re-invention of the feminine, but it must be able to resist the tendency to create new conventions." (*Theory, A Sunday,* 48-49).

distinguished by its imaginative plays on words. In her essay for *La théorie, un dimanche* Bersianik suggests that literary critics had to learn how to read feminist writers. In particular, they needed to understand feminist writing not as ideology but as a powerful practice and praxis of language.[33] To fail to do so, Bersianik maintained, is to fear feminist writing instead of appreciating its effort towards change. This would be change not only in literary form and practice, Bersianik emphasized, but change in society, notably change to the social, economic, and political structures that privilege some and marginalize others.

Like Brossard, Scott, and Bersianik, poet Louise Dupré, the fourth contributor to *La théorie, un dimanche*, links writing with space, movement, and multiplicity. Writing makes it possible to conceive of feminism as a space for discussion, interrogation, and change, Dupré writes in "Quatre Esquisses pour une morphologie"/"Four Sketches for a Morphology".[34] Feminist writing is a territory that is open, manifold, and moving.[35] Like Scott, Dupré places emphasis on community and its potential to trans*form*. She plays with the word "form" as that which can bring together aesthetics and ethics, social convention and individual style, at the same time that it can point to the visual

---

33 "non comme *idéologie* … mais comme pratique signifiante" (*La théorie, un dimanche*, 98). "I don't mean feminism as *ideology* … but rather feminism as *signifying practice*." (*Theory, A Sunday*, 77).

34 "L'écriture permet de concevoir le féminisme comme un espace de discussions, de remises en question, de changements." (*La théorie, un dimanche*, 133). "Writing allows for a conception of feminism that would be a space of discussion, questioning, change." (*Theory, A Sunday*, 101).

35 "un territoire mouvant, ouvert, multiforme. Un movement." (*La théorie, un dimanche*, 133). "feminism as it actually is: a territory in motion, open, polymorphous. A movement." (*Theory, A Sunday*, 101).

arts and literary forms.[36] Feminist writers' search for new forms, blending theory and fiction, poetry and prose, as in the contributions to *La théorie, un dimanche,* constitutes for Dupré the morphology of a slow but steady transformation of form into force,[37] understood as energy and resistance to the static, linear vision in which history has enclosed women.

Louise Cotnoir picks up on the "historic place" of women in her essay for the collection, "Des Rêves pour Cervelles humaines"/"Dreams for Human Brains." For Cotnoir, too, writing is a place, a territory where the "I" can take up space, a place of strength where a woman can assert her humanity.[38] In the eyes of History, Cotnoir continues, recalling both Brossard's and Dupré's essays, she is as a woman illegible, immaterial, and illegitimate—an *un*reality that she opposes and resists with force.[39] In women's relationship to language, however, there is

---

36 "Réunit également éthique et esthétique… régulation du processus social, des formalités pour respecter la vie en commun mais aussi arts plastiques, *dessin, ligne, trace,* et, en littérature, *expression, style.*" (*La théorie, un dimanche*, 129). "Form also brings together ethics and aesthetics. As a concept indicating *ways of acting,* conventional rules, it implies the regulation of social processes, practices for the maintenance of communal life. But it also, in terms of the visual arts, means *sketch, line, outline,* and, in terms of literature, *expression, style.*" (*Theory, A Sunday,* 98).

37 "une énorme capacité de résistance, une enérgie lente et résolue." (*La théorie, un dimanche,* 135). "An immense capacity for resistance, a slow and resolute energy." (*Theory, A Sunday,* 102).

38 "territoire où 'je' peut prendre place, une place forte, quand je m'affirme en représentante du genre humain." (*La théorie, un dimanche,* 150). "Writing becomes the territory where 'I' can take place, a strong place, whenever I affirm myself as a representative [répresentante] of the human race." (*Theory, A Sunday*, 112).

39 "Dans L'Histoire, je suis l'illisible, l'ombre, le vide. Contre ce plaçage symbolique sur le prétendu réel qui fonde la legitimité mâle, opposer notre force de résistance." (*La théorie, un dimanche,* 150). "In History

positioning in the public place, ways of inscribing oneself in reality (161).[40] Reiterating the concept of writing as a space of women's self-realization, Cotnoir declares writing to be the place where a woman can exist as herself.[41] Writing, then, as place and presence for women, rather than absence from history and time. This notion, now familiar but then still emergent, resonates in the sixth and final essay of the collection—poet and novelist France Théoret's "Eloge de la mémoire des femmes"/"Elegy for the Memory of Women."

In a poignant exploration of the difference between what she refers to as her ideal and real selves Théoret recalls simply but profoundly how feminism addressed her actual self rather than her idealized self.[42] The latter, she writes, has no basis in reality, nor in action or agency.[43] Théoret's account of discovering an entire generation's demands, desires, and determination

---

I am the unreadable, the shadow, the void. Against the symbolic veneer of the alleged real that grounds male legitimacy, we oppose the force of our resistance." (*Theory, A Sunday*, 112).

40 "Dans le rapport d'une femme au langage, il y a cette 'exposition du sujet', cette montre sur la place publique incluant aussi les revendications pratiques et concrètes. Une manière de se figurer dans la réalité." (*La théorie, un dimanche*, 161). "A woman's relationship to language necessitates this exhibition of the subject, this public display that also includes practical and concrete demands – a way of imagining oneself in reality." (*Theory, A Sunday*, 122).

41 "le lieu où 'je' femme peut 'exister' en tant que TELLE." (*La théorie, un dimanche*, 153). "The place where 'I' woman can 'exist' *per s(h)e*." (*Theory, A Sunday*, 115).

42 "le féminisme s'adress[ait] au moi-réalité plutôt qu'au moi idéal." (*La théorie, un dimanche*, 185). "A feminism that speaks to the reality-ego rather than the ego-ideal." (*Theory, A Sunday*, 138).

43 "aucun fondement dans la réalité, c'est-à-dire dans l'action" (*La théorie, un dimanche*, 179). "No basis in reality, that is to say, in action." (*Theory, A Sunday*, 133).

to change social reality[44] rounds up the key themes and content of the collection.

La théorie, un dimanche expressed a decade's analysis of a symbolic and social order in which women's views, in particular feminist views, were kept largely on the margins of a central, public, intellectual space. The collection was an "intervention" into that space. The essayists' primary focus was still on issues of gender, especially in relation to language, more than on issues of race and class; these appear in later work that they—and other Canadian and Quebec women novelists and poets—publish during the 1990s.[45] In the 1980s, however, Canadian and Quebec feminist writers, specifically the six contributors to *La théorie, un dimanche*, were developing writing as a space for shared interests, communication, and community, and developing the essay genre as a place for public commentary and critique. Their essays, like so much of the essay writing discussed in *Her Own Thinker*, took up and expressed early on issues and ideas that in many cases—the environment being an example—remained under the radar of general public attention for lack of more supportive critical response at the time. A review of *La théorie, un dimanche* by Jean-Roch Boivin in *Le Devoir* (28 June 1988) entitled "Ceci n'est pas une critique et la théorie a

---

44 "attitude de revendication, [un] désir de s'engager pour une cause et une volonté de changer la réalité sociale." (*La théorie, un dimanche*, 186). "The spirit of making demands, the desire to commit oneself to a cause, and the desire to change the outside world." (*Theory, A Sunday*, 139)

45 Writers like Dionne Brand (*Bread out of Stone*, 1994 or *A Map to the Door of No Return*, 2001), Himani Bannerji (*Returning the Gaze: Essays on Racism, Feminism, and Politics*, 1993), M. NourbeSe Philip (*Frontiers: Essays and Writings on Racism and Culture*, 1992), and Lee Maracle (*Telling It: Women and Language Across Cultures*, 1990 – another collaborative work, with Sky Lee, Daphne Marlatt, and Betsy Warland).

ses limites" (This is not criticism and theory has its limits), is dishearteningly representative of the very style of critical reception that Louky Bersianik deplored in her essay. Nicole Brossard, Boivin claimed, used virile ("vachement virils") vocabulary, referring to the words motivation, decision, and concentration. Poet and short story writer Louise Cotnoir's essay, he asserted, was intellectually cramped ("intellectuellement rebarbative"). Only France Théoret's contribution met Boivin's approval, for what he described as its greater accessibility to readers of all genders and levels of culture ("plus large accès aux lecteurs de tous sexes et niveaux de cultures")—a measure of the critical engagement there was, and to some extent still is, with a collection of feminist essays such as *La théorie, un dimanche.* Bringing this work forward in *Her Own Thinker* is not to credit it with more than it contributed. As noted, the collection predates the 1990s' greater attention to issues of race. Rather, it is to suggest once again that essay writing by Canadian and Quebec women writers of fiction and poetry deserves a place of more prominence in the country's literary history and public intellectual space.

Gail Scott—*Spaces like Stairs*

The analogy between women's writing and space is central to novelist Gail Scott's collection of essays, *Spaces like Stairs* (1989). Like Marlatt, Scott contributed extensively to the development of fiction theory and the renewal of the essay genre. Scott moved to Montreal from Ontario as a professional journalist and became involved in the city's writing scene, in particular the feminist writing community and the *Theory, A Sunday* group. In *Spaces like Stairs*, Scott describes her essay writing as "a writer's journey among the literary, theoretical, political signposts" of 1980s Quebec ("Preface," 11). In her position as "a minority anglophone writer in a largely French milieu," she perceived one of a writer's most important tasks to be "a constant, rigorous criticism of her nation's dominant culture" ("Virginia and Colette: On the Outside Looking In," 30).

Scott's essays offer unique perspectives on relations between English- and French-speaking Canada, politically, culturally, and historically. They consider the comparative roles played by language and religion in Quebec and English Canada, for example, and the different perspectives these two parts of the country have on shared historical events, such as the 1970 October Crisis ("A Visit to Canada," 45). The events that rocked Quebec during the fall of 1970—notably the kidnapping and death of Quebec Minister of Immigration and Labour, Pierre Laporte— were, from the point of view of many Anglophone Canadians, acts of terrorism intended to break up the country. From the perspective of supporters of the militant Quebec independence movement, the events were attacks on English colonialism and capitalism. When the federal government invoked the War Measures Act on October 16, 1970 to contain the crisis, there was protest in both English- and French-speaking communities.

Gail Scott's life and work experiences in Quebec influenced the language and form of her writing. In her own words, "The French in my ear, a French coloured by the politics and struggles of *les Québécois(es)* over two decades, has altered my English 'line' of thinking, and in the process somewhat collapsed other genres into my prose" ("A Visit to Canada," 46). Lianne Moyes characterizes Scott's essay writing as a project "to open up the sentence, to unhinge or unbind the sentence" (Moyes, 222). From the individual sentence to the shape of a text as a whole, writing is a key focus for Scott and, as the title of her essay collection indicates, writing involves space in a variety of ways. Writing wedges "spaces between the established genres of a male-dominant literary canon" (*Spaces like Stairs,* 10) "where a new female subject might emerge in all her difference" ("A Feminist at the Carnival," 124). It makes space in language, which is seized and used in new ways and forms like fiction theory. Writing is the "space" between mind and body, a gap closed by writing "with the body" ("Red Tin + White Tulle," 21). It is space for "the integral other," for those of ethnic, racial, regional differences as well as white feminists ("A Visit to Canada," 54, 53). The multiple, open nature of writing applied well to the essay form as used by Scott. For the journalist in her, it was "precisely where the poetic and the personal enter the essay form that thought steps over its former boundaries" ("Spaces like Stairs," 106). This boundary-breaking, thought-provoking capacity of the essay is what made the genre so attractive to poet and novelist Lola Lemire Tostevin as well.

Lola Lemire Tostevin—*Subject to Criticism*

Lola Lemire Tostevin's collection *Subject to Criticism: Essays* (1995) compiles essays, reviews, interviews, and correspondence that she produced between 1984 and1993. Born in Northern Ontario, Lola Lemire Tostevin grew up in a Franco-Ontarian family. A sojourn in France in the early 1970s was instrumental in her development as a writer and in her interest in the new critical thinking of post-1968 Paris. This was particularly the case for the work of French feminist writers whose essays Tostevin was able to read in the original French, facilitating her connection with the theory and writing of Quebec feminist writers.

Fluent in French and familiar with French feminist theory and Quebec feminist writing, Tostevin was able to offer readers a succinct account of their complex interaction, impact, and influence in *Subject to Criticism*. The collection features an excellent introductory overview of the use of the essay genre by her contemporaries. Tostevin explains how feminist thinking, theory, and writing were generating so many new ideas that new writing forms were called for—the essay being a case in point. "Some of us began to cross genres, interweave different levels of discourse," she recalled; "The essay was suddenly invaded by poems, personal anecdotes, autobiographical fragments. Abstract and master concepts were displaced" ("Introduction: Criticism as Self-Reflection," 10). Language wordplay, puns, rhyme, and etymological breakdown of words, all became strategies by which many women writers found a new relationship to language in their fiction and essay writing alike.

Tostevin is clear-eyed and confident in her assessment of theories and writers in critical and literary vogue during the 1970s and 1980s: structuralism, semiotics, deconstruction, postmodernism, and Jacques Lacan, Jacques Derrida, Roland Barthes, Julia Kristeva, Luce Irigaray, and Hélène Cixous, among others. Like Gail Scott, Tostevin perceived a resistance to theory in English Canada, "a reluctance to accept intellectual ideas around writing" ("Fred Wah: In Conversation," 66). This was regrettable in her view as "new readings of psychoanalysis, mythology, theories about language and feminism are but a few disciplines that have changed the face of literature in recent decades" ("Sylvia Fraser: Afterword to *Pandora*," 132). Tostevin herself was drawn to the language-oriented texts of women from France, Belgium, and Quebec, "because language in its power to express the most fundamental dimension of both personal and universal realities also has the power to transpose, to transform" ("Breaking the Hold on the Story: A Feminine Economy of Language," 36).

Transformation and change are what interested Tostevin—and the writers whose work she discusses throughout the essays in *Subject to Criticism.* These include Daphne Marlatt, Phyllis Webb, Anne Hébert, Sylvia Fraser, Elizabeth Smart, and Smaro Kamboureli, as well as Fred Wah, bpNichol, and Christopher Dewdney. Tostevin identified language as the central story of her contemporaries' writing and highlighted the recurring themes of writing and the body, "a body encompassing a mind, an intellect that strives toward freeing itself from its historical and socio-symbolic contract" ("Breaking the Hold on the Story: A Feminine Economy of Language," 35). New perspectives on language and on the "writing body" allowed feminist writers to break through old concepts and constructions of self and others in their essay explorations. This undertaking, so central to Tostevin's *Subject to Criticism,* is also central to Erin Moure's collection *My Beloved Wager.*

Erin Moure—*My Beloved Wager: Essays from a Writing Place*

The subtitle of Erin Moure's *My Beloved Wager* signals writing as a core concern for her. Published in 2009, the collection gathers essays from earlier years in Moure's writing life. The essays present her thoughts on the practice of writing, both hers and those of some of her Quebec contemporaries throughout the 1980s. Born in Alberta, Moure moved to Montreal and pursued her career as a poet, translator, and essayist in Quebec's French language context.

Moure describes her writing as "a practice of contingency and permeability, rather than representation, a practice in and of language as social space, as social spacings in which embodiment and speech both play a role" ("Shaggy Mammal Intervençao," 264). This description places Moure's essays on a continuum of collections in which writers explore their craft and use of language, and envision writing as making space for women, both metaphorically and literally. Like Gail Scott, Moure's experience as an Anglophone writing in French-language Montreal had significant impact on her use of English as well as on her view of the world. In an observation akin to Scott's, Moure remarked that "to write in Quebec in English is to feel one's English opened up, split, and in constant motion" ("Re-çiting the Citizen Body," 219). Writing in English while surrounded by French also affected her world view and philosophical outlook. For Moure, "philosophy in French, along with French theatre, feminisms, everyday politics, and ways of seeing," were closest to her personal philosophy and view of the world ("Re-çiting the Citizen Body," 220). Feminist and critical theories coming out of 1970s and 1980s France were of particular influence. Like Scott, Tostevin, and Marlatt, Moure brings the work of French and Quebec feminists Hélène Cixous, Luce Irigaray, and Nicole Brossard into her essays.

Beyond "the historic French/English binary," Moure identifies and situates herself within a third culture, one "that rubs up against the borders of many cultures" ("Re-çiting the Citizen Body," 219). This "in between" location combines with language, structure, and sound in shaping her work. Moure describes structure as the "jewel" of writing, and sound as the poetry and risk of writing. Poetry demands listening. "Listening is key," Moure insists; "I learned what poetry was for ... to query, listen to language itself ... Poetry isn't about creativity or lifting people but about risk, great risk, hurtling oneself at the boundaries of language, ears pressed to the borders of the structure and hearing its constraints" ("Poets Amid the Management Gurus," 148).

Structure is more critical than form for Moure. Form, she contends, is "a cultural artefact"—"a principle giving unity to the whole" ("The Anti-Anaesthetic," 22). Structure is the relation and interrelation of parts within the whole. Moure is intrigued by how structure "relates to our bodies and physical presence and, thus, to the social order" ("The Anti-Anaesthetic," 22). For her a key interest in writing is "how subjectivity works and how we are persons: how our being is socially and culturally constructed, and constructed in and through technology(ies) that flatten and twist notions of space / time" ("Speaking the Unspeakable: Responding to Censorship," 99). Moure writes to break down the constructed social self ("Breaking Boundaries: Writing as Social Practice, or Attentiveness," 56) and make room for identity, where identity is understood in terms of relationality ("A New Bird Flicker, or The Floor of a Great Sea, or *Stooking*," 114). The concept of relationality allows better understanding of identity in all its dimensions and expressions, including sexual identity. This, too, "grows out of all relationality," Moure asserts; sexual identity "is not sited just in sex" ("A New Bird Flicker, or The Floor of a Great Sea, or *Stooking*," 114).

Moure is adamant that "writing is always and forever a social practice" ("Breaking Boundaries: Writing as Social Practice, or Attentiveness," 49) and must always be "engaged in some way" ("I Learned Something about Writing from You in the Sports Pages of *The Montreal Gazette*: A Conversation with Joshua Lovelace," 86). She is critical of societies and social structures that privilege some people more than others. In Canada, she points out, "First Nations people, gays, lesbian families are still less-thans … they're not just outside a discourse; they're outside in economic and social senses as well (health-benefit plans, pensions, clean water, housing, etc.)" ("Breaking Boundaries: Writing as Social Practice, or Attentiveness," 51). Essays in her collection respond to issues of social and political mistreatment. "Speaking the Unspeakable: Responding to Censorship" confronts the censorship of gay and lesbian material. "It Remained

Unheard" critiques the 1988 "The Spirit Sings" exhibition in
Calgary's Glenbow Museum and condemns government dispossession of lands belonging to the Lubicon Lake Cree. And
"Poetry, Memory, and the Polis" echoes concerns expressed
earlier in Margaret Laurence's essays about nuclear testing and
chemicals in food production, their impact on health, and the
failures of modern immune systems.

Elsewhere in *My Beloved Wager* Moure takes exception to
Canada's cultural policy on translation for being limited to
French and English projects. Herself a translator working with
the Galician, Portuguese, and Spanish languages, Moure sees
prioritizing French-English translation as a dimension of Canadian multiculturalism of which she is critical. Canadian multiculturalism, she states in "Translation as Absence, Bookended
as Gift" is a way of "demarcating 'otherness' merely so as to
contain it, thus reinforcing, not so surprisingly, an overwhelm-
ingly white, anglo and bourgeois state" (197). Moure proposes
a new concept of community as well as a new understanding of
citizenship.[46] In "Poetry, Memory, and the Polis," she argues for
community based on a "sense of 'with'-ness, 'joint'-ness" (62)
as an "alternative to problematic notions of difference and belonging, where difference is mere opposition and belonging is
passive" (61). In "The Public Relation: Redefining Citizenship

---

46 In her fiction writing, too, *O Cidadan* being a case in point. This work,
Moure writes, is "an argument against purity in which essay surges as a
form proper to poetry, and one that promulgates lyric as a form or force
that lives in poetry irrevocably. In its forms, *O Cidadan* enacts what it
speaks of, to insist that the crossing of borders, that leakages in borders,
is what makes entities (countries, persons, communities) possible" (263).
O Cidadan maintains that "identity finds its stability in the fluidity of
limits, in the 'not yet'" (219).

by Poetic Means," she discusses citizenship as "a mode of en-
actment, not belonging. It is a way of comporting oneself. It is
a public relation. It is sited, but not rooted in soil or in soil's
versions, and its terms are open to the possibility of movement
beyond the 'already constituted,' remain open to *constitution*
itself as an open act, an act of *co-situating*" (164).

Citizenship, community, culture, language, writing—in
these, indeed in all areas, Moure stands by the central role of
poetry, of words: "the force of words, sounds, and signification,
as well as the relation between the parts or particles, the interrelation of parts in the whole" ("The Anti-Anaesthetic," 22). She
draws deliberate attention to "missing words, repetitions, mis-
spellings, and jarring representations" ("For Scoping Girls," 95).
She emphasizes that her work interrogates itself ("My Relation
to Theory and Gender," 87); it asks "what does it mean to exist,
to communicate, to love alongside each other? What part does
a social framework play? What are the limits of 'the person,' of
grace, of honesty, of speech? How do we situate ourselves as
entities, organs in the *civis*, in *civil* society?" ("One Red Shoe,"
224). The questioning character of Moure's essays, the philosophical nature of her enquiries, and the poetic quality of her
writing make for challenging reading, with more questions
raised than answered. But questions fuel Moure's writing and
energize her essays. Questions are equally energizing for poet
Betsy Warland's essay writing as well.

Betsy Warland—*Breathing the Page*

Published in 2010, Betsy Warland's *Breathing the Page: Reading
the Act of Writing* brings together essays written over an earlier
period of twelve years. Each essay begins with a "hook question"
("Proximity," 58), Warland's way of entering into the "state of

consciousness" of writing ("Heartwood," 26), in which she explores the act of writing.

Warland credits essays by Phyllis Webb and Margaret Atwood for getting her "hooked on the essay form" ("Acknowledgements," *Breathing the Page,* 167). Phyllis Webb's "On the Line" (*Talking,* 1982) and Margaret Atwood's "The Page" *(Murder in the Dark,* 1983) prompted "a state of consciousness about the act of writing," Warland explains, "and opened a parallel, embodied world of thinking and writing about writing" ("Acknowledgements," 167). Ultimately, they inspired her to collect a selection of twenty-four of her own essays in *Breathing the Page.*

In addition to the subject of writing and the related subjects of language, the body, imagination, and risk, a number of topics in *Breathing the Page* connect it to specific collections by other Canadian women essayists. For example, Warland shares Moure's particular attention to the importance of listening, the primacy of poetry and sound, and the materiality of words and language. "Deep listening takes time. Lots of it," Warland remarks, and "as a poet, it is absolutely essential to sound out your poem over and over throughout the inscription, composition, and revision processes" ("Embodiment," 34).

Contiguity is another shared topic. Moure described contiguity as the "relationality" that was critical to her as part of what defined her "as a body, as present in space, as conscious, as imbricated" ("Speaking the Unspeakable: Responding to Censorship," *My Beloved Wager,* 99). Warland perceives contiguity as a contemporary way of life that, as readers, we experience through contiguous forms of narratives, "blended braided, text within a text, collage, and parallel text narratives" ("Spatiotemporal Structural Strategies," *Breathing the Page,* 97), or that, in more recent times, we experience through technology (surfing the web, hundreds of television channels). She views her 1987 *serpent (w)rite* as "a contiguous long poem that investigates and retells the first three chapters of Genesis" ("Spatiotemporal Structural Strategies," 97). Both Warland and Moure conceive of form as content—Moure, in her essay "I Learned Something about Writing from You in the Sports Pages of *The Montreal Gazette*" (*My Beloved Wager*, 79), and Warland, in "Intrinsic Form," where she references Aristotle's distinction between form and structure and declares "Form = Content / Content = Form" (*Breathing the Page*, 119).

Stylistically, Warland's essays depart from Moure's and other more experimentally adventurous essays; hers are more straightforward in sentence structure and composition. Indeed, parts of the collection read, as Warland intended them to be read, as "how-to"s or guides to writing, or as light-hearted but thought-provoking tributes to the lowly pencil or the familiar writing table.

> A pencil on average writes 45,000 words. It signals time's passage, urging us on to the next word, the next page. Our hand intimately knows a particular, curious, accumulating sadness as pencil becomes smaller, smaller, until it is too small to hold. Reluctantly, we throw pencil stub away. Wonder what its final two inches might have enabled us to write.
>
> ("The Pencil," *Breathing the Page*, 29)

> As writers, the table is our familiar. It is upon this intimacy with the table that we write our way into the public world … The desk, though more practical, is also more armoured: defended. I prefer a table with its embodiment of negative and positive space. Prefer its more inclusive lineage. (…) In the wood of the table we meet tree, as we meet it in pencil, page, chair, rooms, and books. This is a writer's lineage. *Tree, deru, truth.*
>
> ("The Table," *Breathing the Page*, 76)

From essays exploring spaces and places of writing (tables, desks, and writing rooms), to essays about tools of the trade (pencils and computers), concerns of composition (lines, commas, and structural strategies), and sources (memories) and influences ("Quote-tidians") of writing, Betsy Warland's *Breathing the Page* spans the concrete, practical "how-to"s of writing and writing's less tangible but compelling drive toward truth.

Di Brandt—*So this is the world & here I am in it, Dancing Naked*

A different take on "how-to" and an alternate writing toward truth are presented in poet Di Brandt's essays. Brandt's non-fiction writing comprises three volumes, *Wild Mother Dancing* (1993), a revised version of her PhD dissertation, and the essay collections *Dancing Naked: Narrative Strategies for Writing across Centuries* (1996), and *So this is the world & here I am in it* (2007).

Like her contemporaries, Brandt was keenly interested in the modern critical theories of the feminist writers who inspired her peers—Julia Kristeva, Luce Irigaray, Hélène Cixous, Adrienne Rich, Mary Daly, and Marianne Hirsch—and, like her peers, she engages with their theoretical work in her essays. She also interacts with the work of Canadian Anglophone writers such as Margaret Laurence, Adele Wiseman, Dorothy Livesay, Mavis Gallant, Margaret Atwood, Daphne Marlatt, Joy Kogawa, and Francophone writers Nicole Brossard and Jovette Marchessault. She identifies commonalities in these writers' different cultural backgrounds and narrative concerns:

All, for example, agree on the fact of the mother's oppression and silencing under patriarchy. All share in the political/artistic struggle to bring her back into story, and hence into public/

social discourse. Each of these writers also, in her own way, affirms the metaphorical (and biological) connection between maternal narrative and concern for children and the environment.
("Coda," *Wild Mother Dancing*, 157).

Patriarchal power, the maternal experience, the environment, social and political issues, all are writing subjects that Brandt shares with her contemporaries. She writes critically about the experience of mothers in patriarchal society, the use of pesticides, the genetic modification of foods, the hyper-industrialization of the Great Lakes region, colonialism and the treatment of Canada's Indigenous peoples. In confronting these concerns, she believes, like Moure, in the central role—and risk—of writing, in particular writing poetry: "how deeply political and potentially transforming poetry can be: how much power it holds on shaping the imaginative life of a society" ("Foreword," *Dancing Naked*, 11).

A distinguishing feature of Brandt's work is its examination of her traditional Mennonite cultural background and how she not only rebelled against it but dared to write about her rebellion. Brandt describes the impact of Mennonite culture on her life as "the trauma of breaking through the strict codes of separatism and public silence" ("Foreword," *Dancing Naked*, 9). Breaking away from her Mennonite upbringing marked the beginning of writing for Brandt. Her essay "Letting the Silence Speak" traces her difficult journey from silence to writing. In this, the 1983 Women and Words conference in Vancouver was a critical turning point in helping her dare to do what no Mennonite woman she knew had ever done: become a writer. "My culture was traditional, patriarchal and separatist," Brandt wrote; "we weren't supposed to read books, never mind write them" ("Letting the Silence Speak," 19). The road to reading and writing was open for men in Mennonite communities, and writers like Rudy Wiebe and Patrick Friesen took to it, although not without pitfalls along the way. For his novel *Peace Shall Destroy Many* (1962), Wiebe, for example, had to step down as editor of the *Mennonite Brethren Herald*. For Mennonite women, Brandt found, to write was to experience "nakedness as speakers in public against our heritage of silence" ("Dancing Naked: Narrative Strategies for Writing Across Centuries," 38).

Not only did Brandt dare to write about the impact of Mennonite culture and community on her life and work, paving the way for Mennonite women writers like Miriam Toews to follow, she wrote about Mennonite impact on Indigenous peoples and communities as well. The opening essay of *So this is the world & here I am in it* acknowledges the part played by Mennonite communities in the dispossession of Indigenous lands: "This stolen land, Métis land, Cree land, buffalo land. When did I first understand this, the dark underside of property, colonization, ownership, the shady dealings that brought us [settlers] here, to this earthly paradise? ("This land that I love, this wide, wide prairie," 1). The essay, which dates from 1997, expresses Brandt's realization of the extent to which the Mennonite community in which she grew up was implicated in Canada's colonialism and disregard for its Indigenous peoples. She recognized that her Mennonite "colonialist farm upbringing ... immigrant settler project" (192) was a beneficiary of the Canadian government's agricultural project that became one of the reasons for the Métis rebellion ("This land that I love, this wide, wide prairie," 2).[47] She perceived that treaty negotiations were unfair,

---

47   She credits fellow writer James Reaney for bringing "a growing sense of First Nations indigenosity and immigrant multiculturalism into our academic and public literary discourses (in the 1950s and 1960s in Manitoba)" (141), adding: "What is striking, in light of the current eco-crisis,

that Indigenous and Métis communities had resisted the take-over of their lands and livelihoods, and that treaties were signed under duress "with strangers who practiced duplicity" ("This land that I love & here I am in it," 9). This history of duplicity had severe consequences for Indigenous communities and for the land—"this slow dying prairie," Brandt wrote ("This land that I love & here I am in it," 10):

> In a little more than a hundred years, we, the immigrant set-tlers of this beautiful land, have managed to poison the land and our food sources and our own bodies so drastically as to jeopardize the future of all life in this country.
>
> ("This land that I love, this wide, wide prairie," *So this is the world & here I am in it*, 7)

Moreover, she added:

> We still occupy land that belonged to indigenous people not long ago. Can history ever be fixed up or atoned for or un-done? We haven't even begun to memorialize the cultural cost of occupying Turtle Island, let alone negotiate amends.
>
> ("Berlin Notes," *So this is the world & here I am in it*, 94)

Brandt's essays draw attention to past and present challenges faced by Indigenous communities, such as the "Oka Crisis," that is, as Leanne Betasamosake Simpson and Kiera L. Ladner explain, the resistance at Kanehsatà:ke:

---

is Reaney's prescient rage about its coming horrors well before the topic became generally fashionable in North American lit circles, as it is begin-ning to be now" ("Souwestoegg on Winnipuzz: James Reaney's Winnipeg," *So this is the world & here I am in it*, 146).

Although the "Oka Crises [sic] is known to most Canadians as the "Oka Crisis," the term is offensive to many involved in the struggle because it refers to the non-Native town, and because the term was manufactured by the mainstream media. We agree. However, in editing a collection from a group of such diverse writers, we have left the language up to individual writers. Like it or not, Indigenous or Canadian, people identity with the term "Oka Crisis" in far greater way than they do to phrases such as "the resistance at Kanehsatà:ke" or the "standoff at Kanehsatà:ke and Kahnawà:ke." Still, we feel it is important to disrupt colonial labels, and have encouraged writers to decolonize their use of language where appropriate.

(*This is an Honour Song: Twenty Years since the Blockades*, 8-9)

Brandt's essays pay homage to Indigenous women writers who speak up about these and other matters in their essays and fiction. The regard for the land that writers like Jeannette Armstrong, Lee Maracle, Kateri Akiwenzie-Damm (Anishinaabe), Paula Gunn Allen (Laguna), and Louise Halfe (Cree)[48] express in their work led Brandt to reflect on how her Mennonite cultural upbringing, oppressive as it was to her as a woman and a writer, had attached her to the land and to values of community. The essay "*Je jelieda, je vechieda*: Canadian Mennonite (Alter) Identifications" is a complex reflection on cultural difference stemming from growing up in a Mennonite community.[49]

---

48 See *So this is the world & here I am in it* (pages 70, 184, 194, and 197) for references to these writers.

49 Brandt suggests that Mennonites practised a kind of "indigenosity," "a sense of ethnicity that puts high stakes on embodied physicality, ancestral loyalty, wild-minded communal interdependence, separatism from the rest of the world, and an intimate relationship to land" (126). The suggestion

Di Brandt offers readers strong, intelligent, and accessibly written essays. Stylistically, she employs various postmodern techniques that characterize the work of Moure, Marlatt, and others. But she does so without forgoing the use of punctuation and capital letters. Her use of theory is clear, her ideas are insightful, and she is thoughtful about Indigenous history and experience in Canada. For a voice from within that history and experience, however, there is the powerful essay writing of Stó:lō poet and novelist Lee Maracle, whose too-early death in November 2021 renders her collections all the more invaluable.

Lee Maracle—*I Am Woman*; *"I am an Indigenous feminist." (Memory Serves, 149)*

Given the publication of two post-2000 collections, *Memory Serves: Oratories and Other Essays* (2015) and *My Conversations with Canadians* (2017), Lee Maracle's essay writing readily takes its place in more than one chapter of *Her Own Thinker*. Her essay publications date back to the 1980s when she published *I Am Woman: A Native Perspective on Sociology and Feminism* in 1988. Maracle's was a vitally important voice heard, if insufficiently listened to, decades ago.

I Am Woman marked a departure from the style of much 1980s essay writing by Canadian women poets and novelists. The volume does not feature the deconstructed sentences and syntax of essays by writers like Daphne Marlatt or Erin Moure. This is not to suggest that *I Am Woman,* or subsequent collections

---

of an "Indigenous-minded aspect" (129) to Mennonite culture arises in her "quarrel" with theorists of ethnicity and postcolonialism who "valorize hybridity as the solution to tribal and ethnic misunderstandings and hostilities" (*So this is the world & here I am in it,* 129).

and works by Maracle, are stylistically traditional. Rather, it is to distinguish the oral dimension of her writing. Orality, characteristic of much Indigenous writing, is integral to Maracle's writing.

Maracle was at the forefront of and a prominent spokesperson for the recognition of the distinct nature of Indigenous writing in Canada, rooted in the influence of Indigenous oral traditions and storytelling on the written text. "Our orality is not simply about our stories," Maracle explained; "It is about our sociology, our science, our horticulture, aqua culture, our medicine, our law, our politics, and, lastly, our story" ("Reconciliation and residential school as an assimilation program," *Conversations*, 141). Maracle adamantly rejected the infantilization of the oral nature of Indigenous knowledge and repudiated the notion that Indigenous knowledge and writing did not deserve "the same recognition and protection as written knowledge" ("Appropriation," *Conversations*, 103).

Maracle's writing is integrally informed by the orality of her Stó:lō culture, "its rhythm, its ease, the way we can slip into poetry, story, even song and dance, break the tedium with a joke, particularly an anti-colonial joke," she wrote (*Memory Serves*, xii). These elements of her writing produced "a new kind of prose, what is fashioned when oratory is written down" (*Memory Serves*, xii). Maracle's essays exhibit the traits and story structures of the Salish longhouse. In the longhouse, she described, "there are gaps in the storytelling process. Not everything is fleshed out (…) the scenes are open-ended; they direct the listeners to consider their own journey through this long dance of colonization and de-colonization" ("Dancing my way to Orality," *Memory Serves*, 221). Moreover, Maracle added, in the longhouse a story is normally told by more than one person, "so sometimes the voice changes and the story shifts just slightly because maybe an elder is talking the story" ("Dancing my way to Orality," 219).

In her writing Maracle could "shift and write in the voice of the elders translating and transforming English into a shape that is purely Salish" ("Dancing my way to Orality," 219). A "collective" understanding of writing such as this puts the notion of individual genius and authority into a different perspective:

> Indigenous peoples have historically hesitated to create books such as this [collections of essays] because they express the views of individuals presenting thoughts on the whole. The individual cannot represent the whole in that way in our communities. We don't assign anyone that kind of authority. I derive my understanding of social theory, of our logic, our processes for thought, discovery, consultation, and learning from stories I have heard and from having witnessed thousands of oral discussions with youth, elders, middle-aged people, even children. As a witness I pay attention to how these discussions unfold, how each individual engages the whole, the subject in question, and how they play with it. I have been witnessing for as far back as my memory serves, but this does not make me an expert on our people. (*Memory Serves*, xiv)

The significance and understanding of these and other aspects of Indigenous writing largely eluded the reading and critical public that Maracle encountered when she began writing in the 1970s. Her audiences at that time, she recalled, were "mostly white men," and they questioned not only what she wrote but who had written it for her, as if she herself could not possibly be a writer ("Meeting the Public," *Conversations*, 13, 14).

Among other contributions to cultural and political discussion in Canada, Maracle put the issue of voice appropriation squarely on the table. At the 1988 Third International Women's Book Fair in Montreal, she famously advised women writers, indeed the feminist movement as a whole, to "move over" ("Appropriation," *Conversations,* 99). With these two words, Maracle captured and articulated early on an issue that has grown more critical and acute with each passing year: cultural appropriation. At the time, it was a subject only beginning to be grasped and understood by established arts and cultural communities. It went on to become a topic for society at large to understand, and remains a pressing, political, and complex issue today.

Maracle's directive to the feminist community in 1988 to "move over" expressed the concern of many Indigenous writers, then and now, that writers who are not part of their communities are speaking for them. Indigenous writers, Maracle declared, can speak for themselves. A case in point, she noted, was *Daughters of Copper Women.* Published in 1981 by the feminist collective Press Gang Publishers, this book drew on stories, myths, and legends that author Anne Cameron heard from Indigenous elders. It became a best-seller and enjoyed multiple re-printings. While Maracle did not specifically ask Cameron to move over, she did ask her to "stop stealing our stories" ("Appropriation," 99). "Like other people (white people)," Maracle explained, Cameron "thought if some elders asked her to write our stories down that it was okay with the rest of us" ("Appropriation," 99). As Maracle would reiterate for years to follow, it is not. Stories, she made clear, are "keys to the national treasure known as our knowledge," underscoring the seriousness of their appropriation—their theft—by non-Indigenous people ("Marginalization and reactionary politics," *Conversations,* 40).

Drawing on her experience and knowledge of story as a Stó:lō woman, Maracle further clarified the understanding of story as belonging to the story teller, in the same way that personal clan or family identity, inheritance or wealth, belong to a named individual. A story keeper is recognized as the owner of knowledge to be passed along to children as their rightful inheritance. Stories are "what our inheritance is about," Maracle emphasized ("Appropriation," 103). Stories are private property, comparable to homes, passports, birthright, or even the Bible in non-Indigenous societies. Stó:lō and other Indigenous stories, songs, and names are "who we are and what we believe, where we have been and where we are now," Maracle wrote ("Appropriation," 100). For non-Indigenous people to appropriate and use Indigenous stories is tantamount to theft: "the person doing the appropriating has no prior authority or birthright or permission to access the item and no permission from its original owner to use or benefit from the item," Maracle explained ("Appropriation," 101). This is stealing; it is "where the issue of appropriation of culture comes into play," she specified; "We want our sensibility about ownership honoured by the Outsiders and we also want our children to pick up their cultural bundles and access their birthright" ("Appropriation," 116).

As Maracle stated at the Montreal book fair, non-Indigenous writers had "to stop stealing Indigenous people's stories" ("Appropriation," 99). They had to start understanding, appreciating, and respecting the critical place and role of story and storytelling from Indigenous perspectives. In many Indigenous cultures, stories are not fiction in the sense of being made-up or imaginary; nor are they myths in the Western sense of the word.[50] Stories are real in the way that Nicole Brossard perceived fiction

---

50 Maracle at times aligns story, storytellers, and writing with myth, myth makers, and mythologies: "Most Canadians think mythologies are false, are fiction, but as all writers know, fiction is often the source of profound truth. (...) Mythology contains truth. We use fantastic stories to engage our children in the search for truth through mythology. The story of the 'hole in the sky' by Ojibway people has plenty of truth" (Conversations, 58).

as more real than reality. "I believed our elders when they said *reality is always false*," Maracle remarked ("Indigenous Women and Power," *Memory Serves*, 137; italics in the original). Stories are historic and present at the same time; they are witness to life and powerful truths, and they lead to "right living, to the good mind, to relationship with one another and the land" ("Appropriation," *Conversations*, 119). Stories help determine how to "make it right with creation," Maracle added; "This kind of discourse is about the lessons, the teachings, meanings and the conduct that we must arrive at personally and collectively" ("Toward a National Literature," *Memory Serves*, 204). Lessons and teaching do not make Indigenous stories and storytelling all seriousness, and humour and laughter figure prominently in Indigenous storytelling, Maracle's included.

Maracle's Montreal declaration reverberated across Canada in subsequent events and statements of protest against "speaking for others," most notably against white middle-class feminists speaking for women from Canada's Indigenous and Black communities. Moreover, the matter of cultural appropriation was relevant beyond the field of writing.

In Calgary, host to the 1988 Winter Olympics, an exhibition at the city's Glenbow Museum called "The Spirit Sings" ignited protest across the country, from different communities, for different reasons and perspectives.[51] That same year at the Women's Press in Toronto, an anthology that included stories about Black women written by white women divided the

---

51 Joe Norton, then Grand Chief in Kanehsatà:ke, for example, protested the inclusion of an Iroquois face mask. The Lubicon Cree from northern Alberta, who were battling the fossil fuel industry, protested Shell sponsorship of the exhibition. Not all Indigenous people agreed with the protests; some Blackfoot elders, for example, were in support of the exhibition.

country's first feminist press when Black authors took their writing elsewhere. M. NourbeSe Philip recalled:

> African Canadian women … did not view The Women's Press as a particularly friendly place for their work. It was, in my opinion, no different from the other mainstream presses … they held themselves out as being feminist and therefore representative of *all* women, when in fact they represented a very specific group – white, middle class women. And to be brutally frank, when the issue of racism exploded at the Press and became public, my first gut response was: "It's about time – they've had it coming for a long time!"
>
> ("Gut issues in Babylon," *Frontiers: essays and writing on racism and culture*, 214–215).

As if nothing was learned from the 1988 "The Spirit Sings" exhibition at Calgary's Glenbow Museum, in 1989 Toronto's Royal Ontario Museum exhibition "Into the Heart of Africa" ignited protest as well. Lack of sufficient consultation with and involvement of Toronto's Black communities resulted in an exhibit that some saw as accepting of the imperial conquest of Africa. Protest was also part of the 1989 international PEN[52] congress in Toronto, co-hosted with Montreal that year. The Toronto gathering of writers was picketed by the group Vision 21. Its members sought to draw public attention to the underrepresentation of minority writers in the various areas of PEN Canada's activities, from adjudication committees to

---

52 Originally poets, essayists, and novelists, hence the name PEN, though it now welcomes playwrights, editors, and writers of multiple forms, such as journalists and historians.

the nominees and recipients of grants and awards. The protest sparked a public exchange between poet M. NourbeSe Philip and PEN Canada's incoming president at the time, journalist and author June Callwood, which generated national newspaper and media coverage and drove division among members of the writing community.[53]

Meanwhile at the 1989 meeting of the Writers' Union of Canada, Lenore Keeshig-Tobias (Anishinaabe) and Daniel David Moses (Delaware) called for a task force on artistic appropriation and accessibility. An *ad-hoc* committee was created and the issues were taken up at various events in the 1990s. These included a three-day retreat in 1992 on the topic of The Appropriate Voice, protests in 1993 against the Toronto staging of the American musicals *Miss Saigon* and *Show Boat,* and the consequential 1994 Writing Thru Race conference. Carol Tator and Frances Henry detail these and other race-based events in 1980s-1990s Canada in their book *Challenging Racism in the Arts: Case Studies of Controversy and Conflict* (1998). These events inspired significant essay writing in the 1990s and renewed discussions about cultural appropriation, as we will see in the next chapter.

---

53 The exchange in question involved an expletive with which Callwood responded to Philip's call for greater minority representation within the organization. A social activist as well as a writer, Callwood was known for her work for vulnerable, disadvantaged, marginalized communities in Canada, helping to establish women's shelters, centres for teenagers, and the country's first HIV/AIDS hospice. She and Philip might well have shared perspectives on numerous issues, but the exchange that day revealed importantly different perspectives, positions, and experiences as well.

Debates on cultural appropriation and the marginalization of "minority" writers marked the beginning of long overdue attention to Indigenous and racialized voices in Canadian literary and intellectual circles. Maracle would write extensively on the subject of appropriation and would remind readers that "in order for me to be marginalized in your mind, you must be further convinced that you are at the center of the universe" ("Response to empathy from settlers," *Conversations*, 127).

> The notion of marginalization is conjured up by those who believe we want to be a part of this racist, colonial, patriarchal world that is struggling to maintain its grip on our continent and on the former colonies, particularly Africa. ("Marginalization and reactionary politics," *Conversations,* 48)

In the decades that followed, Maracle and other Indigenous writers would introduce readers and critics whose understanding of literature was based largely on works by British and American writers, to writing based on "another way to be, to think, to know," as Maracle put it (*Memory Serves*, xiv). "When Canadians witness another way," she added, "perhaps colonial domination can begin to end" (*Memory Serves,* xiv). In the meantime, other ways of writing, being, and thinking, had yet to be embraced by a predominantly Anglo-focused Canadian reading and critical community. The 1980s saw Canadian literary criticism turn toward the significant body of writing—both literary (novels, poetry, short fiction) and academic (scholarly books, articles, theses)—on multiculturalism, a stage of Canadian cultural and intellectual discourse that writing by two "multicultural authors," novelist Aritha van Herk and poet Kristjana Gunnars, serves briefly to discuss here.

Multiculturalism and Canadian literary culture

Multiculturalism was declared an official government policy in Canada in 1971 and has become a major multidisciplinary field of study explored by sociologists, demographers, political scientists, historians, and literary critics, among other scholars.

Multicultural writing in Canada predates official multicul-turalism. It has been part of Canadian literary culture since the beginning, developing in tandem with the country's evolving immigration policies and the demographic changes these poli-cies have generated.[54] Post-World War II policies, for example, under which displaced peoples of Eastern Europe were able to come to Canada in greater numbers, resulted in the growth of earlier established Jewish communities which supported writers such as Adele Wiseman and Miriam Waddington, and many others such as A.M. Klein, Irving Layton, Mordecai Richler, and Leonard Cohen.

Historically, multicultural writing, drawing from the notion of two founding nations, has been taken to be that of immi-grants of non-British and non-French background, and often that of their Canadian-born descendants as well. At times, it has even been used in reference to the work of Indigenous writers as part of a general but inaccurate perception of multicultural writers as anyone "culturally different" from dominant Anglo-phone or Francophone culture.

The 1980s saw intensified study of multiculturalism. It be-came the subject of extensive debate within a larger discussion

---

54 In my chapter for the book *Immigrant and Ethnic-Minority Writers since 1945: Fourteen National Contexts in Europe and Beyond* (Verduyn, 2018), I present an in-depth account of this relationship and its literary "outcomes".

in Canada about immigrant, ethnic, diasporic, minority or mi-
noritized Canadians and "Canadian culture." In its earlier stages
the discussion revolved around ethnicity, broadly understood
to be that of immigrants of European background whose ethnic difference was "invisible" because "white," as in Aritha van
Herk's Dutch background and Kristjana Gunnars's Icelandic
background. As multiculturalism discourse evolved, ethnicity
was "fine-tuned" to distinguish between majority/minority ethnicity and invisible/visible ethnicity, with the former referring
to Canadians of Scottish, Irish, British, and mainly northern
European backgrounds, and the latter—visible minority—serv-
ing as "code" for racialized, meaning non-white, Canadians.

The immigrant or ethnic perspectives that van Herk and
Gunnars explore in their essays are those of invisible minority
experience—very different from the experiences of visible minority difference and its consequences, namely racism, the focus of much of the essay writing discussed in the next chapter.
While Gunnars's and van Herk's ethnic difference was "invisible," it nevertheless generated a good deal of "visible ink"—to
play on the title of van Herk's collection *InVisible Ink (crypto-
frictions)* (1991). As its subtitle, suggests, there was "friction" in
being "different" from mainstream Anglophone and Francophone Canada, in being "strangers at the door," to evoke the
title of Gunnars's collection, or the earlier Laurence collection,
Heart of a Stranger.[55] Even invisible cultural difference was often
best kept secret during the early decades of developing

---

55 Perhaps also, and critically, J.S. Woodsworth's 1909 *Strangers Within our
Gates*, which he claimed was "an attempt to introduce the motley crowd of
immigrants to our Canadian people and to bring before our young people
some of the problems of the population with which we must deal in the
very near future" (5).

multicultural awareness in Canada. One might be better advised to commit one's difference to writing, to keep one's foreign accent silenced, one's tongue frozen, the title of van Herk's second collection, *A Frozen Tongue* (1992) suggests.

With Aritha van Herk and Kristjana Gunnars, complexities of ethnic or immigrant identity and experience deepen the complexities of gender and sexuality, language and writing, reality and imagination, and the theoretical underpinnings of these topics. Like Brandt, Moure, Warland, Tostevin, and Marlatt, van Herk and Gunnars write about these and other subjects from a variety of modern theoretical perspectives—feminist, poststructuralist, postmodern, and in particular here, "multicultural."

Aritha van Herk—*Writing the Immigrant Self*

While born in Canada, Aritha van Herk's experiences growing up in an immigrant family—her parents were part of the post-war emigration from the Netherlands—became the subject of extensive reflection and writing about the deeper dimensions of the experience of immigration and being an immigrant. Her essay "Writing the Immigrant Self: Disguise and Damnation" in *InVisible Ink* is a prime example.

This essay is vintage van Herk—inventive, thought-provoking, and fun. Like the characters in her novels and short stories—"fictioneers", "buccaneers", travelling nudes, picaros and picaras—the voices in her essays are lively and engaging, addressing readers directly, drawing us into discussion. The narrative "I" in "Writing the Immigrant Self"—a writer and daughter of immigrants—is struggling to write "the immigrant novel." The essay's "I" begins with disclaimers: "I" is neither a historian nor a sociologist, but a novelist—"a writer of fictions" who has been daunted by the challenge of writing "an immigrant novel". She is aware of the profound displacement of immigration but at the same time she is alive to the opportunity it offers for "disguise and damnation," for reinventing one's story—the real story replaced by a new story, secrets swept under the carpet, silenced. For her, the immigrant is a sort of "magician of the self" and the act of immigration presents all the rich and wonderful potential of an act of imagination. For the immigrant parents, by contrast, the story is simple and straightforward—"it happened, period" ("Writing the Immigrant Self," 175)—and the writer's ideas are utterly incomprehensible to them:

> The plot thickens! What does she think she's doing? Here she's got a fabulous story to write, a natural story that any writer would give her and his right arm for, and she's talking about the curse of realism! Fiction, realism – it happened, period. Why doesn't she just write it down? ("Writing the Immigrant Self," 175)
>
> What is she trying to prove? Why can't she just tell the story? That's the way it happened. Compliance and justification! The plot thickens! These damn writers always want to make things complicated. It's an action story, a potential movie, a straightforward accounting of what people did. Enacting their own transformations! Nonsense! They were trying to get from point A to point B. Perfectly simple in any language. Just call it "Travelling to Canada."
>
> ("Writing the Immigrant Self," 180)

The writer recognizes that her ideas are next to blasphemous for many immigrants who offer "every official pre- and post-immigration argument for their displacement" (174). But she insists on the fiction that stories contain, and argues that stories of immigration are no exception. There is the story that is told, and there is the story that is silenced; there is the overt story and there is the covert story.

The overt story recounts how Holland after World War II was a country in ruins following Nazi occupation. The economy was in tatters, the people poor, the country congested. Canada, by contrast, was spacious and growing; it had room and need for more people. The covert story, on the other hand, is "much more complex and multi-foliate" (177). It is also much less noble about why people immigrate, why they displace themselves. The covert story is one of financial debts, love affairs, family feuds, collaboration with the enemy, and other "silenced" stories.

Overt and covert stories—both are temptations for the writer. The overt story, its "plot summary ready" (178), its "identifiable iconographic moments" (182) recognizable from myriad accounts, appeals with its "myths and popular refrains, an inevitable rousing of sentimental emotion" (178). Any suggestion that imagination or fiction, let alone magic, play any part in this story, invites denial and anger (183). The overt story "construes the greatest temptation of the two," the writer admits (178). But it is the covert story that she cannot resist. Complicated, complex, and by comparison to the larger political and social story, personal and unofficial, the covert story suggests itself as "potentially 'true' in the great fiction of immigration," the writer finds (184). This is the story that both offers and draws the imagination.

Van Herk's essays join those of other writer-essayists in affirming the crucial role of the imagination—and of language and writing for expressing the imagination. Language in Aritha van Herk's work is not only Daphne Marlatt's theory-informed mother tongue—"the beginning," as Marlatt wrote in "musing with mothertongue." It is not only "tied to the mast of gender," "the wonderful and unbridled tongue of women" (*A Frozen Tongue*, 21, 23). Language in van Herk's essays is also, and importantly, an immigrant language—Dutch, "that obscure language" (*A Frozen Tongue*, 19), "with its idiosyncratic voice and cultural nuance" (*Invisible Ink*, 129), "the original language of blood and bone" (*A Frozen Tongue*, 19), and the source of her writing. "No one used *my* language," van Herk reflects, "so, I began to write myself" (*A Frozen Tongue,* 32). Entering her Grade One classroom for the first time after a childhood on the family farm where her parents spoke Dutch, the young writer understands within seconds "how different" she is. In that moment and understanding, van Herk writes, fiction took hold.

> When you are a by-product, a hybrid, an off-spring of transience, you learn the limits of facts and replace them with fabrications.
>
> (…)
>
> I learned that the world was fiction and fiction was refuge … In language, in words, one could find the outlines of a world. I became, out of a love of lies and a desire for truth, a writer of fiction.
>
> It is language, after all, that accomplishes displacement … language that made me aware of my displacement … my first language … Dutch.
>
> ("Placing Truth or Fiction," *A Frozen Tongue,* 46-47)

The role played by the Dutch language in van Herk's essays has an encore in Canadian poet Sadiqa de Meijer's 2020 Governor General award-winning *alfabet/alphabet: a memoir of a first language.* For de Meijer, too, Dutch, "with its idiosyncratic voice and cultural nuance," as van Herk describes the language, is a source for her "essai" explorations of cultural identity, difference, belonging, and writing. In Van Herk's essays, these explorations fuse language and feminist theory. The essay "Of Viscera and Vital Questions" in *InVisible Ink* pinpoints the patriarchal power of language that excludes and simultaneously binds women to "think and write within" it (129)—"a male m(y)nefield of difficulties, words capable of inflicting so much pain, and also so much pleasure" (129). But van Herk has access to other languages, including her first language—Dutch, the language of her desire—fiction, and the "most mysterious language of all"—silence (129). Silence is the language that the feminist writer first shatters in writing her own voice, and then adopts in listening to other voices. Declaring her feminism and the difference her immigrant background has made ("an immigrant daughter, poor and *different*," 137), acknowledging the privilege of her invisible cultural difference ("I am not black or native, so as feminist or fictioneer I'm not sure I should appropriate difference," 133), van Herk proposes, along with Maracle and Moure, stepping aside and creating space for the silent others.

Imagination claims the spotlight in "Writing the Immigrant Self" but the narrative "I" recognizes that "politics and economics and social questions enter into the act," and "yes, inevitably religion and God do too" (174). Van Herk's essays take up these subjects in critical ways. On the politics of cultural difference van Herk writes that we—Canadians—"congratulate ourselves on our tolerance" ("Im/migration and Writing: A Coming," *A Frozen Tongue*, 37), reducing multiculturalism to "painted Easter eggs and various ways of cooking cabbage, clothing and alternative ways of saying 'prosit'" ("Im/migration and Writing," 37). The "ethnic tag, the hyphenated definition" have "frozen us," she remarks:

"Ethnic" has been co-opted as a piece in the jigsaw of Canada's identity, a fossilated means of trying to put an amorphous place in a glass beaker and "identify" it into stasis ... we must rebel.

("Im/migration and Writing: A Coming," *A Frozen Tongue,* 38)

Matters of faith, religion, and spirituality are for van Herk "a gender problem, a tongue-tied difficulty" ("Women and Faith: the Reach of the Imagination," *A Frozen Tongue,* 107), shared with other women who were "told both bluntly and subtly that [they] have no business talking about faith, God, or the church" ("Women and Faith," 108). Like Di Brandt's father, van Herk's "read to his family every day of every week of every year ... a chapter of the Bible" ("Women and Faith," 108). This inscribed stories on her imagination. "No one can deny that the Bible is the source of innumerable and archetypal stories," van Herk states ("Women and Faith," 109). The biblical stories she retained were of women—Eve, Sarah, Rachel, Leah, Miriam, Ruth, Esther, Mary, Deborah, Judith—stories that she rewrote in novels and in essays that critique religion's exclusion of women's words and imagination.

Van Herk's essays offer critical commentary on religion and social and political "reality"; they insist on the place of the imagination, and warn that "colonization of the imagination is the most powerful of occupations" ("Women and Faith," *A Frozen Tongue,* 113); and they prioritize the act of writing, notably writing in new ways.[56] Her collections are notable for inventive,

---

56 See, for example, the riotous essay "Blurring Genres" in *InVisible Ink.* It presents a humorous exchange between a "fictioneer" and a "buccaneer"; compares literary genre to coffins "ready to slam their lids down on you" (22); proposes ficto-criticism as "a necessary departure from genre and its expectations" (23); portrays footnotes as textual lurkers (30-31); treats

witty explorations of writing, for word-y resistance to rules of essay writing and literary criticism, and for generous essays about Canadian writers, from Margaret Atwood to Bronwen Wallace, and along the way Marian Engel, Margaret Laurence, Gwendolyn MacEwen, Nellie McClung, Carol Shields, Jane Urquhart, Sheila Watson, among others—all "Women Who Made a Difference," the title of the final essay in *Frozen Tongue*.

Kristjana Gunnars—*Stranger at the door*

Recognition of other women writers and their work is a distinguishing feature of Kristjana Gunnars's *Stranger at the Door: Writers and the Act of Writing* (2004) as well. Gunnars immigrated to Canada from Iceland in her early twenties, settling on the prairies where her work as a poet and fiction writer unfolded in a steady production of publications throughout the 1980s. While *Stranger at the Door* appeared in 2004, the collection addresses theoretical issues that preoccupied Gunnars during the final two decades of the 20th century. In her essays Gunnars brings a chorus of national and international voices to the ongoing discussion and exploration of writing and theory, language and imagination, and the growing focus on the cultural difference of immigrant, diasporic, "minority" Canadians. "We need the constant reminder that there are other peoples, other cultures, other languages," Gunnars urges in *Stranger at the Door*, "and that the hegemony of our own literary culture

---

readers to the adventures of Hannike Buch, her refuge in theorist Maurice Blanchot (38), her Porsche pursuit of a pick-up truck carrying a coffin (41), and last but not least includes the author's declaration that "the most interesting critics at work in Canada today are … authors and poets *first*" (39).

can be examined—that ours are not the absolute methods and solutions" ("Theory and Fiction: The Mixed Bag of Postmodern Writing," 64).

Gunnars joins her feminist contemporaries in a practice of fiction theory and postmodern writing techniques as a means for expressing multiplicity and dialogue. For Gunnars, "it is dialogical writing that takes into account the other voices in the community and interacts with them, even at the time of writing" ("Theory and Fiction: The Mixed Bag of Postmodern Writing," 64). *Stranger at the Door* is very much a collection of essays in conversation with essays by other writers on the recurring topics of writing, theory, language, difference, imagination, and their combined interrogation of "reality."

The challenge to reality, so central to the work of the Canadian women essayists in *Her Own Thinker*, is at the heart of Gunnars's collection. Indeed, *Stranger at the Door* makes clear the extent to which Canadian women writers' interrogation of "reality" was part of an international re-imagining of reality. From Chinua Achebe to Christa Wolf, Hannah Arendt to Eudora Welty, Gunnars finds that writers have written compellingly about fiction being more real than reality and about how we are "deceived by what we think of as our phenomenal reality" ("The Art of Solitude," 11). Canadian women writers take their place alongside these and other international writers whose essays argue the need to, in Italo Calvino's words, "look at the world from a different perspective, with a different logic and with fresh methods of cognition and verification" (Calvino, *Six Memos,* 7, qtd in Gunnars, 10). In this, the act of writing is as crucial and critical as the act of imagining. Achebe deemed the life of the imagination a vital element of human nature, Gunnars recalls ("The Truth of Fiction," *Hopes,* 147, qtd in Gunnars, 12), while Calvino declared that the writer must "deconstruct language and image and reality ... and then start to construct again from a clean slate" (*Six Memos*, 95, qtd in Gunnars, 11).

For Gunnars, the life of the imagination necessarily includes the imagined, imaginative lives of "strangers at the door"—the immigrant, the "ethnic," the "other." Her essay "The Diasporic Imagination: Writers' Perspectives" traces the link between the diasporic or immigrant experience and the experience of writing for a host of writers. The dislocation so familiar to the immigrant is comparable to the dislocation that writing requires, Gunnars reflects. Indeed, dislocation is the writer's condition, she proposes, pointing to Edmond Jabès and Salman Rushdie among numerous other writers whose work she explores in *Stranger at the Door*.

Gunnars's essays are part provenance of these explorations and part products of conversations with students in her creative writing classes. Throughout *Stranger at the Door*, from the opening essay "The Art of Solitude" to the closing essay "Poetry and the Idea of Home," she aligns Canadian writers—women as well as men—with writers around the world, as she discusses different dimensions of the life of writing and the imagination with her readers and students. She explores the solitude and space for writing and imagination that a home may offer a writer like Marguerite Duras, while another writer, like George Jonas, may prefer or have no choice but to write in the busy bustle of public cafés. The essay "The Home and the Artist" traces back to Gunnars's first reading encounter with Virginia Woolf and Woolf's essay "Professions for Women." Gunnars considers the case that Woolf makes for artists, especially women, to have "a room of one's own." She then considers Montaigne's essay on the study as a desirable space for writing. The idea of the study "sounds very patriarchal," Gunnars comments, "meant to allow the patriarch to check out of the domestic scene without leaving the home" (38).

From spaces and places of the writing life, Gunnars turns to voices of writing and to the issue of literary and cultural appropriation. In "Transcultural Appropriation: Problems and Perspectives" she foregrounds Lee Maracle's powerful words and steadfast writing on the issue, particularly Maracle's 1989 essay "Native Myths: Trickster Alive and Crowing." As seen earlier, in Maracle's view voice appropriation is far more than literary dishonesty; it is racist and criminal. Appropriating Indigenous people's stories under the guise of freedom of the imagination, Maracle maintained, is "just so much racism" ("Native Myths," 314, qtd in Gunnars, "Transcultural Appropriation," 45). Gunnars brings the Stó:lō writer's thinking and words into conversation with those of other writers in Canada and around the world, presenting a "panorama of theoretical concerns that branch into issues of creative writing, of postmodernism, of postcolonialism, cultural studies, and linguistic-semiotic studies—among others" ("Transcultural Appropriation," 53). In "Transcultural Appropriation: Problems and Perspectives" Gunnars delivers a nuanced essay on a challenging literary and cultural issue that continues to call for attention today.

In "Theory and Fiction: The Mixed Bag of Postmodern Writing," Gunnars takes her place alongside "fiction theory" writers like Gail Scott, Daphne Marlatt, Erin Moure, and other authors of "experimental" writing," defending the use of literary theory in writing fiction (56). While she refers to "theory fiction" rather than "fiction theory," Gunnars shares the perspective that the inclusion of theory in fiction, along with deconstruction of text and genre and intense investigation of language, have demythologizing impact and social and intellectual value (57). This is especially the case for the woman writer, Gunnars writes: "There is a certain pressure imposed on women writers that their work should be 'moving,' emotional, and therefore that it should exclude the intellect. It is harder, in other words, to be accepted if what you do is intellectual, because that is not expected of you if you are a woman" (65). But, she counters, "engaging the intellect along with the poetic is a healthy thing to do," and asks "Why would you not want to engage the whole mind, all parts of it, rather than just your emotions?" (65). Theorized writing, whether referred to as theory fiction or fiction theory, is about interrogating the present, Gunnars states; it is about "intervening in current textual practices, about resisting the kind of canonization that society sanctions and the market economy encourages. Such writing interferes with ideas and habits and practices that are forced on us, until we no longer remember what we thought about things—until we forget there are counter-ideas" (64). This connects directly to Gunnars's position that opening up writing, theory, and the imagination, opens the door to the realities of other peoples, languages, and cultures—to the "strangers" at the door.

For Gunnars, as for her feminist contemporaries, the writer's imagination and act of writing are "blueprints" for different realities, in which "there is spiritual, social, political, and cultural value to shared imaginary 'worlds' and … alternatives to what is far too often a tortuous reality" ("The Diasporic Imagination: Writers' Perspectives," *Stranger at the Door*, 24). Writing to argue for a world of shared spiritual, social, political, and cultural values is the impetus behind much of Bronwen Wallace's essay writing.

Bronwen Wallace—*Arguments with the World*

A Kingston-based poet whose life was cut short by cancer at the age of 44, Bronwen Wallace's posthumous collection *Arguments with the World: Essays* (1992) stands out for the distinctly political and grounded character of her essays. Written in large part for the newspaper column "In Other Words" that Wallace contributed to the Kingston *Whig-Standard* from May 1987 to February 1989, they address topics of public concern in a style that blends elements of both the Bacon and Montaigne essay traditions. On the one hand, they present factual information with a practical purpose for political, social, and economic action and impact. On the other hand, they display the personal dimension of Wallace's belief that "it is in the explanation, in the interpretation of events, *in the way that we use them in our personal lives* that history begins to matter" ("The Cuban Missile Crisis and Me," 27; emphasis in the original).

Organized into three groups, the forty essays in *Arguments with the World* are preceded by a Foreword and an Introduction, and followed by a "Coda: Blueprints for a Larger Life." The Introduction comprises two interviews with former CBC Radio Morningside host Peter Gzowski, and the Coda consists of a speech that Wallace delivered on International Women's Day, 1989. Together with the essays, the different components of *Arguments with the World* express the political and literary thrust of Bronwen Wallace's life and writing. As editor Joanne Page states in the Foreword to the collection: "Writing, politics, her own life: all were synthesized in her nonfiction" (*Arguments with the World*, 6).

Wallace engaged with a great many of the concerns of writers in both the present and previous chapters. Her essays recall Wiseman on the environment, Laurence on nuclear power, and Rule on homophobia, and they recognize the preoccupation with theory, language, patriarchy, the mother figure, and related themes of essays by Marlatt, Moure, Brandt, and other writers in this chapter. Wallace directed attention to experiences specific to women's lives and bodies, from motherhood to infertility to abortion. She discussed and distinguished between "power over" and "power to" and how these played out differently for women than for men in the contexts of patriarchal society and culture. For women to have control of their physical realities and bodies required social change—both collective and individual, Wallace maintained. It also required feminism—"as a political force [and] because it connects the individual and the collective, the private and the political" ("Coda," 224).

Feminism aligned with Wallace's adamant and outspoken spirit. As a student at Queen's University in 1963, she joined CUCND (Combined Universities Campaign for Nuclear Disarmament) and attended meetings of various left-wing groups on campus. In 1967, she participated in her first women's meeting during a SUPA meeting (Student Union for Peace Action) and in May 1970 she disrupted a House of Commons debate on abortion. Her perspectives and arguments were grounded in the politics of everyday. By "the politics of everyday" Wallace meant politics that involve "every aspect of our 'ordinary' lives, from the food we eat to the choices we make about education or jobs" ("The Politics of Everyday," 39). Everyday life was anything but ordinary as Wallace saw it, especially for the "men and women who worked in the factories, people who worked with their hands" about whose daily realities she wrote ("Foreword," 8). In her various jobs at co-ops, daycares, and a Kingston shelter for women and children, she witnessed everyday realities of financial stress, poverty, food banks, housing, daycare, healthcare, physical limitations, homophobia, racism, violence, abuse, incest, rape, and abortion. The politics of everyday, Wallace argued, meant realizing that these are not "givens" to be accepted; rather, they are "created out of certain historical developments and they can be changed" ("The Politics of Everyday," 40). They meant "a commitment to change that recognizes how the politics of class and race affect feminism" ("Coda: Blueprints for a Larger Life," 224).

On the politics of class and race, Wallace was keenly aware of her privilege as "female, white, middle-class, university-educated and heterosexual" ("The Politics of Everyday," 39). She recognized that "all of these attributes have a political significance" ("The Politics of Everyday," 39) and that they resulted in chances and opportunities that had less to do with her as an individual than "with politics, with the everyday politics that we often think of as 'just natural' or 'the way things are'" ("The Politics of Everyday," 39):

> One of the stories our society particularly likes to tell is the story of the individual. "Individual rights," "individual opportunity," "individualism," are some of our favourite words. … The story of the individual is a great story…. But it is not the only story. For many cultures, including many native cultures in this country, it is not even the most important story.
>
> ("Celebrating the Cadence of a Particular Voice," *Arguments with the World*, 90)

It was important for Wallace that the stories of others be heard. "Now, more than ever, we need such voices," she urged ("Celebrating the Cadence of a Particular Voice," 91). Essays in *Arguments with the World,* such as "The Diversity of Women's Experience," expressed her awareness of identity politics and the concrete realities of power and exclusion. She drew attention to a collection of essays by American author Nancy Mairs, *Paintext: Deciphering a Woman's Life,* for including pieces such as "On Being a Cripple," and she supported a friend's suggestion of the word TABS (Temporarily Able Bodied) to refer to people who, like Wallace, still enjoyed the full use of her limbs—use that her friend, newly quadriplegic, had lost. "I like what it makes me remember about my own frailty, my own limitations,"

Wallace wrote. "I like how it challenges me to recognize that we are all 'whole' – and all 'broken.' None of us is complete or completely able" ("When Jesus Becomes More Than a Word and Enters the World of Human Beings," 44).

As a feminist, Wallace was conscious of the need to "enter the harder, more complex regions where women's experiences begin to diverge and differ" ("The Diversity of Women's Experience," 48). As a writer, she saw it as her job "to give expression to as much human experience as I can. Since I am a woman, much of this experience will be female and for that reason a lot of it will be previously *un*expressed experience" ("Pornography and Ways of Dealing with It," 71; italics in the original). Wallace conceived of feminism as a journey "into places where women have been absent, the blank spaces in history, psychology, science, literature, art, music, religion, anthropology, and politics where women's lives have not been adequately recorded" ("Feminists, Like Explorers, Spend Their Lives Venturing into Unknown Territory," 107). "There's a lot of unknown territory out there," she wrote, "new routes have to be charted, whole countries named" ("Feminists, Like Explorers, Spend Their Lives Venturing into Unknown Territory," 107).

In setting about this work, Wallace's perspectives and arguments were firmly grounded in concrete issues and politics. She wrote about schools and educational materials, affirmative action and the law, the treatment of animals and the environment, the waste of water and the lack of it in other parts of the world, collaborative city gardens, in short, everything from "the politics of power and exclusion, goddesses and reproductive rights, women lost and found, nurturing children and the crafting of poems, and much more" (Foreword, 10). She was aware of the theory and language work that questioned "reality," and she acknowledged the feminist challenge to language and the use of postmodern and deconstruction literary techniques to disrupt patriarchal discourse. She had concerns, however, about experimental, deconstructionist feminist writing and theory—"quibbles, reservations and disagreements," as she described them to Erin Moure in a series of letters that the two poets exchanged between 1985 and 1987. The letters were subsequently edited by Susan McMaster and published in 1994 as *Two Women Talking: Correspondence 1985 to 1987 Erin Moure and Bronwen Wallace*.

Two Women Talking is a discussion of feminist theory. The letters chart Moure's and Wallace's "two paths of the discussing, their crossing, their incessant explaining, objecting, tripping, excitability" about theory (*Two Women Talking*, "Preface"). For Moure, this was "part of the process of thinking itself" ("Preface"); "consideration of theory [was] vital, vital, vital," and she took it up "excitedly as a new opening" (letter dated 20 February 1986). Feminist theory was equally important for Wallace, indeed vital to rethinking the many dimensions of women's lives. But theory in general, she found, was limited in its own way for explaining "all that we have to tell about ourselves" ("Why I Don't (Always) Write Short Stories," 175). This included feminist theory, in Wallace's view. "Much of the feminist theoretical work that has been done in Canada – and the U.S.," she wrote, "reflects the experience of white, middle-class women" ("The Diversity of Women's Experience," 47). This did not mean that it was "wrong" or valueless, she added; it simply meant that, in her view, it was limited, "and that feminists who ignore those limitations have some re-thinking to do" ("The Diversity of Women's Experience," 47). For Wallace, theory, like language and writing, had to come from "the concrete, historical ways that women have made space for ourselves" (letter dated 3 January 1986), from "women's lives and the stories they told" (letter dated 12 March 1986).

Arguments with the World concludes with the text of a speech that Wallace delivered on International Women's Day 1989: "Coda: Blueprints for a Larger Life." Blueprints, she explained, involve both "the ability to express imaginatively ... what we want to create" and the need to pay attention to "physical realities" ("Coda," 215). The physical realities in Wallace's coda are "the bodies of women" ("Coda," 215). Together with the importance ascribed to the imagination and questioning reality, they place Wallace's "coda for a larger life" on the continuum of Canadian women's essay writing during the 1980s.

"Blueprints for a Larger Life" was Wallace's last public address; cancer claimed her life on August 25, 1989. Her untimely death coincided with the end of the decade that has been the focus of this chapter. As Joanne Page wrote in the foreword to *Arguments with the World*, "Bronwen's voice resonates like a struck bell through the issues of her day, issues still ours" (7). Chief amongst these issues were considerations of race and class, central concerns in the essay collections considered in the next chapter.

CHAPTER IV

Refiguring

It is difficult, if not impossible, for Black female writers in the West today to ignore issues of racism or sexism in their work ... The challenge today for Black women writers is to subvert those restrictions that subtly, and not so subtly, suggest we should only write about certain topics, in certain ways.
 —M. NourbeSe Philip, "Journal Entries Against Reaction," *Frontiers: Essays and Writings on Racism and Culture* (64)

Slavery, and then colonialism, erased or distorted so much of our lives that we have had to learn to write ourselves into the story in any way we can.
 —Lorna Goodison, "The Caribbean imaginary," *Redemption Ground: Essays and Adventures* (74)

Essay collections considered in this chapter brought discussions about invisible minority experience and Canadian multiculturalism back to writing about realities of racism in Canada. These realities had been raised earlier by writers from Indigenous and racialized communities and in debates about cultural appropriation. But in the 1990s, writers like Himani Bannerji, M. NourbeSe Philip, and Dionne Brand directed pointed attention to the experiences of racialized Canadians. Their essays probed the cultural codes, stereotypes, and social relations that structured Canadian society, and called out the "common sense" that masks racism and sexism in everyday life (Bannerji, "In the

Matter of 'X': Building 'Race' into Sexual Harassment," *Thinking Through: Essays on Feminism, Marxism, and Anti-Racism,* 132).

These and other authors of collections introduced in this chapter still shared the preoccupations with language foregrounded in the collections discussed in the previous chapter. Experimental syntax and composition, however, are of lesser focus in their collections. As M. NourbeSe Philip suggests in her essay "Interview with an Empire," in the face of the realities that she and other racialized writers examine in their essays—in particular racism—"playing with language appears almost frivolous" ("Interview with an Empire," *Bla_k*, 58). Moreover, as Margret Brugmann (1993) noted, "the deconstructionist style" involved "playing with existing discourse," and as such could not "address the socio-political concept of societal change" (78).

Several important anti-racism events in Canada and the world at large formed the backdrop of collections considered in this chapter, such as the 1994 Writing Thru Race conference, #MeToo (2006), Idle No More (2012), Black Lives Matter (2013), ongoing debates concerning appropriation,[57] and

---

57 Paralleling the appropriation debates and Writing Thru Race conference in English Canada, in Quebec the 1997 Sroka-Larue *pure laine* debate and the 2007 Hérouxville affair raised issues of racist attitudes around Quebec identity, belonging, and cultural place. Patricia Smart provides an account of the former in "The 'pure laine' debate" (*Canadian Forum,* 76 (864):15-19). A short essay by novelist Monique LaRue on Quebec literature and pluralism, *L'arpenteur et le navigateur* (Montreal: Fides/CETUQ, "Les grands conferences," 1996. 30 pp), was criticized by Ghila Sroka, then editor of *La Tribune Juive*, in an editorial entitled "De LaRue à la poubelle" (*Tribune juive*, vol. XIV, n° 3, mars 1997, p. 4-5). Smart characterizes LaRue's essay as "a call for greater openness to 'the other,'" the non-Québécois (15). For Sroka, it was a "racist discourse [suggesting] that Quebec had produced only sublime *Québécois pure laine* writers and that all the others can be dismissed" (quoted in Smart, 16). The term *pure*

Indigenous cultural "renaissance."[58] Essays by Canadian women novelists and poets during these eventful years offer some of the most cogent and compelling examinations of these and other racialized events and experiences in Canada.

The first half of this chapter looks at 1990s collections by Himani Bannerji, M. NourbeSe Philip, and Dionne Brand.[59]

---

laine or *Québécois de souche* refers to a "dyed-in-the-wool" or old-stock Québécois having French ancestry as descendants of the first French colonists, as distinct from Québécois of immigrant background.

A decade after the *pure laine* controversy, the Hérouxville affair sparked controversy about "accommodation" and led to the creation of a commission to examine the issue. "In January 2007," Diana Brydon explains in "Negotiating Belonging in Global Times: The Hérouxville Debates" (*Crosstalk: Canadian and Global Imaginaries in Dialogue*, Diana Brydon and Marta Dvořák, editors. Waterloo ON: Wilfrid Laurier University Press, 2012, 253-271), "a small town in Quebec posted a declaration of 'norms' for immigrants on the town website as its contribution to an ongoing controversy in the province regarding the accommodation of religious and cultural minorities. This act became a media event" (253). It led to the Commission de Consultation sur les Pratiques de l'Accommodement Reliées aux Différences Culturelles/Consultation Commission on Accommodation Practices Related to Cultural Differences. Chaired by Gérard Bouchard and Charles Taylor, it resulted in the report *Building the Future: A Time for Reconciliation* (2008).

Since these events, Quebec's Bill 21, "An Act respecting the laicity of the State," has fueled community discord. Passed in 2019, the bill disallows public workers from wearing religious symbols while on duty and requires uncovered faces of all Québécois for specific public services, with particular impact on the lives of Muslim women and other minority groups in Quebec.

58 This phrase circulates in reference to Indigenous art, writing, music, and other artistic and cultural practices that are less "born anew" than "newly noticed" by non-Indigenous critics and members of the general public in recent years. Indigenous cultural practices date back to well before today's "renaissance."

59 Other nonfiction works by these authors include Philips's *Showing Grit: Showboating North of the 44th Parallel* (Toronto: Poui Publications, 1993) and *CARIBANA: African Roots and Continuities - Race, Space and*

Philip and Brand have both published post-2000 collections, Philip's *Bla_k: Essays and Interviews* (2017) and Brand's *An Autobiography and the Autobiography of Writing* (2019). These more recent publications segue to discussion in the second half of this chapter of post-2000 collections, both by earlier-published essayists like Lee Maracle and more newly published poet-novelist essayists Alicia Elliott, Leanne Betasamosake Simpson, and Tessa McWatt. The combination of anti-racist and feminist theories and perspectives in the essays of these writers, both before and after 2000, puts Canada and Canadian experience in new and critical light.

Himani Bannerji—*Writings on the Wall*

A prolific essayist throughout the 1990s, Himani Bannerji produced three collections: *The Writing on the Wall: Essays on Culture and Politics* (1993), *Thinking Through: Essays on Feminism, Marxism, and Anti-Racism* (1995), and *The Dark Side of the Nation: Essays on Multiculturalism, Nationalism and Gender* (2000). Born in India, Bannerji came to Toronto as a student in 1969. Her literary studies inform her essays both in terms of their subject matter and in the elegance of her writing. Herself

---

the Poetics of Moving (Toronto: Poui Publications, 1996). And Brand's *Rivers have sources, trees have roots: speaking of racism,* with Krisantha Sri Bhaggiyadatta (Toronto: Cross Cultural Communications Centre, 1986); *No Burden to Carry: Narratives of Black Working Women in Ontario, 1920s-1950s,* with Lois De Shield (Toronto: Women's Press, 1991); *A Kind of Perfect Speech: The Ralph Gustafson Lecture Malaspina University-College,* 19 October 2006; and *We're Rooted Here and They Can't Pull Us Up: Essays in African Canadian Women's History,* with Peggy Bristow, Linda Carty, Afua P. Cooper, Sylvia Hamilton, and Adrienne Shadd (Coastal Research Publishing, 2008).

a published poet, Bannerji's essay collections include pieces on the poetry of Ernesto Cardenal and Dionne Brand, on Bengali theatre and the theatre of Utpal Dutt, and on novels by Sunil Gangyopadhyay. They also include essays on cultural politics and political culture, feminism and anti-racism, nationalism and multiculturalism.

Of her first collection, *The Writing on the Wall: Essays on Culture and Politics* (1993), Bannerji is forthright in declaring that the essays are "not in the genre of a recent (through the 1980s up to now) tradition of radical cultural theorization," clarifying that "they are not a critique of colonial discourse" (x). An unapologetic Marxist-socialist (viii), Bannerji's essays emerge from a tradition of commitment to class struggle and liberation movements (x), and from her interest in the possibilities that culture presents for resistance. They are in her words "attempts to make sense of culture's (for example theatre, literature, cinema) relationship to … the political and the historical" (ix). For Bannerji, the "colonial subject" is a "colonial object" (xi), and rather than allocate more space and time to "the colonizer's construction of us as 'others'" (xi), she chooses to begin from "her own end"—"from a 'third' world that exists in its many dimensions outside of the colonizer's grasp" (xi).

> In these spaces, in other societies and histories, fully formed subjects exist, grow, struggle, make their mistakes, win their victories, without caring what the so-called West thinks of them or without asking its permission. (xi)

Like Kristjana Gunnars in *Stranger at the Door*, Bannerji reaches out well beyond Canadian examples in her first collection of essays. Her intent is to counter stereotypes of the "Third World" as places and peoples to be "pitied and rescued, even as victims of the West" ("Introduction," *The Writing on the Wall*, xiii). At the same time, in Montaigne mode, she sees her essays as a way of making her "own political statements ... [on] a whole range of political positions, images, testimonials to one's having been there, a witness to events of our time in history" ("Introduction," *The Writing on the Wall*, xiv). Bannerji maintains that personal experience, in particular the personal experiences of the socially marginalized, is essential to knowledge. Far from mere feeling or physical reflex, the experience of the marginalized constitutes an "originating point of knowledge" (*The Dark Side of the Nation*, 12). This stance is strengthened in her second collection.

Published two years later in 1995, essays in *Thinking Through* address issues of feminism, anti-racism, and violence as Bannerji "thinks through" her experiences in Canada. Her account is disturbing and uncomfortably still relevant over a quarter century later, as evidenced by the movements Black Lives Matter (BLM) and Missing and Murdered Indigenous Women and Girls (MMIWG). Bannerji recalls her first months in Canada as "full of denial, rejection and ... inexplicable and downright hatred" ("Introduction," 7). Violence, humiliation, fear, and "a continual sense of non-belonging" (8) are dominant memories. The histories of Black and Indigenous peoples and the anti-colonial work of theorist Franz Fanon helped Bannerji understand her own racialized experiences—both "big and trivial"—as those of the violence of racism (11).

Thinking through the interconnected workings of race, gender, and class led Bannerji to writing about personal and political agency and to essays arguing for "situated critique" and transformative knowledges (13). Situated critiques pay attention to the greater social structural context of individual experience and circumvent arguments about "isolated incidences" by illustrating how "individual" experience in fact applies to all similar persons within the context. This re-directs critique to the broader context, in this case Canada, rather than narrowing it to a singular case of individual experience. "In the matter of 'X': Building 'Race' into Sexual Harassment," an essay about a Black woman's experience of sexual harassment in a large pharmaceutical company, Bannerji demonstrates clearly how intersecting social forces construct sexist, racist experience for racialized Canadians.

Another powerful essay in the collection, "Re: Turning the Gaze: An Act of Disassociation: The Private and the Public Self," explores what dissociation looks and feels like from the inside, through the experience of a racialized university faculty member—Bannerji herself. "The social relations of teaching and learning are relations of violence for us, those who are not white," Bannerji reflects, "who teach courses on 'Gender, "Race" and Class,' to a 'white' body of students in a 'white' university" (102). The gaze of white students, colleagues, and staff causes Bannerji to "disassociate" from herself, mediate the anger she feels at sexist and racist comments she hears, and turn rage into careful, smooth explanations to challenge the comments and to pedagogically "exact a teaching moment" (105) out of the experience. "How can I not disassociate?" Bannerji asks, when "institutional and everyday practices of conceptual cultural racism have pre-organized the conditions of my alienation and reification" ("Re: Turning the Gaze," 118).

In "thinking through" her essay writing, Bannerji uncovers racism and sexism in Canadian workplaces, including her own experiences of these as a university professor. She brings the same thorough thinking to other areas of Canadian experience, such as immigration policy, economic history, globalization, and imperialism, in a third collection of essays: *The Dark Side of the Nation: Essays on Multiculturalism, Nationalism and Gender* (2000).

Toward the end of the 1990s, the culture component of Bannerji's essays encompassed increased political critique and focus on the Canadian state, in particular "the political practice of the state and the ruling classes and their ideologues in Canada and elsewhere" (3). *The Dark Side of the Nation* charts an intensified exploration and criticism of Canadian multiculturalism.[60] "We need to think through the different discursive articulations and uses of multiculturalism," Bannerji urged ("Introduction," 5). Official multiculturalism "sidelined the claims of Canada's aboriginal population" (9), she pointed out, reduced political demands to cultural demands (9), and "replaced the emphasis on race and racism with an emphasis on cultural diversity" ("The Paradox of Diversity: The Construction of a Multicultural Canada and 'Women of Colour,'" 18).

Canada's treatment of Indigenous peoples is a recurring subject of criticism in *The Dark Side of the Nation*. The James Bay Project, the Meech Lake Accord, "Oka," Gustafson Lake, Ipperwash, unsettled land claims, and the fight for self-government, all are examples of Canada's colonial relations with Indigenous communities that Bannerji discusses in her essays. In both English Canada and Quebec, she finds, "there is a remarkable and a determined political marginalization of the First Nations" ("On the Dark Side of the Nation: Politics of Multiculturalism and the State of Canada," 92), and "the role that 'race' has played

---

60 Bannerji does not limit her analysis to multiculturalism. She tackles the then still developing discourse of globalization, which she sees as "both an economic and a cultural imperialism" ("Introduction," *The Dark Side of the Nation*, 3). She puts pen to paper on ongoing issues of immigration, a euphemism, she states in no uncertain terms, for "racist labour and citizenship policies" (4). And she takes the labour movement to task for having "repeatedly displayed anti-immigrant sentiments" (8).

in the context of colonization is obvious" ("Geography Lessons: On Being an Insider/Outsider to the Canadian Nation," 75).

In an early usage of the phrase "white settler society," Bannerji names that sector of Canadian society ("Introduction," 5). Given divisions of gender, class, and patriarchy in Canadian society, she questions the concept of "community" and "the nation" (10). She sees official, or elite "invisible minority" multiculturalism as an "ideological state apparatus ... a device for constructing and ascribing political subjectivities and agencies for those who are seen as legitimate and full citizens and others who are peripheral" (6). Multiculturalism's perspective is "from above, whether conducted by the state or the national elite, its organic intellectuals" (7), Bannerji writes. For her, multiculturalism has to be based on "antiracist and feminist class politics" (5), not on discourses of tolerance and cultural diversity, nor on the two nations/two solitudes (French and English) account of Canada, as in Charles Taylor's work, *Reconciling the Solitudes* (1993) and *Multiculturalism: Examining the Politics of Recognition* (1994).

In Bannerji's analysis, the concept of Canada as a "dual monocultural entity" might accommodate a "surface" or "first level" French-English diversity but not the more profound differences or the "deep diversity" of Indigenous or visible minorities in Canada (*The Dark Side of the Nation*, 98, 99). Taylor's two nations/two solitudes view of Canada eclipses the country's first nations—Indigenous peoples—who should be more accurately seen through the clearer lens of colonialism. The project of multiculturalism simultaneously enhances and erodes Taylor's politics of recognition, Bannerji argues (101). Recognition would mean empowering "deep diversities" and acknowledging "the social relations of power that create the different differences" (102). Taylor's multiculturalism, she states, overlooks "real politics, of real social, cultural and economic relations of white supremacy and racism" (102):

> Thus he leaves out of sight the relations and ideologies of ruling that are intrinsic to the creation of a racist civil society and a racializing colonial-liberal state. It is this foundational evasion that makes Taylor's proposal so problematic for those whose "differences" in the Canadian context are not culturally intrinsic but constructed through "race," class, gender and other relations of power.
>
> ("On the Dark Side of the Nation: Politics of Multiculturalism and the State of 'Canada,'" *The Dark Side of the Nation*, 102)

Multicultural policy effectively creates the category of "visible minorities" (immigrants, refugees, non-white people of colour), Bannerji maintains, and must be examined for its assumptions of cultural (comm)unity. Multiculturalism, she continues, reduces and neutralizes difference as diversity of cultures and identities, rather than as colonial ethnocentrism and racism ("On the Dark Side," 96). Indigenous cultures, languages, and land claims bring in another dimension altogether, she notes, one "so violent and deep that the state of Canada dare not even name it [racism] in the placid language of multiculturalism" ("On the Dark Side," 96). Only "real social equality and historical redress" (103) will make a difference, Bannerji declared, a statement that would echo decades later in voices for Missing and Murdered Indigenous Women and Girls and Black Lives Matter.

Bannerji's examination of multiculturalism, indeed of the many issues she takes up in her collections of essays, counts among the most overlooked contributions to public intellectualism in Canada. Whether or not one agrees with her views, as an essayist Himani Bannerji has presented important and insightful analyses of the country and of issues that remain very much of concern today.

M. NourbeSe Philip—*Frontiers of Resistance*

The 2017 publication of M. NourbeSe Philip's most recent collection of essays, *Bla_k*, places it organizationally in the second part of this chapter. But I begin with it here because *Bla_k* reprises many of the essays from Philip's first collection, *Frontiers: essays and writings on racism and culture 1984-1992* (1992). This drives home the relevance decades later of Philip's essay writing and, unfortunately, the fact that many of the issues that she addressed years ago—racism and cultural marginalization to name just two—are still at work in Canada today. It also points to the general inattention to Philip's work as an essayist. This, perhaps more than anything, bears out the central argument of *Her Own Thinker* for greater attention to what Canadian women poets and novelists have had to say in their essay writing and to the importance and value of their collections.

Like Himani Bannerji, M. NourbeSe Philip immigrated to Canada as a young woman. From Trinidad/Tobago she settled first in London, Ontario, where she took graduate degrees in political science and law, and then in Toronto, where she practised law. In 1983, she left law practice to pursue writing full time. A succession of publications have followed: five collections of poetry, including the award-winning *She Tries Her Tongue, Her Silence Softly Breaks* (1989), two novels, two plays, and five collections of essays, counting the recent *Bla_k*.

The new material in *Bla_k* includes "codas," Philip's term for short reflections that she offers on the essays published in earlier collections. There are also newly written essays, beginning with the collection's opening piece "Jammin' Still." This essay presents a sort of *mise en abyme* of the project in *Her Own Thinker*: looking back over Philip's earlier essay writing, it highlights key themes and concerns as well as how long these have been at issue—in many cases over twenty-five years. The sheer number of years since Philip first wrote about racism in Canada is a sobering, repeated observation in *Bla_k*.

The collection's title is doubly meaningful. It is both *Black* and *Blank*, Philip explains ("Jammin' Still," *Bla_k*, 27), evoking the blackness of the night sky, which is "often read as blank but which is filled with unseen and yet unexplained activity" ("Jammin' Still," *Bla_k*, 28). The lives of Black people, too, she elaborates, are often "seen as blanks or cyphers onto which others project their desires, suspicions and at times ignorance" (28).

"Jammin' Still" traces a trajectory from the 1990s anti-Black Yonge Street riots and Indigenous protests at Ipperwash that Philip wrote about in *Frontiers: essays and writings on racism and culture 1984-1992* (1992), to movements twenty-five years later in support of Black Lives Matter and Missing and Murdered Indigenous Women and Girls. "Make no mistake," Philip writes, "if Black lives truly mattered, or if Indigenous lives mattered … we would, indeed, be living in an altered universe" ("Jammin' Still," 18). Instead of change, the measures called for by promissory actions like the Royal Commission on Aboriginal Peoples (RCAP, 1991-1996) or the Truth and Reconciliation Commission (TRC, 2008-2015) remain slow to actualize. In Black, Indigenous, and other racialized communities across the country, systemic racism continues all too real. "What is clear is that in the last twenty-five years racism has remained an issue manifesting in old and new ways," Philip states ("Jammin' Still," 22).

In "Echoes in a Stranger Land," the essay that introduced her 1992 collection *Frontiers: Essays and Writings on Racism and*

Culture 1984-1992, Philip examined how culture traditionally has garnered less attention than housing, employment, education, or police relations as areas of racial contestation (*Frontiers*, 12). Nevertheless, culture—in particular writing—has remained Philip's front-line approach to examining these matters. Her essays tackle some of the most important issues of the past fifty years in Canada. For example, two essays—"Gut Issues in Babylon: Racism & Anti-Racism in the Arts" ("Gut Issues") and "The Disappearing Debate: Or, How the Discussion of Racism has been Taken Over by the Censorship Issue" ("The Disappearing Debate")—illustrate her analysis of the controversy of cultural appropriation and how in 1988 it divided The Women's Press, Canada's first feminist press.

First published in *Frontiers* and reprinted in *Bla_k*, "The Disappearing Debate"'s subtitle—"How the Discussion of Racism has been Taken Over by the Censorship Issue"—expresses a key point that Philip makes about cultural appropriation, namely that it has largely been represented as a debate about freedom of the imagination and censorship, mainly of white writers. Philip counters that cultural appropriation is better understood in the wider and deeper context of racism ("Gut Issues," *Frontiers*, 213). Racism, she states, was how members of the Black community experienced The Women's Press's project to publish a collection of short stories by women—*Imagining Women*. None of the submissions by Black authors made the final selection, yet the collection included stories representing Black lives and experience—as imagined by non-Black authors. This was not only a matter of appropriation, Philip argued; it was an example of racism, and for her and other Black women writers it was a "gut issue": "the apparent freedom of whites to appropriate as their own whatsoever they wished" ("Gut Issues," *Frontiers*, 219), in this case the experiences and voices of Black women in stories submitted to and selected for the collection by white women.

For reasons convincingly explained in her essay "The Disappearing Debate," Philip did not advocate for a law against authors writing in voices other than their own. In the first instance, she pointed out, such a law would be essentially unenforceable. Nor, in a second instance, would it do much, if anything, to address the systemic racism at the root of the obstacles to publication that face marginalized writers; addressing racism would require more far-reaching structural change. Thirdly, as the essay's subtitle implied, the issue of censorship "disappears" the discussion of racism in the arts, redirecting attention to debates about freedom of the imagination—for white writers ("The Disappearing Debate," *Frontiers*, 276).

The imagination, Philip countered in her essay, is both free and unfree: "Free in that it can wander wheresoever it wishes; unfree in that it is profoundly affected and shaped by the societies in which we live" ("The Disappearing Debate," *Frontiers*, 278). To state the obvious, she pointed out:

> In a racist, sexist and classist society, the imagination, if left unexamined, can and does serve the ruling ideas of the time. (…) The danger with writers carrying their unfettered imaginations into another culture—particularly one like the Native Canadian culture which theirs has oppressed and exploited— is that without careful thought, they are likely to perpetuate stereotypical and one-dimensional views of this culture.
>
> ("The Disappearing Debate," *Frontiers*, 278)

For writers, Philip maintained, freedom of the imagination entailed responsibilities, particularly with regard to writers' privilege and use of voice—their own voice and those of others. Writers must ask themselves "hard questions" before writing about another culture, she stated. These questions apply to all writers, in her view, white writers, for starters, but also, she added, "Black middle class writers writing about the Black working class; or the upper class Asian writing about the Asian peasant" ("The Disappearing Debate," *Frontiers*, 284). It is a writer's responsibility, Philip insisted, to understand the privilege of voice and its use. Should that use extend to another culture, it is the writer's further responsibility to proceed with utmost respect and humility. "Writers must be willing to learn," Philip held; "they must be open to having certainties shifted, perhaps permanently" ("The Disappearing Debate," *Frontiers*, 284).

The appropriation debate at The Women's Press in 1988-89 was a significant event in Canada, one in which women writers like Philip played a major role. She queried its absence from renewed discussions in 2016-2017 about cultural appropriation and novelist Joseph Boyden when journalist Jorge Barrera raised questions about the Indigenous identity of the author of the award-winning *Three Day Road* (2005), *Through Black Spruce* (2008), and *The Orenda* (2013). Boyden's response left questions for many when he acknowledged his primary Irish Scottish heritage without disavowing family connection to Indigenous identity. For Philip, the renewed discussions about cultural appropriation posed a different question. Why, she asks in *Bla_k,* given the extent to which the appropriation debate at the Women's Press had gripped the literary and media scene in Canada over a dozen years earlier, why was it so overlooked when the debate resurfaced in connection with Boyden?

In reply, Philip explains in the "coda" "Spot the Difference" that the "new" discussions once again sidelined the larger contextual issue of racism (*Bla_k,* 104). The cultural appropriation debate, Philip reiterates, is about more than identity, belonging,

or freedom or censorship of the imagination. Cultural appropriation raises issues and difficult questions "from quantum blood
rules to why people read books from cultures other than their
own" (*Bla_k*, 105). For Philip, the Boyden controversy illustrated once again her argument of decades earlier for the need,
indeed the requirement, to approach other cultures with respect
and humility. Rather than decree that writers cannot or should
not write about other cultures, or other "genders, ages, abilities,
sexual orientations, historical times, or universes" (*Bla_k*, 108),
Philip calls again for larger, deeper discussion of responsibilities,
research, preparation, and protocols when approaching another
culture. It is more useful, indeed vital, in Philip's view, to focus on
voices of, and venues for, writers from other cultures (*Bla_k*, 108).

Philip repeats these points in "Race-Baiting and the Writers'
Union of Canada," another new essay in *Bla_k*. Here she looks
at cultural appropriation through the lens of another firestorm
in the Canadian literary world, which involved the Writers'
Union of Canada's magazine, *Write*. The magazine's May 2017
edition was a special issue on and mostly by Indigenous writers.
The introductory editorial, however, written by a non-Indigenous author, included "a flippant and uninformed piece about
appropriation," Philip notes (111). Reaction was swift and
critical, with ensuing resignations and recharged public debate.
Once again, Philip emphasizes in her essay, the debates tip-toed
around the discussion of racism in yet another example of "how
systemic racism functions and how we can all be baited to par-
ticipate in a debate that hides even as it reveals" ("Race-Baiting
and the Writers' Union of Canada," *Bla_k*, 113).

At issue, Philip restates, were racist power structures, which
are as present in the cultural sphere as in the country's social,
political, economic spheres. Within these structures, the issue
of appropriation is more a matter for white writers who feel

challenged by writers from marginalized communities, than it is for Black or other writers who deal with racism on a daily basis. This was Philip's observation at the time of The Women's Press debate in 1988, and it is her observation once again in 2017 about the debate reignited by the editorial of The Writers' Union's magazine *Write*.

Cultural and intellectual discussion in Canada has been deepened and sharpened by M. NourbeSe Philip's essays on voice appropriation and on other topical issues and events in Canada, among them the 1989 PEN Canada meeting ("Disturbing the Peace," *Frontiers*, re-printed in *Bla_k*); the 1989 ROM exhibition "Into the Heart of Africa" ("Social Barbarism and the Spoils of Modernism," *Frontiers,* re-printed in *Bla_k*); the 1988 Glenbow Museum exhibition "Spirit Sings" ("Museum Could Have Avoided Culture Clash," *Frontiers,* also re-printed in *Bla_k*); the 1990s Toronto productions of the American musicals, Miss Saigon and Show Boat ("Six Million Dollars and Still Counting," *Bla_k*[61]); and the 1994 Writing Thru Race conference, which is the subject of several essays.

As noted earlier, the Writing Thru Race conference in 1994 marked a critical moment in public recognition of racism in the Canadian cultural domain. For Philip and for writers from marginalized communities generally, Tator and Henry point out in *Challenging Racism in the Arts: Case Studies of Controversy and Conflict* (1998), the conference was "an affirmation and recognition of their identity as critical participants in … redefining what it means to be Canadian, redefining what it means to be a Canadian writer, redefining the literary landscape of Canada"

---

61 This is also the last chapter in Philip's book *Showing Grit: Showboating North of the 44th Parallel*; for detailed analysis see Tator et al. (1998).

(107). Organized by a coalition of community members and members of the Writers' Union of Canada, the conference featured day-time sessions for racialized and Indigenous writers to focus on issues and experiences of concern to them. Evening sessions were open to public participation. This, however, was not enough for some Union members who charged that limiting day-time sessions to Indigenous and racialized writers constituted reverse discrimination. They were joined in the charge by some members of the Canadian public. This drew national and international media attention, which, as Philip had commented earlier of public portrayal of The Women's Press, side-stepped the matter of racism. The Writing Thru Race conference revealed the pressing need to open the gates of Canadian culture to writers from the country's Indigenous, immigrant, racialized, and other marginalized communities.

In other essays,[62] Philip turned her attention to topics and themes prominent in collections discussed in Chapter III, including language, the experience of being a writer, and Canadian feminism and multiculturalism.

In Philip's essays, language is examined less through a "psychoanalytic" lens and more in relation to the value and place of "nation language" or the Caribbean demotic ("Father Tongue," *A Genealogy of Resistance,* 129). Nation language is valorized and valued over standard English in Philip's work where it highlights the role of the English language in the colonization process. For Philip, as for feminist writer-essayists discussed elsewhere in *Her*

---

62 Such as "Who's Listening? Artists, Audience & Language," "Women and Theft," "Journal Entries Against Reaction: Damned if We Do and Damned if We Don't," in *Frontiers*; and in *Genealogy*: "The Absence of Writing or How I Almost Became a Spy," "Dis Place – The Space Between," and "Earth and Sound—The Place of Poetry."

Own Thinker, English is experienced as a "father tongue," an imperial, white, oppressive tongue ("Father Tongue," *A Genealogy of Resistance,* 129). But where other women writers drilled down to a pre-lingual, psychoanalytic level of "mothertongue", Philip foregrounds English as not only a father tongue but also a foreign tongue and a language of anguish. This is powerfully shown in her celebrated poem "Discourse on the Logic of Language" (*She Tries Her Tongue – Her Silence Softly Breaks,* 1989). In her essays, Philip's resists the pain of English's patriarchal imperial colonizing power by opting in part or in entire essays to write in nation language— "some say patwa, some say dialect, others say nation language and still others bad English" ("Father Tongue," *A Genealogy of Resistance,* 129). "African Roots and Continuities: Race, Space and the Poetics of Moving" in *A Genealogy of Resistance,* for example, an essay about Toronto's annual Caribana celebration, is written fully in the demotic.

In writing about the experience of being a woman writer, Philip fixed firmly on the Black woman writer in Canada. For her, this has been an experience of being underrepresented, if not "disappeared," in the country's literary and art worlds, from funding, grant, and prize committees to the publishing industry in general. Feminist publishing outlets have been no exception. Like other mainstream presses, Philip pointed out, "they held themselves out as being feminist and therefore representative of *all* women, when too often they represented a very specific group—white, middle class women" ("Gut Issues in Babylon," *Frontiers,* 214-215).

Philip looked askance at 1980s-1990s feminism in Canada. Like Himani Bannerji, she regarded feminism without class analysis as not very useful ("Who's listening? Artists, audience and language," *Frontiers*). In her analysis, Canadian feminism in the 1980s-1990s sidestepped issues of class in the same way that it skirted matters of race and Indigenous experience in Canada, especially in the cultural domain. Multiculturalism's "white-wash" of the arts in Canada, like white middle-class feminism, evaded realities of racism ("Why Multiculturalism Can't End Racism," *Frontiers*). Canadian culture had to make room for and respect the "other" within the country's borders ("Echoes in a Stranger Land," *Frontiers*, 16). Without respect, there could be no belonging, no being "at home," whether or not a person held a Canadian passport. There was only being "othered" despite Canada's claim to "m/othering all her peoples," Philip stated; "all Canadians—African, Asian, European and Native" ("Echoes in a Stranger Land," *Frontiers,* 23; 25). This was why she wrote, Philip announced in her epigraph to *Frontiers*: "For Canada, in the effort of becoming a space of true be/longing."

In *Frontiers* (1992), Philip described the position from which she wrote in Canada as one of exile.[63] Constant exile was the legacy of colonialism and imperialism that first cut Africans off from their ethnicity and culture ("Echoes in a Stranger Land," *Frontiers,* 10). In her second collection of essays, *A Genealogy of Resistance* (1997), Philip explored a sense of belonging to the is-land of her birth, Tobago. In 1991 she returned to the island for a year. The essays in *A Genealogy of Resistance* are the outcome

---

63 Morrell, 154. In addition to the theme of exile, Donna Bailey Nurse (1992) identifies the following themes in *Frontiers*: colonial education, Canadian racism, white middle-class feminism, the aesthetics of modernism, the Royal Ontario Museum's *Into the Heart of Africa* exhibition, the "whitewash" of multiculturalism in Ontario's arts funding system, the underrepresentation of African, Asian, and First Nations Canadian writers at the fifty-fourth PEN Congress, the politics of not publishing "minority" writers, TV Ontario's interviewing politics, the politics of the Gulf War, and the dismissal of the problem of racism in the debate over appropriation of voice and "freedom of the imagination."

of her experiences and reflections that year. More personal and poetic in content, the essays are also more creative and less formal in style. The opening essay, for example, traces her family background, much of which remains uncertain or unknown to Philip due to the history of slavery. "The Absence of Writing or How I Almost Became a Spy" is an imaginative and creative account of the challenges in becoming a writer when one is from a place historically dominated by British culture, like Tobago. This was a challenge Philip rose to during her time on the island:

> I personally made my writing possible by turning away from a career in law—family, immigration and criminal (juvenile)—which I practiced for seven years in Toronto, Canada, and plunging naively and bravely, as only the fool rushing in can do, into the life of being a poet. Had I known then what I know now, I would not have left the practice of law as easily as I did.
> ("Father Tongue," *A Genealogy of Resistance*, 132).

The importance of place is central to the essay "Earth and Sound: the Place of Poetry" and to its follow-up "Dis Place: the Space Between." These essays and the collection *A Genealogy of Resistance* as a whole establish how important Tobago is to Philip's life and how essential writing is as well. Writing is her way of being in the world, the way to view the social, political, economic, and cultural contexts in which one finds oneself. For Philip as a writer, Black experience, in particular hers as a Black woman, is the key context:

> One Black woman's attempt over time and space to grapple with and understand through writing how and why the simple and profound fact of being remains insufficient in our world; how and why being continues to be contingent on so

much—race, colour, gender, class, sexuality, ability, age; and how, through one's life work, to make a difference, however small for the better.

("Jammin Still," *Bla_k*, 27)

This passage from *Bla_k* echoes the opening essay of Philip's first collection *Frontiers*—"Echoes in a Stranger Land"—in which she explores the theme of exile and how it applies to her experience as a Black woman writing in Canada. "I remain exiled," Philip writes in "Jammin Still" (*Bla_k*), and "count myself among the 'unbelonged'" (15), an "unembedded, disappeared poet" of "multiple identities—Black, African-descended, female, immigrant (or interloper) and Caribbean" ("Jammin Still," 13). Twenty-five years, Philip repeats, and the meaning of *Bla_k's* opening essay title comes glaringly clear: "we keep movin', jammin'... still. Always. In the face of tremendous odds" ("Jammin' Still," 35).

Dionne Brand—*Bread out of stone, doors to no return, & autobiographies of writing*

M. NourbeSe Philip observed that for most writers "an issue chooses you—in my case it was language"—adding that "if one is engaged on the project of language, then one has to be concerned with power" ("Father Tongue," *A Genealogy of Resistance*, 131, 130). Her observation definitely holds for Dionne Brand, a long-time explorer of language and the politics of power.

Like Philip, Brand immigrated to Canada from Trinidad/Tobago and settled in Toronto. A poet and novelist, she is also a documentarian and an essayist. Her work has been recognized by numerous awards and honours, including the Governor General's Award for Poetry (for *Land to Light On*, 1997), the City of Toronto Book Award (for *What We All Long For*,

2006), the Griffin Poetry Prize (for *Ossuaries*, 2011), and, in 2021, the American Windham-Campbell Literature Prize for her work as a whole. Brand's novels and poetry are widely studied, her essays less so, except perhaps for the collections *Bread out of Stone: Recollections on Sex, Recognitions, Race, Dreaming and Politics* (1994) and *A Map to the Door of No Return: Notes to Belonging* (2001).

Brand's 2020 *An Autobiography of the Autobiography of Reading* provides a useful vantage point from which to approach not just her fiction writing but her essay writing as well. In this *essai*—a 60-page print publication of her 2019 University of Alberta Henry Kreisel Lecture—Brand exposes the colonial narrative of the English literature that she read growing up. She examines the embedded relations of power and race in the English literary texts of her education, and what she calls English literature's vehicular language—"what it transmits, the state of being it describes, the mind, the philosophical orientation of the speaker" (*Autobiography*, 20). This was literature with a "pedagogy of colony" underpinning its stories of white class and gender and concealing the stories of Black, Indigenous, and "other" lives (*Autobiography*, 27). It was "a narratively constituted imaginary," "repeated, reinforced politically and socially, rewritten in every novel either as embedded or as dug up to examine difference or those outside the narrative … a code that considers itself ever changing but is in fact ever elaborating itself as primary" (*Autobiography*, 27). Disseminated around the English-speaking world in enormous production, the colonial narrative dictated "not only the way to live but also the way to imagine and the way to write" (*Autobiography*, 24). Reflecting on her journey to reading and eventually to writing counter narratives, Brand recalls "the difficult work of narrativizing the life of Black people, as that life … is located in the racist schema that capital and white power describe" (*Autobiography*, 41). Her essay writing is integral to that work:

> The task of the writer, whether of fiction or non-fiction, or of casual or bureaucratic texts, is to narrate our own consciousnesses, to describe a Black life in the register of the social and the political.
>
> (*Autobiography*, 41)

For Brand as essayist, this task began with *Bread out of Stone: Recollections on Sex, Recognitions, Race, Dreaming and Politics* (1994). The collection's subtitle intimates the range of topics she takes up in the essays from both personal and analytical perspectives. They include immigration and politics, racism and sexism, stereotypes and violence, Black women's experience, music, literature, cultural appropriation, literary theory, and writing. Like M. NourbeSe Philip, Brand addresses "this country," that is to say "the European nation-state of Canada," as she refers to it in her essays ("Notes for Writing thru Race," *Bread out of Stone*, 173).

The collection opens with the titular essay "Bread out of Stone," a phrase Brand learned from her mother and applies to her own writing: "There is only writing that is significant, honest, necessary—making bread out of stone—so that stone becomes pliant under the hands" (23). The essay is a clear-eyed look at Canada—"this country's legacy of racial violence" (9), "its pathological hate for Native people" (10). This is a country "that never talks about race," Brand declares, "but about immigration and self-government, meaning people of colour and First Nations' people, meaning anybody who ain't white" ("Brownman, Tiger …", *Bread out of Stone*, 118). The collection closes with the equally unblinking "Notes for Writing Thru Race." The notes outline the country's racist culture—its "elastic whiteness," which gathers non-English and non-French, but still white groups like Ukrainians or Germans, under Canadian "multiculturalism" (174). Between these bookend-essays, Brand discusses some of the same issues and events in 1990s Canada addressed by writers of other essay collections in this chapter: the appropriation debates, the ROM exhibition "Into the Heart of Africa," the 1994 Writing Thru Race Conference, Caribana, and Showboat; she also introduces others, such as the 1992 Yonge Street insurrection and the 1994 Just Desserts robbery and shooting.[64]

Brand joins Philip in naming English Canada's resistance to "cultural interventions from people it does not recognize as fitting into its imposed norms" ("Notes for Writing thru Race," *Bread out of Stone*, 179). How else to explain, she asks, "the white frenzy over a conference of First Nations and writers of colour—the almost weekly diatribes, the editorial vitriol, the white rage, the leaps in logic, the *obsession* for god's sake of white commentators?" (178; italics in the original). She describes Canadian culture as existing in "stasis" where "in 1994 its artists and social commentators refuse to admit the existence of an ideology some five hundred or more years old" (180), "a

---

64 The Yonge Street insurrection, Brand explains (*Bread out of Stone*, 154) in retort to a column by Michael Valpy in *The Globe and Mail* (4 May 1993) was young people who took to the streets against police brutality and killings of Blacks both in the US (Rodney King in Los Angeles) and in Canada (Michael Wade Lawson, Raymond Lawrence, Lester Donaldson, Albert Johnson and Buddy Evans (*Bread out of Stone*, 74). The Just Desserts shooting, 5 April 1994, involved an attempt by three men to rob patrons of the café, ending in tragedy when a woman on the premises was fatally wounded. While the three men had grown up in Canada, their Jamaican origin led to calls from some quarters for stricter immigration and deportation measures.

culture where the dominant forces are still recapturing or repatriating what they perceive as their original cultural ideals, those of the motherland from which they were cast out or that they had to leave to make their fortunes" (173). She argues that "access, representation, inclusion, exclusion, equity" are all "other ways of saying race in this country without saying that we live in a deeply racialized and racist culture which represses the life possibilities of people of colour" (176).

Access, representation, inclusion, and equity are examples of how words can become "bureaucratic glosses for human suffering" (176). Brand suggests using "cultural imperialism," from the book *Return to the Source* (1973) by African intellectual and political activist Amilcar Cabral, as a more accurate articulation of cultural appropriation. Cultural appropriation, she states plainly, is not about her or other writers like her from Black, Indigenous, and other racialized and marginalized communities. It is a white people's expression and problem. Cultural imperialism more precisely expresses the permanent, organized repression of the cultural life of dominated populations. "Imperialist domination, by denying the historical development of the dominated people, necessarily also denies their cultural development," Brand writes (158) citing Cabral (1973, 39), "imperialist domination requires cultural oppression." There can be no question, she adds, that "Canadian culture has marauded the cultural production of the First Nations not to speak of their spiritual myths and icons and their land" ("Whose Gaze, and Who Speaks for Whom," *Bread out of Stone*, 162).

The final essay in *Bread out of Stone* is a short declaration of the importance of poetry, a tribute to the "room to live" that poetry provides Brand, the relief it brings in the face of the events and issues she discusses in essays, and the hope it allows her to hold on to.

Poetry may be a first choice of genre for Brand but her non-fiction essay writing continued with *A Map to the Door of No Return: Notes to Belonging* (2001). Closer to the French *essai*, this publication is an extended piece of writing, aptly described by Noah Richler as a "set of meditations about writing, reading, race and identity" (Richler, 2003). The word meditations should not evoke writing of inward calm or quietude, however. As Donna Bailey Nurse (1997) comments, *A Map to the Door of No Return* harshly indicts "Canadian racism, along with patriarchal oppression and the world-wide legacy of imperialism." Social class is a concern throughout the collection, including in Brand's essays about her travels to the Caribbean, South Africa (Johannesburg), London, Australia, Germany, and Amsterdam, and in essays about her three years living in rural Ontario's Burnt River (150). The theme of writing ties together these travels, the importance of language and poetry, writing by and about other writers (listed at the end of the book), the genesis of her own writing (58), and Brand's experience as a writer, in particular a Black writer. "Any representation of blackness interests me," she declares (129)—Black lives and experience, Black diaspora and belonging, the Black body, notably the Black female body, sensuality, and sexuality.

The Black body is a major focus in Brand's examination of the long lingering impact on the Black diaspora of the transatlantic slave trade—the Middle Passage—the trauma upon which the "door of no return" opened. The Door of No Return—"a place, real, imaginary and imagined" (19)—"transformed us into bodies emptied of being," Brand writes (93); "I am, we are, in the Diaspora, bodies occupied, emptied, and occupied" (94). Still today, Brand argues, the Black body remains occupied by the racism, violence, economic exploitation, sexism, and sexualization that followed passage through the door of no return. Throughout the diaspora, the door of no return is part of Black lives' stories—Black biographies and autobiographies.

This actuality is developed with deft and deep meaning by Brand in *An Autobiography of the Autobiography of Reading* (2020)—its title weighty with significance, as she explains:

> I call this essay "An Autobiography of the Autobiography of Reading," leading with the indefinite *An Autobiography*, which leaves open the possibility of multiple autobiographies, that this is but one iteration; it is particular but not individual. An autobiography gestures to the world of a reading self. It signals the complicated ways of reading and interpretation that are necessary under conditions of coloniality. It suggests that coloniality constructs outsides and insides—worlds to be chosen, disturbed, interpreted, and navigated—in order to live something like a real self. The definite article of the second clause *the Autobiography* identifies the subject who is supposed to be made, through colonial pedagogies in the form of texts—fiction, non-fiction, poetry, photographs, and governmental and bureaucratic structures. This subject situated at the meeting of violent pasts and futures of coloniality is hailed ambiguously in these texts to simultaneously be mastered and elide to mastery as something other than violence, erasure, and absence.
>
> (*Autobiography*, 8)

From *Bread out of Stone* (1994) to her recent *An Autobiography of the Autobiography of Reading* (2020), in her nonfiction *essai* writing as in her poetry and novels, Dionne Brand has wielded language and literary genres with exacting and poetic precision to reveal the long reach and ravages of colonialism in the lives of Black and other racialized peoples.

Lee Maracle—*Oratories and Conversations*

Like Dionne Brand, Stó:lō writer Lee Maracle pursued print-form essay publication in the era of online social media, blogging, and tweeting. Two post-2000 collections, *Memory Serves: Oratories and other Essays* (2015) and *My Conversations with Canadians* (2017), underscore her longstanding presence as a thinker about Canada and illustrate the unique oratory nature of her writing.

Memory Serves brings together new and previously published essays. Like M. NourbeSe Philip's *Bla_k*, the forward- and backward-looking perspectives of *Memory Serves* allow Maracle to reflect not only on topics that have recurred throughout her work but also on how they are still issues in Canada today. Of these, none are more salient than colonialism and decolonization ("Preface," *Memory Serves*, xi). As Maracle points out, she has been addressing these topics for decades. Where other writers might well tire of such repeated effort, she considers it part of her responsibility as a Stó:lō writer. Remembering ("memory") and responsibility ("serves") are prominent themes in her post-2000 collections. Remembering, Maracle elaborates, is "connected to our emotionality, our physicality, our spirituality, and our mentality" (*Memory Serves,* 21); each is integral to envisioning a different world ("Oratory on Oratory," *Memory Serves*, 231). They are also intrinsic to other key themes of her writing: story, oratory, and theory; Canadian feminism, patriarchy, and "social maturity"; the importance of relations and relationships, of listening, and of the imagination. Maracle discusses these and other topics in both the oratories turned-essay, as she refers to the contents of *Memory Serves,* and the essays in *My Conversations with Canadians*, published two years later.

"I am an orator," Maracle reminded readers in *My Conversations with Canadians*; "Salish oratory is about thinking, and the story is there to remind us or key up our thoughts" ("Marginalization and reactionary politics," 40). While her writing is rich in stories, Maracle identified not only as a writer and storyteller but also as an orator. "I am much too political to just tell stories," she semi-quips in "Marginalization and reactionary politics" (41); "Even when I don't intend to be political, the direction I come from makes my work *sound* political" ("Who are we separately and together?" *Conversations,* 21). Maracle's writing does not just sound political, however; it puts politics squarely on the page in essays that range in topic from the oppression of Indigenous people to issues of poverty, water, murdered and missing Indigenous women and girls, colonization and decolonization, story, oratory, and theory.

Story and oratory are not the same, Maracle emphasizes in *Conversations*, though "each is the key to the other: the story reminds us of the oratory, and the oratory reminds us of the story" ("Marginalization and reactionary politics," 41). Salish oratory covers "all areas of knowledge: history, sociology, political science, medical knowledge, aquaculture and horticulture, law, science, as well as stories" ("Toward a National Literature," *Memory Serves,* 203). Oratory is "transformative," Maracle explains, a "path of continuous growth and transformation" ("Oratory on Oratory," *Memory Serves,* 235, 236) toward what she discusses as social maturity and growth and relations with all of life's beings: "Oratory is comprised of the complex relations between disparate characters ... [It] is a human story in relation to the story of other beings" ("Oratory on Oratory," *Memory Serves*, 241). It is "word art," equal to literature, she contends ("What can we do to help?" *Conversations,* 54); "simply calling written story 'literature,' as the colonial authorities do, and establishing a tradition of what makes good story and what doesn't ... creates a near impossible conundrum for First Nations people" (Untitled, *Conversations,* 139). Whether in oral or written form, Indigenous oratory and story are in no way to be seen as inferior to print-form knowledge—or to theory as traditionally understood by academia. "As a thinker, an orator, and a Stó:lō," Maracle stated, "I did what other Indigenous speakers do. I blended theory and story together" ("Marginalization and reactionary politics," *Conversations*, 40).

The essay "Oratory: Coming to Theory" in *Memory Serves* profoundly rethinks established concepts of theory, argument, and evidence. Rather than theory as "proposition, proven by demonstrable argument," or argument as evidence, and evidence as demonstrable testimony ("Oratory: Coming to Theory," 161), Maracle tenders oratory, understood as "place of prayer; to persuade," with proof "in the doing," where doing is "some form of social interaction" (161).

In this conception of theory, story plays a vital role. Story is a "persuasive and sensible way" to share the thoughts of a people and the knowledge of a storyteller, Maracle maintained ("Oratory: Coming to Theory," 161). Like story, theory is collective in nature and in process. Theory allows the orator to share collective knowledge. "The web of relations" that Maracle establishes, Smaro Kamboureli observes in her Afterword to *Memory Serves*, "epitomizes how storytelling as the foundation of oratory operates as critical discourse" (259). Instead of theory as an abstract system or paradigm of conceptual thought, Maracle's understanding and practice of theory is a constant "coming to theory" (259) grounded in the experiential and expressed in oratory. Her 1988 book *I Am Woman: A Native Perspective on Sociology and Feminism,* Maracle asserted, is a theoretical text, "rooted in my theoretical perceptions of social reality and it is tested in the crucible of human social practice. (…) *I Am Woman* is empowering and transformative (…) filled with story and [it is] guided by theory presented through story—the language of people" ("Oratory: Coming to Theory," *Memory Serves,* 166). Maracle opposed theory written in language that only a hierarchical minority understands. "European knowledge keepers are referred to as intellectuals, academics, professors, teachers, experts, etc.," she commented ("Preface," *Memory Serves,* xiii), but for her, Salish *si`yams* are the knowledge keepers, thinkers, law keepers, spiritual logicians, and historians. "*Si`yams* know something and we recognize their knowledge" ("Preface," xiii-xiv).

At the 1988 International Women's Book Fair in Montreal Maracle had called for women in the feminist movement to "move over" and make room for Indigenous women. Despite her criticism of 1980s feminism as largely a white, middle-class movement, Maracle did not consider it irreconcilable with her feminism as an Indigenous woman and she remained open to Western feminist approaches. She believed in the value and importance of relationship, connection, and engagement, and she shared the critique of patriarchy, one of several oppressions that she lay firmly at the feet of colonialism. "We are besieged by a patriarchal settler state," Maracle wrote ("Indigenous Women and Power," *Memory Serves,* 129), and Indigenous women have been stripped of the status and respect they had in their communities before colonization. "The matriarchal aspects of our systems destroyed, the door was opened to inequity between men and women, and shame and violence became our lot" ("Indigenous Women and Power," *Memory Serves,* 133).

In consensus with other Indigenous women, Maracle charged the patriarchal colonial settler state as responsible for the breakdown of Indigenous cultural and governance structures—most notably the positions and powers of women within Indigenous communities. Colonization disrupted Indigenous governance and women's roles in their cultures and communities. "The colonial reality for Indigenous men is loss of power in their relationship with Canada," Maracle observed, but for women the reality of colonialism is "loss of power over the social relations inside our families and the internal world of our nations" ("Indigenous Women and Power," *Memory Serves*, 138-139). Ultimately, "the reality for everyone is systemic breakdown" ("Indigenous Women and Power," *Memory Serves*, 138-139).

Maracle did not refrain from pointing to the part played by Indigenous men in this breakdown: "I believe we have been lied to not just by Western colonialists but by our leaders as well," she wrote ("Indigenous Women and Power," 133). Recognizing colonialism's role in this, Maracle saw the need for twofold restoration: "the restoration of matriarchal authority and the restoration of male responsibility to these matriarchal structures to reinstate respect and support for the women within them" ("Indigenous Women and Power," 149). "Rematriation and decolonization must be our response," she asserted ("Indigenous Women and Power," 130). This for Maracle was Indigenous feminism. "*I am an Indigenous feminist*," she declared, emphasizing her statement with italics ("Indigenous Women and Power," 149), and challenging men to "make real their commitment to the matriarchal and co-lineal structures of the past" ("Indigenous Women and Power," 151). "*This is a feminist act*," she declared, using italics again to emphasize her stance.

In the final paragraph of "Indigenous Women and Power" Maracle clarifies that while her feminism does not contradict Western feminism, "the restoration of our nations is going to require a deeper kind of feminism" (*Memory Serves*, 152). Maracle's "deeper kind of feminism" was intersectional in vision and presaged the metafeminism that Marie Carrière is "cautiously hopeful" for in *Metafeminist Writing in Canada* (2020), a feminism that, going forward, will exhibit "an always intersectional praxis that remains self-aware of its past, present, and possible futures" (6).

Intersectionality emerged out of Black feminists' challenge to feminism as a predominantly white middle-class movement and put a name to the complexity of identity. The term itself is attributed to the American academic and activist Kimberlé Crenshaw, who used it in a 1989 address and paper that she wrote for the University of Chicago Legal Forum, "Demarginalizing the Intersection of Race and Sex: A Black Feminist Critique of Antidiscrimination Doctrine, Feminist Theory and Antiracist Politics." Crenshaw argued that a Black woman's experience could not be understood in terms of being Black and being a woman as separate, but rather as two identities interacting. What began as an exploration of the oppression of Black women within society based on gender, race, and class grew to the recognition of oppression on multiple bases of multiple identities. As a term, intersectionality identifies oppressions beyond gender, race, and class—from multiple cultural and sexual identities, including but not limited to lesbian, gay, bisexual, transgender, gender-variant, sexually diverse and intersex people, nor to identities related to ability, age, religion, white privilege, colonialism, geography, and other "dimensions" of identity. Intersectionality identifies the complicated intersections of structural discrimination and systemic institutionalized oppressions—racism, sexism, homophobia, transphobia, ableism, xenophobia, classism, and others—and offers a theoretical framework for developing critical theory as well as a conceptual and analytical tool for confronting serious issues of social justice and power.

Metafeminism, as Carrière discusses it in *Cautiously Hopeful: Metafeminist Writing in Canada,* 7), is intersectional and encompasses "methodologies, social concerns, aesthetic features, ethical thought, and political positions that have characterized its past and now determine, though often differently, its twenty-first-century incarnations" (7). Maracle's Indigenous feminism and her essays exploring colonialism's impacts on Indigenous lives in Canada, particularly the lives of women, are powerful examples of Carrière's definition of metafeminism. They are also an expression of the "social maturity" and transformation that Maracle envisioned within Canada's reach:

> Salish study looks for the obstacles to growth, both in the external and internal worlds. Once an understanding is achieved … hope leads humans toward social maturity and growth. The assumption here is that growth and maturity are capable of inspiring intervention and will lead to the transformation of the dichotomous social arrangements in Canada.
>
> ("Oratory on Oratory," *Memory Serves,* 231)

Maracle's essays convey her own cautious hope for a less socially divided, more socially just Canada. "Rejection of white people in their totality is contrary to our inclusive [Salish] history," she pointed out ("Dancing my Way to Orality," *Memory Serves,* 226). Maracle sought "connection and relation with those who are privileged by colonialism ("Dancing my Way to Orality," *Memory Serves,* 227). But this was a connection and a relationship based on "continuum as cultural and social beings alongside others – not under them or over them, but exactly like them, alongside them, different, known and cherished by them" ("Oratory on Oratory," *Memory Serves,* 247). In this lies the unique opportunity for the social transformation and maturity of Canada.

Only when we understand the connections between ourselves and all living things, and connect this to the historical direction we are travelling, can we find the means to develop a clear perspective. Only when we have uncovered the places in which stasis cripples development can we free ourselves to develop a rational and inclusive value system. Only when we see ourselves in our relationship to the whole can we master our lives and govern ourselves in a sustaining way. When we understand the connection between the living world and ourselves, we will begin to study history as the connection between humans and the living world.

("Salmon is the Hub of Salish Memory," *Memory Serves*, 62)

In her preface to *Memory Serves: Oratories* Maracle acknowledged others who joined her in expressing through writing the thinking that comes directly from Indigenous stories. This describes the essay writing of Indigenous authors Alicia Elliott and Leanne Simpson.

Alicia Elliott—*A Mind Spread Out on the Ground*

Haudenosaunee/Tuscarora short story and essay writer Alicia Elliott's collection *A Mind Spread Out on the Ground* was published in 2019 to great acclaim. The collection's title—English for the Mohawk phrase for depression (Wake'nikonhra'kwenhtará:'on)—is also the title of the opening essay. In it, Elliott confronts the experience of depression as she witnessed it in her mother's life and lived it in her own life, and posits depression as the ongoing workings of colonialism in Indigenous communities across Canada. Symptoms of depression, Elliott argues, reflect the effects of colonialism on Indigenous peoples. "Low

self-esteem, self-critical thoughts, tiredness or loss of energy, difficulty making decisions, seeing the future as hopeless, recurrent
thoughts of death, suicidal thoughts? Check, check" (11), she
summarizes. Depression and colonialism, Elliott asserts, have
stolen her language (12).

As her essays and short stories powerfully attest, however,
"things that were stolen once can be stolen back" (12) and in
A Mind Spread Out on the Ground, Elliott makes use of the
English language to confront colonialism. The collection exposes the colonial crimes of racism and sexism, from intergenerational trauma due to the loss of language and culture, to
economic and family breakdown, poverty and social isolation,
physical and sexual abuse, and mental illness and suicide. It also
expresses Elliott's resistance to colonialism and her embrace of
decolonization by refusing colonial narratives:

> This is how I can decolonize my mind: by refusing the colonial
> narratives that try to keep me alienated from my own commu-
> nity. I can raise my kid to love being Haudenosaunee in a way
> my parents couldn't, in a way my grandparents couldn't. This
> is my responsibility as a Haudenosaunee woman.
>
> ("Half-Breed," *A Mind Spread Out on the Ground*, 22)

In her essays, Elliott moves through the pain of "passing" in
the non-Indigenous world ("Half-Breed," 21) to an affirmation
of love ("On Seeing and Being Seen") and of responsibility as
an Indigenous woman, and to taking her place in a community
of Indigenous writers who write with love:

> *That* is what I felt when I read [Leanne Betasamosake] Simp-
> son's stories. That's what I feel when I read the work of Gwen

Benaway, Waubgeshig Rice, Tracey Lindberg, Eden Robinson, Katherena Vermette, Billy-Ray Belcourt, Joshua Whitehead, Lindsay Nixon, Kateri Akiwenzie-Damm, and Cherie Dimaline. That's what I hope Indigenous people feel when they read my work. Love.

("On Seeing and Being Seen," *A Mind Spread Out on the Ground*, 30)

Elliott expresses hope and optimism but not without recalling realities and facts of the past. She remembers that Toronto, for example, was once Tkaronto, and was ruled by treaty: "It was Dish With One Spoon territory: a space that was shared by my people," Elliott writes, "the Haudenosaunee, the Mississaugas of the New Credit, the Anishinaabe, the Huron, the Wendat" ("The Same Space," 49). She recalls other facts and realities, such as the recent deaths of two young Indigenous people, Colten Bouchie (Cree) and Tina Fontaine (Anishinaabe), and the acquittal of the white men charged with their murder, Gerald Stanley and Raymond Cormier ("Dark Matters"). She points out that Indigenous children are up to twelve times more likely to be taken into government child welfare. This reality exists not because there is anything "endemic to First Nations families that would explain a higher rate of placement," she underlines, citing Nico Trocmé, director of McGill University's School of Social Work and researcher for the *Canadian Incidence Study of Reported Child Abuse and Neglect*, but because in social work and police parlance, "'neglect' is another word for poverty" ("Scratch," 87). The fact is, Elliott states, that poverty accounts for the poor nutrition of Indigenous youth across Canada, the reality being that "junk food" is cheaper than nutritious food ("34 Grams Per Dose"). The fact is that "the

biggest indicator of poverty is race," Elliott declares, noting that
with one in five racialized families living in poverty, as opposed
to one in twenty white families, poor, racialized families end up
relying on cheap, unhealthy food ("34 Grams Per Dose," 97).

For Indigenous families in particular, Elliott continues, there
is the factual reality of a history of colonialism and its impact
through the systems of reserves and residential schools on access to traditional Indigenous nourishment, "country foods" of
wild game and wild rice, fish and berries ("34 Grams Per Dose,"
100). Scholars Ian Mosby and Tracey Galloway, in "Hunger Was
Never Absent: How Residential School Diets Shaped Current
Patterns of Diabetes among Indigenous People in Canada," report: "We can now be fairly certain that the elevated risk of obe-
sity, early-onset insulin resistance and diabetes observed among
Indigenous peoples in Canada arises, in part at least, from the
prolonged malnutrition experienced by many residential school
survivors" ("34 Grams Per Dose," 111). Elliott's aim to remain
hopeful is threatened by the evidence of malnutrition's genera-
tional impact, the legacy of "a colonial history that has altered
our very DNA "("34 Grams Per Dose," 115). She steadies her
outlook with nêhiyaw Erica Violet Lee's certainty that "the love
of our ancestors is in our DNA and our bones as well" ("34
Grams Per Dose," 115) and with her own abiding belief in the
power of love ("Bruised Boundaries" or "Crude Collages of My
Mother," among other essays in the collection).

The autobiographical character of *A Mind Spread out on the
Ground* intensifies the collection's critical analysis and insights.
Elliott researches her subjects in depth and is clear and compelling in her critique, which she directs toward a swath of issues
and areas: government policies, decisions, laws, actions, and
inactions, perceived as purposefully aimed at the dispossession

and disappearance of Indigenous communities, through community relocations, lack of implementing commissioned reports, and lack of or difficult access to essentials of life—healthy food, clean water, and safe, affordable housing. Her critique further extends to literary colonialism and its paternalistic assumptions and expectations of Indigenous writing ("Not Your Noble Savage"). She expresses praise and love for Indigenous writers like Leanne Betasamosake Simpson (Michi Saagiig Nishnaabeg) and for Indigenous photographers like Nadya Kwandibens (Anishinaabe/Ojibwe) and Dayna Danger (Métis/Saulteaux/Polish) as well as for non-Indigenous artists like Alison Lapper or Aaron Huey, who work from a place and position of respect, acceptance, and acknowledgment ("Sontag, In Snapshots").

The last essay in the collection, "Extraction Mentalities," is a "participatory essay." Elliott explains: "every so often I will stop this essay to ask you questions. I'll leave space for you to answer. Do with that space what you will. Even blank spaces speak volumes" ("Extraction Mentalities," 195). Questions are a key component of Elliott's writing process. In "The Colonialism-Depression Link," presented online to the international conference "The Poetics and Ethics of 'Learning With': Indigenous, Canadian, and Québécois Feminist Production Today" (27 January 2021), she explained that her essays develop out of questions that she asks herself. At the outset of writing she is unsure where the questions will lead. She knows only that questions are essential and that in her writing it is important to give readers questions to ask themselves. Aspiring writers, Elliott suggests, can try posing a question and exploring what it means to them personally.

A Mind Spread Out on the Ground opened with an essay exploring the experience of depression, which both Elliott and her mother have endured, as the consequence of Canada's history of colonialism, which entire Indigenous communities have endured. The collection closes with an essay that establishes a parallel between abuse at the hands of an individual and abuse by the settler nation-state. The essay "Extraction Mentality" asks readers to think about how nation-states like Canada are formed. It starts with land, Elliott writes, "as the settlers who landed here knew" (212), and it exploits everything on, below, and above the land: "Under capitalism, colonialism and settler colonialism, everything Indigenous is subject to extraction" (213). This includes children and language. Extraction mentality extends nation-state abuse to non-Indigenous citizens as well, Elliott notes, pointing to the history and experience of Black, Chinese, and other communities in Canada (214).

The critique and resistance, hope and love that interweave throughout Alicia Elliott's *A Mind Spread Out on the Ground* thread through Leanne Betasamosake Simpson's collections *Dancing on Our Turtle's Back* and *As We Have Always Done* as well.

Leanne Betasamosake Simpson
– Dancing Resistance and Resurgence

In *A Mind Spread Out on the Ground*, Alicia Elliott names Michi Saagiig Nishnaabeg writer, activist, and musician Leanne Betasamosake Simpson as a key inspiration to her as an Indigenous writer ("On Seeing and Being Seen," 23). In her work, Simpson interlaces stories, songs, poetry, and nonfiction in publications that take a place of their own among the already uniquely non-traditional essay collections of women considered in *Her Own Thinker*. Many of her publications are collaborative;[65] others identify more as fiction than as nonfiction.[66] Given *Her Own Thinker*'s focus on essay collections, my discussion of Simpson's extensive *oeuvre* concentrates on *Dancing on Our Turtle's Back; Stories of Nishnaabeg Re-Creation, Resurgence and a New Emergence* (2011) and *As We Have Always Done: Indigenous Freedom Through Radical Resistance* (2017).[67]

In *Dancing on Our Turtle's Back,* Simpson confronts Canada and its colonial history, policies, and treatment of Indigenous peoples, countering it with the philosophical and theoretical knowledge and practices of her Nishnaabeg ancestry and the resurgence of Indigenous creativity and sovereignty. Inspired in her own turn by Stó:lō writer Lee Maracle, Simpson assumes and asserts sovereignty, both individually on a personal level and politically on a community level. Taking up her "sovereign self," Simpson writes, does not require permission or approval from mainstream Canadian society. It involves instead choosing to live according to Nishnaabe ways rather than Western ways. It looks back to the knowledge and experience of the foremothers and moves forward in their steps toward "Mino Bimaadiziwin"—"the Good Life"—and a society where women occupy the centre, not the margins.

---

65 Such as the edited collections *Lighting the Eighth Fire: The Liberation, Resurgence, and Protection of Indigenous Nations* (2008); *This Is an Honour Song: 20 Years Since the Blockades, An Anthology of Writing on the "Oka" Crisis* (2019), with Kiera Ladner; *The Winter We Danced: Voices from the Past, the Future and the Idle No More Movement* (2014), with the *Kino-nda-niimi Collective*; and most recently, *Rehearsals for Living* (2022), with Robyn Maynard.
66 Like *Islands of Decolonial Love* (2013), *This Accident of Being Lost: Songs and Stories* (2017), and *Noopiming: The Cure for White Ladies* (2021).
67 Simpson has since published *A Short History of the Blockade: Giant Beavers, Diplomacy & Regeneration in Nishnaabewin* (2021), her Henry Kreisel Lecture for the Centre for Canadian Literature at the University of Alberta.

The wisdom, teachings, and truths of the Elders, specifically for Simpson those of Nishnaabeg Nation and the Mississauga Ojibway, form the headwaters of her writing, research, and resistance. She holds out against settler state-sanctioned reconciliation, critical of how it historicizes colonial traumas of the past, as if the consequences were not ongoing realities for Indigenous individuals and communities right across the country. In Simpson's view, reconciliation means more than settler recognition of the dispossession of Indigenous lands, or settler awareness of policies of assimilation, or of continued resource and environment extraction economics. It requires more than settler acknowledgement of the suppression of Indigenous dissent in the past and in the present. For Simpson, reconciliation fundamentally demands decolonization with, as its starting point, a base in Indigenous (Nishnaabeg) understandings, theories, and epistemologies of sovereign communities. From her perspective as a Michi Saagig Nishnaabeg person, reconciliation necessitates nation-to-nation relations between Indigenous and settler peoples, and between individual Indigenous communities and the Canadian settler state.

In her 2017 collection of essays, *As We Have Always Done: Indigenous Freedom Through Radical Resistance*, Simpson reflects on how writing *Dancing on Our Turtle's Back* brought out for her the many Indigenous stories that are not crisis- or victim-based, stories that are instead about self-determination and change from within, not recognition from outside. These stories are about a way of living based on community, relations, empathy, and the present. The essays in *As We Have Always Done* position Simpson in the present and in relation to her ancestors and her relations. They express what she seeks in the present and what she expects for the future. Indigenous freedom is her hard fast point of reference. It is the guiding vision of *As We Have*

Always Done, a manifesto for radical resistance and resurgence. To live in freedom as a Nishnaabekwe, Simpson writes, means refusing to be "tamed by whiteness or the academy" ("Kwe as Resurgent Method," 33). More than political resistance to the settler colonial state it means living Indigenous selfhood in the present and in a space such as the Elders shared with Simpson during her two-year stay with them at Long Lake #58. This present-space is a cognitive, spiritual, emotional, land-based Anishinaabe world and world view ("Nishnaabeg Brilliance as Radical Resurgence Theory," 17).

The essays in *As We Have Always Done* explore Anishinaabe selfhood and Indigenous understandings of nationhood, both of which Simpson observes to be generally misunderstood by mainstream society. Indigenous nationhood radically overturns the concept of the nation-state, she clarifies: "It is a vision that centers our lives around our responsibility to work with our Ancestors and those yet unborn to continuously give birth to a spectacular Nishnaabeg present" ("My Radical Resurgent Present," 10). Indigenous nationhood, Simpson continues, is "a manifesto to create networks of reciprocal resurgent movements with other humans and nonhumans radically imagining their ways out of domination, who are not afraid to let those imaginings destroy the pillars of settler colonialism" ("My Radical Resurgent Present," 10). For Simpson, Indigenous nationhood is the "radical resurgent present," a beginning in which nation comprises relationship, connectivity, and a hub of Nishnaabeg networks, "a web of connections to each other, to the plant nations, the animal nations, the rivers and lakes, the cosmos, and our neighboring Indigenous nations" ("My Radical Resurgent Present," 10, 8). It is "a series of radiating responsibilities" to the land and the environment, she adds (9), clarifying that for her, nationhood does not just radiate outwards: "it also radiates inwards. It is my physical body, my mind, and my spirit. It is our families—not the nuclear family that has been normalized in settler society, but big, beautiful, diverse, extended multiracial families of relatives and friends that care very deeply for each other" ("My Radical Resurgent Present," 9).

Love of land, family, and Indigenous nations forms the backbone of Indigenous resistance and the core of Anishinaabe ways of living, Simpson writes in her essays, emphasizing "how": "*how* we live, *how* we organize, *how* we engage in the world—the process ... *How* is the theoretical intervention. Engaging in deep and reciprocal Indigeneity is a transformative act ... If we want to live in a different present, we have to center Indigeneity and allow it to change us" ("Nishnaabeg Brilliance as Radical Resurgence Theory," 19-20). Where in *Dancing on our Turtle's Back* Simpson discussed this worldview as emergence, in *As We Have Always Done* she sees it as resurgence, "a strategic, thoughtful process in the present as an agent of change—a *presencing of the present* ("Nishnaabeg Brilliance as Radical Resurgence Theory," 20, emphasis in the original).

Resurgence centers the brilliance that Simpson locates in Anishinaabe thinking and worldview, in which story, knowledge, theory, methodology, ethics, politics, and community combine and create a different order of intelligence and way of living that are not based on Western epistemologies and colonial realities. The Elders show Simpson "an alternative Nishnaabeg world existing alongside the colonial reality" ("Nishnaabeg Brilliance as Radical Resurgence Theory," 16). In their world there is no room "for the desire to be recognized and affirmed by the colonizer ... to accommodate and center whiteness" ("Nishnaabeg Brilliance," 17). There is instead "an unfolding of a different present" (18), a "decolonial present" (21) of doing and "rooting the practice of our lives in our homelands and within our intelligence systems" (21). In this, Simpson perceives Dene scholar Glen Coulthard's concept of "grounded normativity" in *Red Skin, White Masks: Rejecting the Politics of Recognition;* in her own words, "ethical frameworks generated by place-based practices and associated knowledges" ("Nishnaabeg Brilliance," 22). Grounding Indigenous practices and knowledges in ethical living and being connected to land and community, this, Simpson argues, is how to resist colonialism; this is radical resurgence.

As we have always done presents the Radical Resurgence project, outlining its steps and stages in successive essays, which are summarized at the outset of the collection in "Kwe as Resurgent Method," and at the end of the collection in "Toward Radical Resurgent Struggle." Within a theoretical framework of Indigenous intelligence and grounded normativity, and proceeding with kwe as method—that is, refusal of colonial heteropatriarchal thinking—the project analyses colonialism as *"a structure of processes"* ("Kwe as Resurgent Method," 35, italics in the original). It conceptualizes dispossession to include "land and bodies as the meta-relationship Indigenous peoples have with the state" and envisions place-based Nishnaabeg internationalism and Nishnaabeg practices of anti-capitalism. It critiques heteropatriarchy and recognizes queer Indigeneity as an expression of Indigenous intelligence. Finally, it valorizes place-based education, acknowledges the resurgent struggle of Indigenous movements, and calls for collective action of everyday acts of resurgence and decolonizing queer politics to reinforce resurgent mobilization ("Kwe as Resurgent Method," 35-36).

The Radical Resurgence project is clear about the need to center Indigenous intelligence in mobilizing collective action, and to create Indigenous community as well as relationships with other resistant groups in Canada and internationally. The central point of *As we have always done*, Simpson states, is that "Indigenous futures are entirely dependent upon what we *collectively* do now as diverse Indigenous nations" ("Toward Radical Resurgent Struggle," 246, emphasis in the original):

> We need to collectively figure out how to instigate and sustain mass resurgent mobilizations within nation-based grounded normativities. We need to radically uncouple ourselves from the state political and education system. We need to be willing to take on white supremacy, gender violence, heteropatriarchy, and anti-Blackness within our movement. We need to be willing to develop personal relationships with other communities of coresistors beyond white allies.
>
> ("Constellations of Coresistance," *As We Have Always Done*, 231).

Radical resurgence, Simpson puts on record, includes recognition and support of Black communities and their struggles in Canada "so both of our peoples could live free ... that's what ... freedom could look like under radical resurgence" ("Constellations of Coresistance," 231).

Simpson's radical resurgence, Elliott's extraction mentality, Maracle's oratories as theory, these and other expressions and explorations of Indigenous resistance to, and critique of, ongoing colonial experience in Canada make valuable and effective use of essay writing as a means for imagining a different country and different ways forward. The importance and power of the imagination in the goal to establish a more equitable world has been a key theme of essay collections in *Her Own Thinker*. It recurs in novelist Tessa McWatt's collection as well.

Tessa McWatt—*Anatomy of Race and Belonging*

Born in Guyana, raised in Toronto after her family immigrated
to Canada in 1962, Tessa McWatt is the author of six novels
and the volume of essays *Shame on Me: An Anatomy of Race
and Belonging* (2019). A finalist for the Hilary Weston Writers'
Trust Prize for Nonfiction, *Shame on Me* takes up topics and
themes discussed by writers such as M. NourbeSe Philip and
Dionne Brand among others. The collection presents a unique
"scientific structure": an opening "Hypothesis" is followed by
an "Experiment," "Analysis," and a concluding "Findings." The
collection's contents, however, challenge its scientific structure,
as one by one the essays question long-held beliefs and givens of
Western science. McWatt interrogates the privilege and primacy
of reason, progress, and other eighteenth century concepts and
measures of human civilization. She probes the racist roots
and historical colonialism of categories and social hierarchies
that place white people above "othereds"—Indigenous, Blacks,
Asians, mixed "race," and others—"Others" like McWatt, according to the question asked by her Grade Three teacher in a
searing moment forever remembered and repeated by the author. Recalling the shameful schoolyard game Adele Wiseman
remembers in her essay collection (*Memoirs*, 16), McWatt's
teacher asks: "What are you, Tessa?" (14).

   This is the central question of *Shame on Me*'s "experiment."
McWatt begins with a "Hypothesis" like no other—seven
vignettes about her forbears: her Chinese grandmother, her
great-great African grandmother and great-great-great Scottish
grandmother, and her Indian, Arawak, Portuguese, and French
Jewish ancestors. The "experiment" ensues in an eight-step
analysis organized around parts of the human anatomy: Nose,

Lips, Eyes, Hair, Ass, Bones, Skin, and Blood. In the "Analysis" stage of the experiment, McWatt exposes the racist ideas, attitudes, and stereotypes about these parts of the anatomy when they are associated with Black and other non-white bodies. The "Double Helix" "findings" of the "experiment" reveal the "scientific racism" ("Ass," 124) and "so-called science in the service of slavery" ("Bones," 141) that has been the history of Black and othered peoples objectified by identity categories defined by dominant society: race, class, gender; place of birth, family history, language. "I understood, without being able to articulate it," McWatt recalls of her painful Grade Three experience, "that language had the power to change me completely with the utterance of one word" ("What Are You?" 15). The word that day was "Negro". "In being asked what I was and realizing I did not know, I set off to find out. I believe it was the moment I became a writer," McWatt remarks ("What Are You?" 15).

The question and moment that led McWatt to becoming a writer also led to her analysis and critique of racism and colonialism. The essays in *Shame on Me* examine the history and operations of "race" in Guyana where she was born, in Canada where she grew up, and in the UK where she moved in 1999. "While there are superficial differences in the conversations about race in Britain and Canada," McWatt finds, "at the centre the issues are the same: violence, displacement, settlement, genocide, citizenship, migration, inequality and more" ("What Are You?" 23). These are issues on a continuum—from Guyana to Canada, and from the essay collections of Indigenous women writers to those of Black women writers. In Guyana, "plantation mentality," McWatt writes, deems some citizens more dispensable than others ("Eyes," 80). Plantation mentality perceives "a hierarchy of human civilizations" ("Eyes," 90), with the white race at the top and Black and Indigenous peoples at the bottom.[68] "This is plantation mentality" and "it trapped me," McWatt reflects, as her analysis of racism and colonialism reveals facts and under-standings aligned with those exposed by Simpson, Elliott, Brand, and Philip in their collections: "Race is a construct, not a reality. It is an expression of power," McWatt writes ("What Are You?" 22). "White is related to skin colour, but whiteness is a state of mind" ("What Are You?" 30), a state of mind that encourages inequality (Hair," 112).

Whiteness may be a state of mind, and race a construct, but the consequences of how a culture uses them are real, as McWatt observes ("What Are You?" 22). Whether in Guyana, Canada, or England, "race becomes an economic construct that governs who gets 'more'" ("Skin," 169), she points out. Race exists "to do the accounting for who will have more and who will have less" and it can operate even within groups of people who share the same skin colour ("Skin," 167). Over the course of her essays and investigations into race, McWatt focuses in on the "material inequality" of race-making: "I had believed in a liberal dream of being self-made. Yet by following that dream, I bought into the plantation hierarchy that established that free-dom would come if I strove to work in the master's house. (...) As Audre Lorde said, the master's tools will never dismantle the master's house" ("Skin," 165). The material structures of the master's house stand sturdy and strong. Citing John Berger, whose 1972 essay and BBC series *Ways of Seeing* were influential in developing the concept of the male gaze, McWatt recognizes

---

68 "A tiny European planter class that dominated not only the Indigenous peo-ple who had survived slaughter by earlier conquerors, but also the enslaved Africans and the Indian and Chinese indentured labourers who arrived over decades to work on their plantations" ("Nose," *Shame on Me*, 41).

that "Race-making was class-making, and inequality happened as soon as there was an 'us' and a 'them'" ("Skin," 170).

The McWatt family encounters "us" and "them" attitudes, structures, and experiences in Canada. McWatt learns that there is a Canadian equivalent to Guyanese colonialism ("Nose," 41): "Canada is also a country with a history of colonialism, slavery, the cultural genocide of Indigenous peoples through the residential system, Japanese internment, the Chinese head tax, the War Measures Act and many of the same pitfalls of border-making that arise in any nation state," she notes in the essay "Eyes" (82).

The theme of belonging, so powerful in collections by M. NourbeSe Philip and Dionne Brand and others, reappears ever stronger and more compelling in *Shame on Me*. In Canada as in the UK, multiculturalism and diversity initiatives exist, McWatt observes, but they do little to change the structures that determine who belongs and who does not ("Skin," 165). McWatt recalls the overwhelming "longing to belong to the mainstream" ("What Are You?" 18) and "striving to be that good immigrant ... that perfect self that will never be achieved" ("Eyes," 90), which she and her family experienced. "New to Canada, we concerned ourselves with survival and assimilation ... Our job was to assimilate ... to catch on to how Canadian life was lived" ("What Are You?" 26). Her brother embraced hockey, playing "his heart out to become a good Canadian" ("Nose," 48) only to find himself the target of more rough play than other team members. McWatt took up track and field, and excelled as a high jumper, aiming "higher and higher" to champion level. "Now I see it as a metaphor for my aspiration," she realizes in *Shame on Me*, "to fit in, to do better, to be not only enough but the best. I see how much I struggled to be accepted ... Achievement in sport is acceptable black attainment" ("Hair," 111), "a way of demonstrating how much I have 'overcome'" ("Eyes," 90).

Achievement in sports, scholarship, and other areas not-withstanding, and despite lighter skin and middle-class status conferring "privilege and mobility" ("Lips," 71), McWatt experienced being both too visible ("What are You?" 15) and invisible ("Nose," 53), being othered both externally and internally.

> To strangers, even friends—on some days also to myself—I am images of violence and oppression. I am the language of shame and destitution, of slavery and indenture, of rape and murder. I am images of power and privilege, of denial and shades of skin, shapes of faces ... belonging nowhere else but in a story.
>
> ("What Are You?" *Shame on Me*, 28)

Race, McWatt determined, is "the story of the self told by a stranger, with 'white' as the primordial narrator" ("Double Helix," 197). Her Grade Three experience had taught her early on "the power of words" ("What Are You?" 15) and that "colour, the lack of belonging, could be made intelligible by words" ("Nose," 46). It also taught her that "the single most powerful tool we have is our language and its ability to reinvent realities" ("Double Helix," 209). The process of writing allowed new realities to be imagined ("Nose," 46), new stories to be told. New stories offered "new ways of seeing. Community action, art and activism ... paths towards new spaces beyond the plantation—place outside both the master's house and the field" ("Double Helix," 200).

Writing provided McWatt with a space of belonging, and her experience as a writer in Canada included several of the race-related events that other Canadian women writers examine in their essays as well: the 1983 Women and Words conference, the 1988 Women's Press appropriation debate, the 1989 PEN meeting and exchange between June Callwood and M.

NourbeSe Philip (94). These experiences, and participating in a 1989 Women's Day march, were instrumental in McWatt becoming "politically black" ("Eyes," 95). Like other racialized women, she witnessed the extent to which whiteness characterized the Canadian feminist movement at the time and that "claiming liberation for all" did not end "erasure and violence" for others ("Eyes," 95). This realization put longing to belong into a new light, and McWatt's politics shifted again from being about "politically black" to being more "about ensuring that those whose stories were suppressed were heard than [about] the politics of group identities" ("Bones," 142).

As the longing to belong diminished, the desire for real change grew for McWatt. As vital as identity politics may have been in the 1970s-1980s, they did not produce the foundational change that she sought, change that would replace the structural politics of "plantation mentality" ("Bones," 143), for example. Plantation mentality, McWatt saw, could accommodate Black owners and leaders, as long as its politics were maintained. "The plantation likes identity politics. It likes us to be divided while it continues to make profits" ("Bones," 151), she remarked. A new longing formed for McWatt: "This is what I long to do: to speak beyond an identity that was named for me" ("Bones," 153). Her identity "was deeper than race, gender, sexuality, class or ability," McWatt wrote ("Bones," 144). "I don't want to belong anywhere on the plantation" ("Double Helix," 208); "I belong in action, in resistance" ("Double Helix," 208). "I have been the obedient 'other'. But it's time for disobedience. For action" ("Double Helix," 209).

Commitment to resisting racism and to contributing to real change galvanized McWatt's critique of Canada's shameful relationship with Indigenous peoples—and of her own as an immigrant trying to fit in, "blind to the fact of the cultural

genocide of Indigenous peoples in Canada" ("Bones," 147).
McWatt does not mince her words: what happened to Indigenous peoples in Canada, she writes, was cultural genocide. The
1876 Indian Act permitted practices that the country's 2015
Truth and Reconciliation Commission deemed cultural genocide ("Blood," 177), from the residential school system and
policies of assimilation to the dispossession of Indigenous lands
and ways of life on them.

These are practices that Indigenous writers like Maracle,
Simpson, and Elliott examine in their collections. McWatt's
essays express a keen awareness that her place as a settler immigrant and her experiences of racism and colonialism as a Black
woman are not those of Indigenous peoples in Canada. Her
critique of Canada's racist colonial treatment of Indigenous peoples consciously acknowledges and firmly respects the difference
between Indigenous experiences and histories and those of Black
and other racialized and marginalized citizens. These are all distinct (hi)stories, McWatt states. They are on a continuum of
Canadian colonialism and racism but, McWatt notes, we are at
a crossroad: "a new moment of reckoning in which the economy,
the environment, technology and our social lives are colliding—
an urgent moment of many walls and few bridges, of history
repeating and identities galvanizing" ("What Are You?" 29).

Shame on Me charts McWatt's resistance to the otherings of
racism and colonialism and her shift away from the question
of "what" she is to "who" she is. This is a shift from identification on the basis of achievement, attainment, success, identity
politics, belonging, or scientific classifications of blood type
or DNA, to "a new language of belonging. A who-am-I space
to gather in with others, rather than the biological 'what' am
I" ("Double Helix," 209). Writing offers McWatt this space
and language of belonging and connection. "Writing feels like

going home, a direct connection to something bigger, outside of myself and yet coming from within me," she comments ("Ass," 123). Writing allows her "to excavate and understand" her African, Chinese, Scottish, Indian, Portuguese, French, and possibly Jewish ancestry ("Bones," 137), "the creolization that made me, that created the complex racial mix and complex social circumstances of my entire extended family" ("Lips," 68-69). Writing reveals that race is a story and that "no single story of race has defined [McWatt]" ("What Are You?" 20). "The reparations my white self needs to make to my black and Indigenous self are not about race at all," she determines; "The reparations have to do with taking action. Now" ("Blood," 192). *Shame on Me* traces McWatt's politics turn toward taking action for self and change.

> My original question—What am I?—is irrelevant ... The more pertinent and ongoing question is *Who* am I? It's a perennial and evolving investigation into what kind of person I am, what change I want to effect and whether my actions hurt other people.
>
> ("Double Helix," *Shame on Me*, 211, emphasis in the original)

Identity and belonging are at the core of Tessa McWatt's essay collection. She shares with other essayists in this chapter a clear critique of colonialism, racism, and social injustice, and a countervailing faith in the power of language, imagination, and writing for resisting and surviving these transgressions of humanity.

Collections considered in this chapter add a lengthening list of topics related to these longstanding subjects of Canadian women writers' essay writing, from mental health, intergenerational trauma, and depression, to food security, resource extraction, new understandings of what constitutes knowledge, spirituality, truth, and reconciliation, and the importance of relationships, both human and non-human. The range and urgency of these topics underscore once again the need for more attention to the thinking that Canadian women novelists and poets share in their collections of essays.

Thinking Ahead

> *The essay form is far from dead. Two challengers of genre earlier in the century produced Stein's* How to Write, *Woolf's* Three Guineas. *I also love the essays of Benjamin and Montaigne for their highly personal side. The two women authors "theorize" in a highly subjective manner on their own experience of writing while being clearly abreast of the progressive ideas of their times. The absence in their work of that deference to authority which obsesses authors of academic essays appeals to me. And the openness regarding form which that absence of deference permits.*
>
> —Gail Scott, *Spaces like Stairs* (106, emphasis in the original)

For the past half-century, a wide array of Canadian women novelists and poets has made substantive use of the essay genre to address significant issues of social, political, and cultural concern while discovering and developing new ways of articulating their views on these issues. There have been three waves of essay development in this regard, which have synthesized the personal, open-ended Montaigne approach with the more rational, formal Bacon approach. The dialectics of this development have generated an extensive production of creative and compelling essay writing by Canadian women fiction writers, which *Her Own Thinker* has introduced and begun to explore.

What comes next for the essay form and its use by Canadian women writers? Recently, writer and editor Emily Donaldson pointed to a post-2000 resurgence in popularity of the essay genre, notably essays by women:

> The 20th century saw the novel displace poetry as the pre-eminent written art form, and these days non-fiction seems to be threatening to do the same to the novel; there is just so much good stuff coming out. This past year in particular was remarkable for the number of quality book-length essay collections by women that got published, so perhaps we can take a minute to appreciate some highlights of the wave that just passed over us.
>
> ("Joan Didion looms large over a wave of talented female essay-writers," *The Globe and Mail*, 14 January 2020)

Donaldson selected Canadian-born Jia Tolentino, staff writer at *The New Yorker* and author of *Trick Mirror: Reflections on Self-Delusion,* as "the essay writer of the moment."[69] She also noted Elizabeth Renzetti's *Shrewed* and Alicia Elliott's *A Mind Spread out on the Ground*, with the rest of her examples non-Canadian and thus outside the focus of *Her Own Thinker.* Echoing Donaldson's observation about renewed interest in the essay genre, the article "New essay collections from Joan Didion, André Aciman and more to ignite, illuminate and inspire," special to *The Globe and Mail*, 5 February 2021, cited the genre's practice by writers Joan Didion, Andre Aciman, Gabrielle Korm, and Karl Ove Knausgaard:

---

69 Tolentino's essay "The Personal-Essay Boom is Over" (*The New Yorker*, 18 May 2017) generated considerable commentary, including Soraya Roberts's "The Personal Essay Isn't Dead. It's Just No Longer White" (*The Walrus*, 20 September 2017), the subtitle of which captures Soraya's argument.

Essay collections are back in the spotlight. After years of damp-
ened enthusiasm for the genre, long-form musings are once
again making must-read lists. Cooped up at home, imprisoned
by winter weather and a pandemic – and profoundly weary
after months of exposure to hot-take Twitter culture – readers
now have both the time and the inclination to join non-fiction
writers on long, meandering literary journeys. In this absorbing crop of titles, luminaries join newcomers in exploring
themes as esoteric as nostalgia and topics as timely as cancel
culture. (Special to *The Globe and Mail*, 5 February 2021)

The named luminaries and newcomers do not include any
Canadians. As I have tried to show in *Her Own Thinker,* there
is a decisive case for them to figure on such lists. The number
of new collections that have appeared since 2000 signals that
the genre continues to attract Canadian women writers. A half-
dozen examples serve to illustrate, including first collections by
Alice Major, M. Travis Lane, Lorna Goodison, Joanna Skibsrud,
and Esi Edugyan, and a second collection by Gail Scott.

Alice Major's *Intersecting Sets: A Poet Looks at Science* (2011)
is an absorbing exploration of the relationship—intersection—
between scientists and poets. "The great age of Western science,
which began around the time of Bacon," Major writes, "was a
great inspiration to poets" ("The Magpie's Eye," *Intersecting Sets*,
xi). Her essays are investigations into theories and 'isms—both
literary and scientific—about which she has questions. Postmodernism is one example: "The more I read about science, the
more I felt that much of postmodernism was based on fossil-
ized ideas from and about science," Major states, "while science
itself *had* changed profoundly and creatively, and had found
useful things to say" ("The Magpie's Eye," xvi, emphasis in the
original). Major is frank about not being fond of the literary

theory she grew up with but she recognizes and acknowledges postmodernism's attempt, like that of science and poetry, to understand the world and "what causes what" (Stallworthy, 2013). Among other concepts she examines in her essays, from both literary and scientific perspectives, are empathy, metaphor, and simile ("the = in mathematics," "Metaphor at Play," *Intersecting Sets*, 41); holographs, geometry, and symmetry; the impact of sound on the brain, and other subjects of science and poetry. Exploring these subjects throughout her essays, Major engages with the work of writers and theorists as eclectic as L.M. Montgomery, Seamus Heaney, and Jacques Derrida.

Intersecting Sets integrates the essay dialectic between Montaigne personal passion and Baconian formal rationalism. Major describes the collection as forming an arc: "It starts very close and personal and as the essays move toward the end of the book they become more public with the social questions about both poetry and science," she explains; "every essay has a kind of metaphor that circles around. Whether it is the idea of a line, or of roses or the idea of animal versus vegetable... The final thing is it is a very personal book" (Stallworthy, 2013). Itself an intersection of essay genre traditions and innovation, Major's collection invites readers to think not only about relationships between science and poetry but also about the essay as a format for thinking.

Poet M. Travis Lane's *Heart on Fist: Essays and Reviews 1970-2016* (2016) collects a sampling of her publications as an active, indeed prolific, reviewer and essayist. The volume's title is inspired by Quebec poet Anne Hébert's 1953 book of poetry *Le Tombeau des rois* (The Tomb of the Kings) and the iconic image in its titular poem—a heart brandished on a fist ("J'ai mon coeur au poing," "Le Tombeau des rois"). The "fisted heart" captures the character of Lane's writing. Her more than 120 reviews of over 250 books by mainly Canadian writers are sensitive and insightful but pack a punch in presenting strong points of view. "I am not charmed by language or ideas that seem to relish horror to the point of exaggeration and fantasy," Lane declares; "Dracula leaves me cold" ("On Reviewing," *Heart on Fist*, 21). In the final section of *Heart on Fist,* "Closing Arguments," Lane offers a commanding commentary on narrative and different forms and functions of poetry, as well as a deeply philosophical reflection on truth and beauty. "A poem is always a clarification," she states in "Alternatives to Narrative: The Structuring Concept," "a small candle … against our darknesses" (*Heart on Fist*, 275). This observation echoes her review of Anne Hébert's poem "Le Tombeau des rois": "The shuddery dawn achieved at the conclusion of 'The Tomb of Kings' is not for those who did not descend to their inner darknesses, 'heart on fist' … poetry must enter, and come out from, our inwardest being" ("Heart on Fist: Three Translations," 186). In "Truth or Beauty: A Manifesto," Lane asserts the centrality of art to both. This collection of essays gathered from previous decades shows that the way forward does not mean neglecting essays written in the past. *Heart on Fist* bids readers' attention for its simultaneously critically direct and nuanced essays and reviews.

Lorna Goodison's *Redemption Ground: Essays and Adventures* (2018) derives its title from a historic market in Kingston, Jamaica, where the author was born and raised before leaving the island nation and making her way to Canada. Redemption Ground was a cholera cemetery before turning into a market space and a meeting place for followers of African spirituality and founders of Rastafarianism ("Redemption is the Key," *Redemption Ground*, 62). *Redemption Ground* the collection is a meeting place as well: Goodison's essays metaphorically gather together some of the many different individuals whose lives intersected with hers in one way or another over the years.

Celebrated as a poet laureate of her country of birth, Goodison is a recognized Canadian writer as well. She moved to Canada in 2000 after years of teaching and writing in the United States. Like other writers in *Her Own Thinker,* Goodison's work calls into question fixed ideas of national identity and cultural belonging, given historical and contemporary exclusions from these on the basis of racism and colonialism. For Goodison, colonial experience began with her British-based education growing up in the Caribbean. Like other school children in the Commonwealth, Goodison was taught that real literature meant poetry, novels, and plays by British-born authors. Real literature, she was given to understand, could not be written locally, "because that sort of writing would have no appeal to international audiences" ("For Keith Jarrett Rainmaker—Iowa City," *Redemption Ground,* 157).

Goodison does not dismiss the work of English or European authors in her essays. But she recognizes in the colonial school curriculum of her day the beginning of her search for writers like herself—Caribbean writers, especially women writers: "Black women poets who might become role models for me" ("Some poems that made me," *Redemption Ground,* 26); "Women writers who would look and sound more like me, whose stories would perhaps help to connect me to a place and a time and a history and to traditions lost in the great watery graveyard of the Atlantic" ("Nadine Gordimer Memorial Lecture," *Redemption Ground,* 37). Goodison's search took her from Caribbean writers to African women writers, whose "sound colonial educations," like hers, "did not take our own opinions as thinking, feeling human beings into account" ("Daffodil-bashing," *Redemption Ground,* 49). In due course, her search led to her own writing, to composing "the poems that I wanted to read, and writing them in a way that sounds more like the language I use" ("Some poems that made me," *Redemption Ground*, 29).

From the Caribbean to Africa, the UK, USA, and Canada, Goodison's essays connect international and Canadian experiences. Like collections by Canadian women writers from Margaret Laurence to Tessa McWatt, *Redemption Ground* perceives Canada in relation to the wider world. This internationalization of Canadian experience is a feature of the collections in *Her Own Thinker* that substantiates the breadth of the perspectives and experiences of their authors and what they bring to Canadian literary and intellectual culture. As a writer, Goodison sees it as her "job to imagine and keep reimagining the past and the future into being, so that the best of what was lost might exist again in the future" ("The Caribbean imaginary," *Redemption Ground*, 76): "I am trying to move past post-colonial," she states; "I am looking forward to the day post-colonial officially ends, so that something new can be made manifest" ("For Keith Jarrett Rainmaker—Iowa City," *Redemption Ground*, 157).

The foregrounding of poetry seen in essay collections by writers like Erin Moure, Kristjana Gunnars, and Dionne Brand, to name just three, describes the essays of poet and novelist Joanna Skibsrud in her collection *The Nothing That Is: Essays on Art, Literature and Being* (2019). Author of the 2010 Giller Prize winning novel *The Sentimentalists,* Skibsrud turns to the essay form to make the case for poetry as an ethics, a way of thinking about the relationship between self and other. Skibsrud's essays ask "is there a way we can allow ourselves to dwell in paradox and contradiction and still find a way to confront what exists beyond language and form?" ("Introduction," *The Nothing That Is*, 9). Essay writing helps her elaborate what she sees as "the fundamental ethical relation implicit within poetic approaches to thinking and being" (9). Poetry, more precisely Skibsrud's essays about poetry, allow her to address the gap between language and material reality, and between self, the world, and others in it; they allow her to draw on the potential of language and thought to imagine beyond language, beyond here and now (10). She is assisted in this by Luce Irigaray's feminist philosophy, which helps her think past white Western masculine perspectives of self/subject and the world/object. Resonances abound between the perspectives of Skibsrud's essays and those in essay collections throughout *Her Own Thinker*. "To write, and to read, poetically," Skibsrud reflects, "is to cast beyond the perceivable limits of language and temporal being" ("The Nothing That Is," *The Nothing That Is*, 13). She explores this idea further in her study, *The Poetic Imperative: A Speculative Aesthetic*, published a year after *The Nothing That Is: Essays on Art, Literature and Being* in 2020.

A first collection of essays by award-winning novelist Esi Edugyan, *Out of the Sun: On Race and Storytelling*, appeared in 2021. Its subtitle expresses two key themes considered throughout *Her Own Thinker*, and the collection as a whole explores the related themes of identity, language, belonging, and the social and political contexts that affect these human experiences. Born in Calgary to parents who immigrated to Canada from Ghana, Edugyan is a two-time winner of the Giller Prize for her novels *Half-Blood Blues* (2011) and *Washington Black* (2018). In addition to a debut novel, *The Second Life of Samuel Tyne* (2004), her publications include *Dreaming of Elsewhere: Observations on Home* (2014), the print version of her lecture for the University of Alberta's annual Henry Kreisel Memorial Lecture series. In similar manner, the essays in *Out of the Sun* issue from her 2021 Massey Lectures, which CBC radio broadcasts as part of its *Ideas* program. Organized into five "chapters," the essays proceed along a geography/theme axis: Europe/seeing, Canada/ ghosts, America/empathy, African/the future, Asia/storytelling.

Edugyan characterizes the essays in *Out of the Sun* as part memoir, part travelogue, and part history, and they are rich in breadth, depth, and detail in all three areas. The collection takes readers from Europe to Canada, America, Africa, and Asia, as Edugyan explores historical representations of Blackness; European, Canadian, and American histories of slavery and the ghosts that haunt those histories; racism and the lines between empathy, activism, and performance (98); the social constructs of identities and complexities of racial passing, authenticity, transracialism (114), and racial fluidity (124); Afrofuturism, coined by Mark Dery, as a term for African American science fiction (140) and what an African nation spared slavery and colonialism might look like (149); and storytelling. What happens, Edugyan asks, "when our once-settled narratives become unsettled? What happens when they begin to shift the boundaries of what we have long believed?" (3). New stories and new storytellers, Edugyan writes in *Out of the Sun*, come out of the shadows and into view.

A new essay collection by Gail Scott combines first-time and previously published essays under the provocative title *Permanent Revolution* (2021). The first half of the volume offers six new essays, a Foreword by Canadian poet and novelist Zoe Whittall, and a Preface by Scott. The second half of the collection reprises five essays from *Spaces like Stairs*: "Virginia + Colette," "A Visit to Canada," "A Story Between Two Chairs," "Paragraphs Blowing on a Line," and "A Feminist at the Carnival." Each is briefly introduced by Scott's reflections upon revisiting her work. The interplay of new and "old" essays works wonderfully in underscoring the enduring ("permanent") place and importance of Scott's essays, and in conveying the innovative ("revolutionary") nature of her earlier essay writing. "A written text or commentary," Scott maintains, "no matter how literary, seems able to function as political intervention" ("Introduction 2020," *Permanent Revolution*, 87-88). Her comments on the five essays from *Spaces like Stairs* underline the significance of their contribution to intellectual discourse at the time of their original publication.

Scott restates the attraction and unique function of the essay genre that she first expressed in *Spaces Like Stairs*: "I love the immediacy of the essay form, its way of intersecting with the period in which it is written," she writes in re-introducing the essays from *Spaces Like Stairs* in the second half of *Permanent Revolution* ("Introduction 2020," *Permanent Revolution*, 87). The essays in *Spaces Like Stairs* date from "a decade of remarkable flowering of feminism in Québec, a decade when the ethical function of the text was underscored in a writing practice greatly concerned with deciphering the effects of social constructs in language, especially for women" ("Introduction 2020," 87). There is a personal ring to Scott's added observation that "the essay, perhaps even more than fiction, shows up this youthful person radiant with hope + intractable enthusiasm. But one also pocked with her + the era's inadequacies" ("Introduction 2020," 87).

These inadequacies of the earlier era are brought into view in Scott's new essays. Foremost among them is the inattention to, and marginalization of, work and writers from Indigenous and Black communities. Writing with heightened consciousness in the 2020 context of "police assassination + other misdemeanours against Black + Indigenous men + women, not to mention ongoing LGBT+ harassment" (76), Scott emphasizes that it is "more important than ever to lend an ear to contingent majority + minority syntaxes + their implications as regards the question of power" ("The Porous Text, or the Ecology of the Small Subject," *Permanent Revolution*, 76). The question repeated in the new essays is once again: "who has the right to speak?" ("The Porous Text," 76). Scott's concern is "that which is not said, is mostly not descripted, that which seeps from the margins of the term + seems, of little consequence to the centre," "the value of the suppressed or hidden" ("Excess + the Feminine," *Permanent Revolution*, 13, 14). She points to the "suppressed Indigeneity" and "shame-filled Montréal site of unceded territory" ("The Sutured Subject," *Permanent Revolution*, 61, 62). But she also turns an unblinking eye on herself: "as one pale of skin + gobs of Western privilege, perhaps the deep conviction of being flawed + of parading this ambivalence (…) is to be attempting obfuscation of the worst crime of all: hypocrisy, guilt's twin!" ("The Porous Text," 81). With an ear to the "oft-repeated conundrum for feminists who write," she acknowledges "white imperialism by working to dismantle a subject formed by the egocentric West" ("Excess + the Feminine," 17). She praises the crucial work of Indigenous writers exploring "identitary issues by foregrounding First Nations knowledge—deploying deeply haunting language" ("Excess + the Feminine," 17), at the same time that she asks herself a hard question: is her praise not in itself colonial comportment? ("Corpus Delicti," *Permanent Revolution*, 55).

Scott is unflinching in her essays—both old and new—in asserting the critical and necessary link between the literary and the social—the "task of retooling the writing subject, embedding her in the social + in the collective effort we call language" ("The Sutured Subject," 60). "The artist's fundamental task," she reaffirms, is "to be a critic of her entire moment, with all its contradicting vectors" ("The Porous Text," 82), adding that "A writer's most important task: to be a critic of one's own culture" ("Virginia + Colette," *Permanent Revolution*, 91). Scott's *Permanent Revolution* traces an artistic trajectory "relating the act of writing to ongoing social upheaval" ("Preface," 5), and confirms the author's belief that "if one wants to think of art as permanent revolution, it can't be single-issue anything" ("Excess + the Feminine," 19). In her Foreword to the collection, Zoe Whittall summarizes Scott's essays as "what she has been *thinking* about" from art, writing, and narrative to community and revolution, revealing her to be "an iconic *thinker*" ("Foreword," 3, emphases added).

Capping this brief overview of additional recent essay collections by Canadian women writers is Margaret Atwood's 2022 *Burning Questions: Essays & Occasional Pieces 2004-2021.* This newest collection by the prolific author continues the sequential coverage of writing periods of her first two collections—*Second Words: Selected Critical Prose 1960-1982* and *Moving Targets: Writing with Intent 1982–2004*—gathering essays from the years 2004 to 2021. Taken together, the three collections represent over sixty years of essay writing—the six decades spanned in *Her Own Thinker*—the postwar 1950s-1960s to present day. In her introduction to *Burning Questions*, Atwood reflects on how her life and writing have intersected and interwoven with the many moments, movements, and matters of protest and change of this period of time, from feminism, to national and international political and cultural upheavals, to environmental and climate crisis today. Her reflection serves as a succinct historical summary and frame not only for her essays but for the essay collections considered throughout *Her Own Thinker* as a whole.

The essays in *Burning Questions* are organized into five parts according to five periods that Atwood perceives in her life and writing between 2004 and 2021: (I) 2004 to 2009: What will Happen Next?; (II) 2009 to 2013: Art is our Nature; (III) 2014 to 2016: Which is to be Master; (IV) 2017 to 2019: How Slippery is the Slope?; (V) 2020-2021: Thought and Memory. Each of these parts, Atwood points out, is marked by an event or turning point. As in her first two collections, Atwood chronicles a number of key events and contexts for her essay writing. In *Burning Questions*, these include, among others: the Iraq war in the aftermath of the Twin Towers attacks; the 2008 financial crash; the American elections in 2009 and 2017; the #MeToo movement; the "culture wars"; the diagnosis of dementia for her partner Graeme Gibson; and the lifelong concern she shared with him about the environment and climate crisis.

It is notable how long concern for the environment has been a focus of Atwood's essay writing, and that of Canadian women writer-essayists going back to Adele Wiseman, Margaret Laurence and others discussed in *Her Own Thinker*. Atwood bookends *Burning Questions* with essays that she wrote about the conservationists Rachel Carson and Barry Lopez. Their work and their post-millennial inheritors, she declares, will only become more important as the future becomes more uncertain in the face of environmental disasters. "Graeme and I were already great fans of Barry [Lopez]'s work ...To meet Barry was to feel we were entering ... the language of our inseparable connection with the natural world. (...) Now that the man-made Sixth Great Extinction is upon us and the Arctic is melting, the centrality of Barry's writing is self-evident" (*Burning Questions*, 444-445). Rachel Carson's 1962 book *Silent Spring*, already essential when first published, is never more so than today, Atwood adds, "in the era of oil, plastics, pesticides and rampant industrial overfishing ... a new era of science denial and a refusal to face facts—not only those about climate heating and the biosphere-killing effects of new insecticides and herbicides, but about more immediately human concerns such as vaccination and vote-counting" (447). Carsons's and Lopez's inheritors—today's post-millennials, Atwood writes, thinking ahead—"will soon grow into positions of power. Let us hope they use their power wisely. And soon" (*Burning Questions*, xx).

Reviews of *Burning Questions*—books by Atwood do elicit review, essay collections included[70]—remark on the seriousness and relevance of the essays and the issues they address: climate change, inequalities of wealth, and threats to democracy, among numerous others. Particular attention is directed to Atwood's 2018 essay "Am I a Bad Feminist?" written in response to criticism she received for adding her name to a petition described in the essay as follows: "an Open Letter called UBC Accountable, which calls for holding the University of British Columbia accountable for its failed process in its treatment of one of its former employees, Steven Galloway, the former chair of the department of creative writing, as well as its treatment of those who became ancillary complaints in the case" (*Burning Questions*, 336). The essay drew further critical response and renewed discussion and debate about the 2016 case that became known as the "Galloway affair" and that divided Canadian literary and feminist communities on the issue of sexual abuse, the legal system, and complainants'—particularly women's—experiences of both.[71] Reviews of *Burning Questions* also comment on the

70 There are sure to be additional and more in-depth studies of the collection to come, but at the time of this concluding section of *Her Own Thinker,* my reference here is to reviews online by Hadley Freeman (2022): "Playing with Fire: Margaret Atwood on feminism, culture wars and speaking her mind," *The Guardian* (February 19); Shahidha Bari (2022): "Burning Questions by Margaret Atwood review – wisdom and wonder," *The Guardian* (March 3); and Marsha Lederman (2022): "Margaret Atwood isn't slowing down, and she's ready to open up," *The Globe and Mail* (March 11).

71 For more about the case and its impact on Canadian literary and feminist communities, the following accounts, among others, may be found online: Kerry Gold (2016): "L'Affaire Galloway," *The Walrus* (September 14):

"occasional pieces"—speeches, keynotes, introductions, obituaries, books reviews, and other selections from the over 500 pieces that Atwood wrote between 2004 and 2021 (Lederman 2022). Some query the inclusion of these "occasional pieces" but at the same time concede the generosity of these inclusions, particularly the tributes to other writers, Canadian women writers such as Alice Munro and L.M. Montgomery; the gracious acceptance of invitations and requests for guest lectures, presentations, and other contributions to public events; and the periodic tongue-in-cheek humour, notably directed at herself.

The "500-page doorstopper," as *The Guardian* reviewer Hadley Freeman (2022) refers to *Burning Questions,* is further confirmation of the place and use of the essay that the genre presents to Canadian women writers, and of the value and importance of their essay writing. The essay continues to offer a means to address social issues, to formulate responses and actions, to experiment and articulate new modes of social and literary expression, and to demand a more central role for those at the margins.

Her Own Thinker has aimed to demonstrate that the contributions and accomplishments of essay writing by Canadian women writers have too long eluded the attention of a large segment of Canada's literary, intellectual, and political establishment. In a column about the essay genre and its practice in Canada, *Toronto Star* literary reviewer Bert Archer wrote: "Essay writing is an art and a skill, an ideal form for writers to draw readers into their way of thinking and seeing the world"

Marsha Lederman (2016): "Under a Cloud: How UBC's Steven Galloway affair has haunted a campus and changed lives," *The Globe and Mail* (October 28); Constance Grady (2018): "Why Handmaid's Tale author Margaret Atwood is facing #MeToo backlash," *Vox* (January17).

(Archer, 1997). Unfortunately, he lamented: "I can't remember the last time I read a good essay published in this country." A decade later another *Toronto Star* writer, Alex Good (2007), wrote a column about public intellectuals in Canada. He rued that no writers of the previous twenty years had come close to the achievements of Harold Innis, Northrop Frye, Marshall McLuhan, George Grant, or Pierre Berton. These were writers of enormous cultural presence and impact, in Good's view, and not just in Canada. At minimum, he argued, "any single one of them had greater influence on our understanding and imagining of Canada than any one of our poets or novelists, alive or dead" ("Woe is us"). "Who has taken their place?" Good fretted. "What has become of the Canadian public intellectual? One supposes the name of John Ralston Saul might make the list today, but even he is more of an inheritor. Looking about the present arid landscape makes us only more aware of what a falling off there has been" ("Woe is us").

Neither author, these articles suggest, had considered essay collections by Canadian women writers. In this, they have regrettably not been alone. Many critics and readers have overlooked Canadian women writers' essay collections. These have been, and continue to be, a generally unfamiliar and undervalued body of work, one that *Her Own Thinker* asserts is in fact substantial and important, deserving of more attention and further study.

Her Own Thinker has introduced and considered some of the many issues, ideas, arguments, and insights that Canadian women novelists and poets have presented, discussed, and shared in their essays. Their interests have ranged widely from the environment, economic and social justice, racism and cultural appropriation, to Canada's history and relations with Indigenous peoples, its policies of multiculturalism and immigration, events such as the Writing Thru Race conference, and movements such as Idle No More. These topics and many others feature in essay collections by women writers from the 1960s to the present, with the subjects of writing and women's lives and experiences as writers, including experiences of colonialism and being an outsider, forming a through-line in the collections and the chapters of *Her Own Thinker* alike.

Looking ahead, ongoing consideration of Canadian women writers' essay writing would further reveal the extent to which they connect Canada to the wider world, in its ties and histories with Africa, Europe, the UK, USA, and the Caribbean. The international dimension of Canadian women writers' essays comprises another generally overlooked contribution that they have made to cultural and intellectual discourse and debate.

In her first collection of essays, *Second Words*, Atwood wrote that writing essays is a way of finding out "what you really think" (13). I have suggested that reading essays works in the same way. It is among the reasons why I have encouraged my students to read more of Canadian women writers' essays, and why I dare hope that ultimately *Her Own Thinker* will encourage readers everywhere to do the same.

Primary Works Cited

Atwood, Margaret (1982). *Second Words: Selected Critical Prose 1960-1982.* Toronto: House of Anansi.

_____ (2002). *Negotiating with the Dead: A Writer on Writing.* Cambridge: Cambridge University Press.

_____ (2004). *Moving Targets: Writing with Intent 1982–2004.* Toronto: House of Anansi.

_____ (2022). *Burning Questions: Essays & Occasional Pieces 2004-2021.* Toronto: McClelland & Stewart.

Bannerji, Himani (1993). *The Writing on the Wall: Essays on Culture and Politics.* Toronto: TSAR.

_____ (1995). *Thinking Through: Essays on Feminism, Marxism, and Anti-Racism.* Toronto: Women's Press.

_____ (2000). *The Dark Side of the Nation: Essays on Multiculturalism, Nationalism and Gender.* Toronto: Canadian Scholars Press.

Bersianik, Louky, et al. (1988). *La théorie, un dimanche.* Montréal: Les Editions du remue-ménage.

Brand, Dionne (1994). *Bread out of Stone.* Toronto: Coach House.

_____ (2001). *A Map to the Door of No Return: Notes to Belonging.* Toronto: Doubleday Canada.

Brandt, Di (1993). *Wild Mother Dancing.* Winnipeg: University of Manitoba Press.

_____ (1996). *Dancing Naked: Narrative Strategies for Writing Across the Centuries.* Stratford: The Mercury Press.

_____ (2007). *So this is the world & here I am in it.* Edmonton: NeWest Press.

Brossard, Nicole (1985). *La Lettre aérienne.* Montréal: Les Editions du remue-ménage. *The Aerial Letter,* Marlene Wildeman (Trans.). (1988). Toronto: Women's Press.

Edugyan, Esi (2021). *Out of the Sun: On Race and Storytelling.* Toronto: House of Anansi Press.

Elliott, Alicia (2019). *A Mind Spread Out on the Ground.* Toronto: Doubleday Canada.

Gallant, Mavis (1986). *Paris Notebooks: Essays & Reviews.* Toronto: MacMillan of Canada.

Goodison, Lorna (2018). *Redemption Ground: Essays and Adventures.* Oxford (UK): Myriad Editions.

Gunnars, Kristjana (2004). *Stranger at the Door: Writers and the Act of Writing.* Waterloo: Wilfrid Laurier University Press.

Laurence, Margaret (1976). *Heart of a Stranger.* Toronto: McClelland and Stewart.

Lane, M. Travis (2016). *Heart on Fist: Essays and Reviews 1970-2016.* Shane Nelson (Ed.). Windsor (ON): Palimpsest Press.

Major, Alice (2011). *Intersecting Sets: A Poet Looks at Science.* Edmonton: University of Alberta Press.

Maracle, Lee (1988). *I Am Woman: A Native Perspective on Sociology and Feminism.* Vancouver: Press Gang Publishers.

_____ (2015). *Memory Serves: Oratories.* Edmonton: NeWest Press.

_____ (2017). *My Conversations with Canadians.* Toronto: BookThug.

Marlatt, Daphne (1998). *Readings from the Labyrinth.* Edmonton: NeWest Press.

McWatt, Tessa (2019). *Shame on Me: An Anatomy of Race and Belonging.* Toronto: Random House Canada.

Moure, Erin (2009). *My Beloved Wager: Essays from a Writing Practice.* Edmonton: NeWest Press.

P.K. Page (2007). *The Filled Pen: Selected Non-fiction.* Zailig Pollock (Ed.). Toronto: University of Toronto Press.

Philip, NourbeSe M. (1992). *Frontiers: Essays and Writings on Racism and Culture.* Stratford (ON): The Mercury Press.

_____ (1997). *A Genealogy of Resistance and Other Essays.* Stratford (ON): The Mercury Press.

_____ (2017). *Bla_k. Essays & Interviews.* Toronto: BookThug.

Rule, Jane (1982). *Outlander: Short Stories and Essays.* Tallahassee (FL): The Naiad Press.

Scott, Gail (1989). *Spaces Like Stairs: Essays.* Toronto: Women's Press.

_____ (2021). *Permanent Revolution.* Toronto: Book*hug Press.

Simpson, Leanne Betasamosake (2011). *Dancing on Our Turtle's Back; Stories of Nishnaabeg Re-Creation, Resurgence and a New Emergence.* Winnipeg: Arp Books.

_____ (2017). *As We Have Always Done: Indigenous Freedom Through Radical Resistance.* Minneapolis: University of Minnesota Press.

Skibsrud, Joanna (2019). *The Nothing That Is: Essays on Art, Literature and Being.* Toronto: Book*hug Press.

Tostevin, Lola Lemire (1995). *Subject to Criticism.* Stratford (ON): The Mercury Press.

_____ (2015). *At the Risk of Sounding: Essays.* Toronto: Teksteditions.

van Herk, Aritha (1991). *In Visible Ink: crypto-frictions.* Edmonton: NeWest Press.

_____ (1992). *A Frozen Tongue.* Sydney (Aust.): Dangaroo Press.

Waddington, Miriam (1989). *Apartment Seven: Essays New and Selected.* Toronto: Oxford University Press.

Wallace, Bronwen (1992). *Arguments with the World.* Kingston (ON): Quarry Press.

Warland, Betsy (2010). *Breathing the Page: Reading the Act of Writing.* Toronto: Cormorant Press.

Webb, Phyllis (1995). *Nothing But Brush Strokes.* Edmonton: NeWest Press.

Wiseman, Adele (1978). *Old Woman at Play* Toronto: Clarke Irwin.

_____ (1987). *Memoirs of a Book Molesting Childhood and Other Essays*. Toronto: Oxford University Press.

Acknowledgements

First and foremost, thank you to the authors—Canadian women novelists, poets, and short fiction writers, whose non-fiction work, in particular whose collections of essays, form the focus of *Her Own Thinker*. I would also like to thank the publishers who took on the publication of the collections, despite the likelihood that sales of these works would be more modest than those of other books on their rosters. Many of the collections in this study came together and were published thanks to the commitment of "small presses" like Arp Books, Book*hug Press, Coach House, Les Editions du remue-ménage, Gaspereau Press, House of Anansi, The Mercury Press, NeWest Press, Palimpsest Press, Quarry Press, Theytus Books, TSAR, Women's Press, among others. To the dedicated individuals behind these publishing venues, some of which are now defunct, grateful thanks for bringing Canadian women writers' essay collections into print. To the publisher of this book, Guernica Editions and its editor-in-chief Michael Mirolla and staff, my greatest thanks and sincerest appreciation.

Many thanks to the students, colleagues, and friends with whom I talked about this project over the years of its gestation. These proved to be more than originally envisioned because of additional and sometimes unanticipated projects and developments along the way. I remain grateful to the Social Sciences and Humanities Research Council and to the Canadian Federation for the Humanities for supporting my research and scholarly projects throughout my career, including *Her Own Thinker* and the conferences it inspired—"Discourse and Dynamics: Canadian Women as Public Intellectuals" (2014), "Speaking her Mind: Canadian Women and Public Presence" (2016), and "Re-Surfacing: Women Writers of 1970s Canada/Refaire surface: écrivaines canadiennes des années 1970" (2018). These conferences may well have sidetracked my writing at times but they were wonderful, productive gatherings of intellectual exchange and mentorship.

Whatever my academic pursuits, initiatives, and distractions over the years, I have had the steadfast support of my family, for which my deepest gratitude. To Robert and our four children, heartfelt thanks for your unflagging interest, encouragement, patience, and good humour, and for making sure that work was always balanced with play, and thinking with doing.

Bibliography

Anonymous (2021). "New essay collections from Joan Didion, André Aciman and more to ignite, illuminate and inspire." *The Globe and Mail*. February 5. https://www.theglobeandmail.com/arts/books/article-essay-collections-to-ignite-illuminate-and-inspire/

Archer, Bert (1997). "The Art of the Essay." *The Toronto Star*. April 5. M16.

Armstrong, Jeannette (1993). *Looking at the Words of our People*. Penticton (BC): Theytus Books.

Armstrong, Sean (Ed.). (1995). *Far and Wide: Essays in Canada*. Toronto: Nelson Canada.

Atwood, Margaret (1972). *Survival: A Thematic Guide to Literature*. Toronto: House of Anansi.

_____ (1982). *Second Words: Selected Critical Prose 1960-1982*. Toronto: House of Anansi.

_____ (2002). *Negotiating with the Dead: A Writer on Writing*. Cambridge: Cambridge University Press.

_____ (2004). *Moving Targets: Writing with Intent, 1982–2004*. Toronto: House of Anansi.

_____ (2008). *Payback: Debt and the Shadow Side of Wealth*. Toronto: House of Anansi.

_____ (2011). *In Other Worlds: SF and the Human Imagination*. Toronto: Signal.

_____ (2017). *The Burgess Shale: The Canadian Writing Landscape of the 1960s*. Edmonton: University of Alberta Press.

_____ (2022). *Burning Questions: Essays & Occasional Pieces 2004-2021*. Toronto: McClelland and Stewart.

Baert, Patrick and Alan Shipman (2013). "The Rise of the Embedded Intellectual: New Forms of Public Engagement and Critique." Peter Thijssen, Walter Weyns, Christiane Timmerman and Sara Mels (Eds). *New Public Spheres, Recontextualizing the Intellectual*. Farnham: Ashgate. 27-51.

Bannerji, Himani (1993). *The Writing on the Wall: Essays on Culture and Politics*. Toronto: TSAR.

_____ (1995). *Thinking Through: Essays on Feminism, Marxism, and Anti-Racism*. Toronto: Women's Press.

_____ (2000). *The Dark Side of the Nation: Essays on Multiculturalism, Nationalism and Gender*. Toronto: Canadian Scholars Press.

Bari, Shahidha (2022). "Burning Questions by Margaret Atwood review – wisdom and wonder." *The Guardian*. March 3. https://www.theguardian.com/books/2022/mar/03/burning-questions-by-margaret-atwood-review-wisdom-and-wonder

Bauman, Zygmunt (1989). *Legislators and Interpreters: On Modernity, Post-modernity and Intellectuals*. London: Polity.

Belleau, André (1980). "Approches et situation de l'essai québécois," *Voix et Images* 3 (Printemps 1980). 537-543.

Benda, Julien (1928). *The Treason of the Intellectuals*. R. Aldington (Trans.). Toronto: George J. McLeod Limited.

Bersianik, Louky, et al. (1988). *La théorie, un dimanche*. Montréal: Les Editions du remue-ménage. *Theory, A Sunday* (2013). New York: Belladonna Press.

Boivin, Jean-Roch Boivin (1988). "Ceci n'est pas une critique et la théorie a ses limites." *Le Devoir*. 28 juin. D3.

Bourdieu, Pierre (2000). "For a scholarship with commitment." New York: *MLA* (Modern Languages Association). 40-45.

Bourque, Dominique (1990). *Canadian Woman Studies/Les Cahiers de la Femme*. Vol. 11, No. 1.107-108.

Brand, Dionne (1994). *Bread out of Stone*. Toronto: Coach House.

_____ (2001). *A Map to the Door of No Return: Notes to Belonging*. Toronto: Doubleday Canada.

_____ (2018). *The Blue Clerk: Ars Poetica in 59 versos.* Toronto: McClelland and Stewart.

Brandt, Di (1993). *Wild Mother Dancing.* Winnipeg: University of Manitoba Press.

_____ (1996). *Dancing Naked: Narrative Strategies for Writing across the Centuries.* Stratford: The Mercury Press.

_____ (2007). *So this is the world & here I am in it.* Edmonton: NeWest Press.

Brossard, Nicole (1985). *La Lettre aérienne.* Montréal: Les Editions du remue-ménage. *The Aerial Letter* (1988). Marlene Wildeman (Trans.). Toronto: Women's Press.

Brugmann, Margret (1993). "Between the Lines: On the Essayistic Experiment of Hélène Cixous in 'The Laugh of the Medusa.'" *The Politics of the Essay: Feminist Perspectives.* Boetcher Joeres and Mittman (Eds.). Bloomington: Indiana University Press. 73-86.

Butrym, Alexander J. (Ed.). (1989). *Essays on the Essay: Redefining the Genre.* Athens and London: The University of Georgia Press.

Cabral, Amilcar (1973). *Return to the Source.* New York: Monthly Review Press.

Cameron, Anne (1981). *Daughters of Copper Woman.* Vancouver: Press Gang Publishers.

Carrière, Marie (2020). *Cautiously Hopeful: Metafeminist Writing in Canada.* Montreal/Kingston: McGill-Queen's University Press.

Coulthard, Glen (2014). *Red Skin, White Masks: Rejecting the Colonial Politics of Recognition.* Minneapolis: University of Minnesota Press.

Crenshaw, Kimberlé (1989). "Demarginalizing the Intersection of Race and Sex: A Black Feminist Critique of Antidiscrimination

Doctrine, Feminist Theory and Antiracist Politics." *University of Chicago Legal Forum*. Vol. 1989, Issue 1. Article 8. 139-167.

De Meijer, Sadiqa (2020). *alfabet/alphabet: a memoir of a first language*. Windsor (ON): Palimpsest Press.

Dewar, Kenneth (2020). "Brain Drain: The loss of intellectuals." *LRC* (*Literary Review of Canada*). Vol. 28, No. 2. (March 2020). 8-9.

Dobrée, Bonamy [n.d.] *English Essayists*. London: Collins.

Donaldson, Emily (2020). "Joan Didion looms large over a wave of talented female essay-writers." *The Globe and Mail*. January 14. https://www.theglobeandmail.com/arts/books/article-joan-didion-looms-large-over-a-wave-of-talented-female-essay-writers/

Elliott, Alicia (2019). *A Mind Spread Out on the Ground*. Toronto: Doubleday Canada.

Freeman, Hadley (2022). "Playing with Fire: Margaret Atwood on feminism, culture wars and speaking her mind." *The Guardian*. February 19. https://www.theguardian.com/books/ng-interactive/2022/feb/19/margaret-atwood-on-feminism-culture-wars

Furedi, Frank (2004). *Where Have All the Intellectuals Gone?* London/New York: Continuum International Publishing Group.

Gauvin, Lise (1994). "Petit essai sur l'essai au féminin." *L'autre lecture: La Critique au féminin et les textes québécois*. Lori Saint-Martin (Ed.). Montreal: XYZ. 117-127.

Geddes, Gary (Ed.). (1977). *Divided We Stand*. Toronto: Peter Martin Associates.

Gold, Kerry (2016). "L'Affaire Galloway." *The Walrus*. September 14. https://thewalrus.ca/laffaire-galloway/

Good, Alex (2007). "Woe is us." *The Toronto Star*. April 8. E3.

Good, Graham (1988). *The Observing Self: Rediscovering the Essay*. London and New York: Routledge.

Goodison, Lorna (2018). *Redemption Ground: Essays and Adventures*. Oxford (UK): Myriad Editions.

Grady, Constance (2018). "Why Handmaid's Tale author Margaret Atwood is facing #MeToo backlash." *Vox*. January 17. https://www.vox.com/culture/2018/1/17/16897404/margaret-atwood-metoo-backlash-steven-galloway-ubc-accountable

Gramsci, Antonio (1971). *The Intellectuals*. Q. Hoare and G.N. Smith (Eds. and Trans.). *Selections from the prison notebooks*. New York: International Publishers.

Gunnars, Kristjana (2004). *Stranger at the Door: Writers and the Act of Writing*. Waterloo: Wilfrid Laurier University Press.

Harvor, Elisabeth (2001). "In her solitude." *The Globe and Mail*. October 20. D4.

Heynders, Odile (2016). *Writers as Public Intellectuals: Literature, Celebrity, Democracy*. Houndmills, Basingstoke, Hampshire (UK): Palgrave Macmillan.

Ignatieff, Michael (1997). "The Decline and Fall of the Public Intellectual." *Queen's Quarterly*. 104 (3). 395-403.

Jacoby, Russell (1987). *The Last Intellectuals*. New York: Basic Books.

Joeres, Ruth-Ellen Boetcher and Elizabeth Mittman (Eds.). (1993). *The Politics of the Essay: Feminist Perspectives*. Bloomington: Indiana University Press.

Johnson, Pauline E. Tekahionwake (1892). "A Strong Race Opinion: On the Indian Girl in Modern Fiction." *Toronto Sunday Globe*. May 22.

Lederman, Marsha (2016). "Under a Cloud: How UBC's Steven Galloway affair has haunted a campus and changed lives." *The Globe and Mail*. October 28. https://www.theglobeandmail.

com/news/british-columbia/ubc-and-the-steven-galloway-affair/article32562653/

_____ (2022). "Margaret Atwood isn't slowing down, and she's ready to open up." *The Globe and Mail.* March 11. https://www.theglobeandmail.com/arts/books/article-margaret-atwood-shows-no-sign-of-stopping/

Kamboureli, Smaro (Ed.). (1996). *Making a Difference. Canadian Multicultural Literatures.* Toronto: Oxford University Press.

Kingwell, Mark (2012). "What are intellectuals for?" *Unruly voices: Essays on democracy, civility and the human imagination.* Windsor (ON): Biblioasis. 137-48.

Kirklighter, Cristina (2002). *Traversing the Democratic Borders of the Essay.* New York: State University of New York Press.

Laurence, Margaret (1976). *Heart of a Stranger.* Toronto: McClelland and Stewart.

Lynch, Gerald, and David Rampton (Eds.). (1991). *The Canadian Essay.* Ottawa: University of Ottawa Press.

Lane, M. Travis (2016). *Heart on Fist: Essays and Reviews 1970-2016.* Shane Nelson (Ed.). Windsor (ON): Palimpsest Press.

Lefebvre, Benjamin (Ed.). (2018). *A Name for Herself: Selected Writings, 1891-1917.* Toronto: University of Toronto Press.

Mailhot, Laurent (2005). *L'essai québécois depuis 1845: étude et anthologie.* Montreal: Editions Hurtubise.

Mairs, Nancy (1992). *Plaintext: Deciphering a Woman's Life.* Tucson: University of Arizona Press.

Major, Alice (2011). *Intersecting Sets: A Poet Looks at Science.* Edmonton: University of Alberta Press.

Maracle, Lee (1988). *I Am Woman: A Native Perspective on Sociology and Feminism.* Vancouver: Press Gang Publishers.

_____ (2015). *Memory Serves: Oratories.* Edmonton: NeWest Press.

_____ (2017). *My Conversations with Canadians*. Toronto: BookThug.

Marks, Elaine and Isabelle de Courtivron (Eds.). (1980). *New French Feminisms: An Anthology*. Amherst: University of Massachusetts Press.

Marlatt, Daphne (1984). *Touch to My Tongue*. Edmonton: Longspoon Press.

_____ (1998). *Readings from the Labyrinth*. Edmonton: NeWest Press.

Mathews, Robin. (1972). "Survival and the Struggle in Canadian Literature." *This Magazine Is About Schools*. Vol. VI, No. 4. 109-24.

Mavrikakis, Catherine (2010). *L'éternité en acccéléré*. Montreal: Editions Héliotrope.

McCarthy, John A. (1989). *Crossing Boundaries: A Theory and History of Essay Writing in German 1680–1815*. Philadelphia: University of Pennsylvania Press.

McDonald, Lynn (1987). "Margaret Laurence and the NDP." *Canadian Woman Studies/Cahiers de la femme*. Vol. 8, No. 3. 23-24.

McMaster, Susan (Ed.). (1994). *Two Women Talking: Correspondence 1985 to 1987, Erin Moure and Bronwen Wallace* (Living Archives of the Feminist Caucus of the League of Canadian Poets). Kingston (ON): Quarry Press.

McLaughlin, Neil and Eleanor Townsley (2011). "Contexts of cultural diffusion: A case study of 'public intellectual' debates in English Canada." *Canadian Review of Sociology*. Vol. 48, No. 4. 341-368.

McWatt, Tessa and Rabindranath Maharaj, Dionne Brand (Eds.). (2018). *Luminous Ink: Writers on Writing in Canada*. Toronto: Cormorant Books.

234 HER OWN THINKER

_____ (2019). *Shame on Me: An Anatomy of Race and Belonging*. Toronto: Random House Canada.

Melzer, Jerry W. and M. Richard Zinman (Eds.). (2003). *The Public Intellectual: Between Philosophy and Politics*. Lanham, Boulder and New York: Rowman and Littlefield.

Morrell, Carol (1993). [Review]. *University of Toronto Quarterly*. Vol. 63, Issue 1. (Fall). 154-156.

Moure, Erin (2009). *My Beloved Wager: Essays from a Writing Practice*. Edmonton: NeWest Press.

_____ and Bronwen Wallace (1994). *Two Women Talking: Correspondence 1985-1987 Erin Moure and Bronwen Wallace* (Living Archives of the Feminist Caucus of the League of Canadian Poets). Susan McMaster (Ed.). Kingston (ON): Quarry Press.

Moyes, Lianne (Ed.). (2002). *Gail Scott: Essays on Her Works*. Toronto: Guernica Editions.

Neumann, Shirley and Smaro Kamboureli (Eds.). (1986). *Amazing Space: Writing Canadian Women Writing*. Edmonton: NeWest Press.

New, William H. (Ed.). (1978). *A Political Art: Essays and Images in Honour of George Woodcock*. Vancouver: University of British Columbia Press.

Nurse, Donna (1992). "A writer perpetually in exile." *The Toronto Star*. December 26. SA2, K19.

_____ (1997). "Writer packs poetic punch / Dionne Brand has always been a fighter of causes, but the pen is now her weapon of choice." *The Globe and Mail*. April 29. C1.

Page, Joanne (Ed.). (1992). *Arguments with the World: Essays by Bronwen Wallace*. Kingston (ON): Quarry Press.

P.K. Page (2007). *The Filled Pen: Selected Non-fiction*. Zailig Pollock (Ed.). Toronto: University of Toronto Press.

Panofsky, Ruth (2006). *The Force of Vocation: The Literary Career of Adele Wiseman*. Winnipeg: University of Manitoba Press.

Philip, NourbeSe M. (1989). *She Tries Her Tongue – Her Silence Softly Breaks*. Charlottetown: Ragweed Press.

_____ (1992). *Frontiers: Essays and Writings on Racism and Culture*. Stratford (ON): The Mercury Press.

_____ (1997). *A Genealogy of Resistance and Other Essays*. Toronto: The Mercury Press.

_____ (2017). *Bla_k. Essays & Interviews*. Toronto: BookThug.

Pollock, Zailig (Ed.). (2007). *P.K. Page, The Filled Pen: Selected Non-fiction*. Toronto: University of Toronto Press.

Posner, Richard A. (2002). *Public Intellectuals: A Study of Decline*. Cambridge, Massachusetts: Harvard University Press.

Przychodzen, Jans (1993). *Un Projet de liberté: L'essai littéraire au Québec (1970-1990)*. Quebec: IQRC.

Queyras, Sina (2006). *Lemon Hound*. Toronto: Coach House.

_____ (2009). *Unleashed*. Toronto: BookThug.

Richler, Noah (2003). "Forgiving Toronto in its time of need: Poet Dionne Brand burrows under the skin of a voracious city." *National Post*. June 12. AL1 Front.

Rule, Jane (1982). *Outlander: Short Stories and Essays*. Tallahassee (FL): The Naiad Press.

_____ (1980). *Contract with the World*. New York: Harcourt, Brace, Jovanovich.

Saïd, Edward W. (1994). *Representations of the Intellectual*. New York: Vintage Books.

Saul, Joanne (2000). *UTQ (University of Toronto Quarterly)*. Vol. 69, No. 1. (Winter 1999-2000). 352.

Scholes, Robert and Carl H. Klaus (1969). *Elements of the Essay*. New York: Oxford University Press.

Scott, Gail (1989). *Spaces Like Stairs: Essays.* Toronto: Women's Press.

_____ (2021). *Permanent Revolution.* Toronto: Book*hug Press.

Shields, Carol and Marjorie Anderson (Eds.). (2001). *Dropped Threads: What We Aren't Told.* Toronto: Vintage Canada.

Silvera, Mikeda (Ed.). (1994). *The Other Woman: Women of Colour in Contemporary Canadian Literature.* Toronto: Penguin Random House Canada.

Simpson, Leanne Betasamosake (Ed.). (2008). *Lighting the Eighth Fire: The Liberation, Resurgence, and Protection of Indigenous Nations.* Winnipeg: Arp Books.

_____ and Kiera L. Ladner (Eds.). (2010). *This Is an Honour Song: 20 Years Since the Blockades, An Anthology of Writing on the "Oka" Crisis.* Winnipeg: Arbeiter Ring Publishing.

_____ (2011). *Dancing on Our Turtle's Back: Stories of Nishnaabeg Re-Creation, Resurgence and a New Emergence.* Winnipeg: Arp Books.

_____ (2013). *Islands of Decolonial Love.* Winnipeg: Arp Books.

_____ and the *Kino-nda- niimi Collective* (2014). *The Winter We Danced: Voices from the Past, the Future and the Idle No More Movement.* Winnipeg: Arp Books.

_____ (2017). *As We Have Always Done: Indigenous Freedom Through Radical Resistance.* Minneapolis: University of Minnesota Press.

_____ (2017). *This Accident of Being Lost: Songs and Stories.* Toronto: House of Anansi Press.

_____ (2021). *A Short History of the Blockade: Giant Beavers, Diplomacy & Regeneration in Nishnaabewin.* Edmonton: University of Alberta Press.

_____ (2021). *Noopiming: The Cure for White Ladies.* Toronto: House of Anansi Press.

_____ and Robyn Maynard (2022). *Rehearsals for Living*. Chicago: Haymarket Books/Toronto: Knopf Canada, Penguin Random House Canada.

Skibsrud, Joanna (2019). *The Nothing That Is: Essays on Art, Literature and Being.* Toronto: Book*hug Press.

Stallworthy, Bob (2013). "A Conversation with Alice Major about Intersecting Sets, A Poet Looks at Science." *FreeFall Magazine*. Vol. XXIII, No. 2. https://freefallmagazine.ca/a-conversation-with-alice-major-about-intersecting-sets-a-poet-looks-at-science/

Stovel, Nora (Ed.). (2020). *Recognition and Revelation: Short Nonfiction Writings – Margaret Laurence.* Montreal/Kingston: McGill-Queen's University Press.

Tator, Carol, and Frances Henry, Winston Mattis (Eds.). (1998). *Challenging Racism in the Arts: Case Studies of Controversy and Conflict.* Toronto: University of Toronto Press.

Tostevin, Lola Lemire (1995). *Subject to Criticism*. Stratford: The Mercury Press.

_____ (2015). *At the Risk of Sounding: Essays*. Toronto: Teksteditions.

Taylor, Charles (1993). *Reconciling the Solitudes: Essays on Canadian Federalism and Nationalism.* Montreal/Kingston: McGill-Queen's University Press.

_____ (1994). *Multiculturalism: Examining the Politics of Recognition.* Princeton: Princeton University Press.

van Herk, Aritha (1991). *In Visible Ink: crypto-frictions.* Edmonton: NeWest Press.

_____ (1992). *A Frozen Tongue*. Sydney (Aust.): Dangaroo Press.

_____ and Christl Verduyn (Eds.). (2021). *HEAR! HEaR! Voices of Canadian Women.* https://mta.cairnrepo.org/islandora/object/mta%3A27096

van Luven, Lynne (Ed.). (2000). *Going Some Place: Creative non-fiction across the prairies.* Regina: Coteau Books.

Verduyn, Christl (2007). "(Es)saying It Her Way: Carol Shields as Essayist." *Carol Shields and the Extra-Ordinary.* Marta Dvořák and Manina Jones (Eds.). Montreal/Kingston: McGill-Queen's University Press. 59-79.

_____ (2012). "Discursive Space: Canadian Women Writers' Essay Writing. *Re-exploring Canadian Space/Redécouvrir l'espace canadien.* Jeanette den Toonder and Bettina van Hoven (Eds.). Groningen (NL): Barkuis Press. 163-171.

_____ (2013). "Giving the Twenty-first Century a Try: Canadian and Québécois Women Writers as Essayists." *Canada and Beyond.* Vol. 3, Nos. 1-2. 289-303.

_____ (2018). "Encountering Canada: Immigrant and Ethnic-Minority Writing." *Immigrant and Ethnic-Minority Writers since 1945: Fourteen National Contexts in Europe and Beyond.* Wiebke Sievers and Sandra Vlasta (Eds.). Leiden/Boston: Brill/Rodopi. 106-150.

_____ et al. (Eds.). (2019). *Resurfacing: Women Writing in 1970s Canada/Refaire surface:* écrivaines *canadiennes des années 1970. SCL/ELC: Studies in Canadian Literature/Etudes en littérature canadienne.* Vol. 44, No. 2. 355 pp.

_____ and Aritha van Herk (Eds.). (2021). *HEAR! HEaR! Voices of Canadian Women.* https://mta.cairnrepo.org/islandora/object/mta%3A27096

Vigneault, Robert (1994). *L'Ecriture de l'essai.* Montreal: L'Hexagone.

Waddington, Miriam (1989). *Apartment Seven: Essays New and Selected.* Toronto: Oxford University Press.

Wallace, Bronwen (1992). *Arguments with the World.* Joanne Page (Ed.). Kingston (ON): Quarry Press.

_____ and Erin Moure (1994). *Two Women Talking: Correspondence 1985-1987 Erin Moure and Bronwen Wallace* (Living Archives of the Feminist Caucus of the League of Canadian Poets). Susan McMaster (Ed.). Kingston (ON): Quarry Press.

Warland, Betsy (2010). *Breathing the Page: Reading the Act of Writing.* Toronto: Cormorant Press.

Warren, Louise (2006). *Bleu de Delft: Archives de Solitude.* Montreal: Typo.

Webb, Phyllis (1995). *Nothing But Brush Strokes.* Edmonton: NeWest Press.

_____ (1981). *Talking.* Montreal: Quadrant Editions.

West, James L. W. III (1988). *American Authors and the Literary Marketplace since 1900.* Philadelphia: University of Pennsylvania Press.

Wiseman, Adele (1978). *Old Woman at Play.* Toronto: Clarke Irwin.

_____ (1987). *Memoirs of a Book Molesting Childhood and Other Essays.* Toronto: Oxford University Press.

Wiseman, Nelson (Ed.). (2013). *The Public Intellectual in Canada.* Toronto: University of Toronto Press.

Woodsworth, J. S. (1909). *Strangers within our Gates: Coming Canadians.* Toronto: F. C. Stephenson.

About the Author

Christl Verduyn works as a scholar and professor of Canadian literature and Canadian Studies, and is the author and editor or co-editor of books, articles, and essay collections focussing on women writers (including *Aritha van Herk: Essays on Her Works*, Guernica Editions 2001), and writers from historically marginalized communities. Professor Emerita of English and Canadian Studies at Mount Allison University, she taught previously at Trent University (1980-2000), where she was of Chair of Canadian Studies and of Women's Studies, and at Wilfrid Laurier University (2000-2006), where she chaired the Canadian Studies Program. Recipient of the Governor General's International Award for Canadian Studies and of the Order of Canada (CM), she is a Fellow of the Royal Society of Canada (FRSC) and a 3M National Teaching Fellow.

Printed in February 2023
by Gauvin Press,
Gatineau, Québec